Lagro U. M. Church

F

AUTHOR Cash, Carey H. Lt.

TITLE A Table in the Presence

DATE

A Table in the Presence

LT. CAREY H. CASH

W PUBLISHING GROUP
A Division of Thomas Nelson Publishers
Since 1798

A TABLE IN THE PRESENCE
By Carey H. Cash

Published by W Publishing Group, a Division of Thomas Nelson, Inc., P. O. Box 141000, Nashville, Tennessee 37214.

ISBN 0-8499-1823-5 (hardcover)

Printed in the United States of America

*Dedicated to the courageous men
of the First Battalion, Fifth Marine Regiment,
who were not afraid to live and die for a just cause;
and to the countless families and friends
back home who unceasingly prayed on our behalf.*

Contents

Acknowledgments

A. W. TOZER WROTE, "The only book that should ever be written is one that flows up from the heart, forced out by the inward pressure . . . The man who is thus charged with a message will not be turned back by any blasé consideration. His book will be to him not only imperative, it will be inevitable."[1]

From the moment I stepped foot back on American soil and back into the lives of my family and friends, I have been driven by what I can only describe as an inward pressure to write about the extraordinary events that our battalion experienced amidst the chaos of the war in Iraq. And yet, as forcible as the pressure was, there were friends and family members along the way who helped to either plant the seed or give much-needed direction, counsel, or shape to what has now become the finished product. It is to these special people that I owe an immeasurable debt of gratitude.

I wish to thank my father-in-law, Captain Larry Ellis, CHC, USN (Ret.); Lieutenant Commander Roger VanDerWerken, CHC, USN; and Susan Forbes for all pointing the way, which at times, I couldn't see. The three of them, unbeknownst to one another, helped me see that the writing of this book wasn't merely an option, but a sacred trust.

ACKNOWLEDGMENTS

Greg Daniel and David Moberg of W Publishing Group heard my vision for this story, only to cast an even greater vision for its relevance in our world today. I deeply appreciate their investment in me and willingness to step out in faith. In addition, I also wish to express my deep gratitude to Ernie and Pauline Owen for their immediate enthusiasm, wise counsel, and added help along the way.

I am profoundly thankful for Lela Gilbert, a godsend, whose passion for writing and editing mirrors her love for the Lord and His truth. As an editor, Lela knew how to encourage and inspire even when the manuscript was, at times, far from where it needed to be. I also wish to thank Elizabeth Runyen for proofing the final draft.

Special thanks are also in order for Mary Hammond and Craig Crawford. Mary's hospitality allowed a frazzled chaplain the time and space to get cracking on his book during twelve days of "working leave." Craig offered unsolicited support and read earlier versions of the manuscript.

There are hardly words to describe how thankful I am for my mom and dad, Captain and Mrs. Roy Cash Jr., USN (Ret.). From the moment that the idea of this book became a possibility, they never stopped praying for me and encouraging me. My greatest hope is that I would always walk worthy of their faithful example. Thanks, too, to my mom's best friend, Peggy Davis, for lifting me up in prayer for the last seventeen years of my life.

Also, I am deeply grateful to Cindy Farnum and the rest of St. John Chrysostom Chuch and School for being our faithful pen-pals from the beginning to the end.

I am especially thankful to all the chaplains and religious program specialists of the First Marine Division. For the past three years, as our world was turned upside down by the events of September 11, they lived as shining examples of courage and spiritual integrity for the men and women they served, as well as for me. Particularly, I wish to express my gratitude to Chaplains Frank Holley, Erik Lee, and Mark Tanis of the Fighting Fifth Marines; and

Jim Edwards of the First Combat Engineers. It was a true pleasure and a special brotherhood to have conducted ministry alongside all of these men.

I also must express how grateful I am for Second Class Petty Officer Redor Rufo. His loyalty, patience, and character, whether in the safety of San Mateo or the chaos of Saddam City, never flagged. I would never have been able to minister to my men in the way they needed me to, had Redor Rufo not helped me the way he did. I am forever grateful for his assistance as a religious program specialist, and his bravery as my personal security guard in the midst of a dangerous war zone.

And finally, for my beloved wife, Charity, and our five precious gifts from God: Caleb, Justice, Phoebe, Nathanael, and Ella Joy. They have been the real heroes in this endeavor. On a starry night in early August 2003, Charity and I walked out on our driveway unsure if we should go forth with the writing of this book. We both understood something of the sacrifice and life adjustment that such an effort would require. After a night of prayer and seeking the counsel of others, we both decided it was what God wanted us to do.

The greatest sacrifice has been the one that she has made. Not only during the war, but for the last twelve years of marriage, she has kept the home-fires lit and warm—home-fires that have glowed on five sweet but tireless little faces. Through it all, she has been the nurturer to the kids, staple of sanity for the home, and chaplain to the chaplain.

Ever, only, all for Thee.

Preface

*Thou preparest a table before me
in the presence of mine enemies. . . .*

KING DAVID WAS A MAN WHO KNEW DANGER. Anyone who even briefly skims the pages of the Bible will see that David all too often found himself in peril, surrounded by evil men determined to do him harm. He knew the anxious moments of the heart that precede battle. He knew the uneasiness of feeling like he was being watched. He knew the stark terror of the arrows that fly by day and the pestilence that stalks by night. He knew intense personal suffering and witnessed the terrible casualties of war. David understood what it was to be in the presence of cruel, unrelenting enemies bent on his destruction.

In the spring of 2003, the men of First Battalion, Fifth Marine Regiment found themselves in the presence of such enemies. "Welcome to Kuwait. You are now within range of Iraqi Scud missiles"—the opening words of our "welcome aboard" session in the northern Kuwaiti desert made that reality all too certain. From the first moments of our arrival in early February to the day we pulled out of Baghdad heading south, our infantry battalion of more than one thousand troops knew the constant threat of real-life, flesh-and-blood enemies. Our unit was the first ground combat force to cross the line of departure into Iraq, saw the first man killed in action at the hands of enemy gunmen, and fought what many believe to have been the most decisive battle in the taking of Baghdad. We had come to know, face to face, the schemes and the power of the enemy.

Yet, there was another power at work in the midst of all the chaos, a power that transcended even the mightiest foe we faced. It was a power that comforted, inspired, delivered, and transformed. It was the power that King David clung to when the night was dark and the hour was difficult. It was the power of the presence of God.

Operation Iraqi Freedom has been a subject of great interest and concern to people all over the world. Much has been written and reported in the media surrounding the intent of the war, its success, and its consequences. However, there is another story, a greater story that must be told. It is the story of how God Almighty revealed His unmistakable presence on the battlefield. As the chaplain to a battalion of front-line combat Marines, I had the unique privilege of witnessing firsthand how God miraculously delivered and even transformed the lives of men confronted by the terrors of war. This book is a chronicle of that awesome experience—the "first fruit" of what I believe has been a stewardship from God. But it is also intended to be an offering of thanks.

While spending the last month of our deployment in the Iraqi city of Ad Diwaniyah, I began to reflect on the outpouring of letters and care packages we had received from people all across our nation. For four months, these letters and packages were a reminder that although we were facing danger day and night, we were also being prayed for around the clock. It occurred to me that those people who prayed needed to know how God had resoundingly answered their prayers on the battlefield. This book therefore, is also a living testimony to God's power in answer to prayer.

Finally, if ever there were a generation that needed to be reminded of the miraculous power and sovereignty of God in the face of overwhelming odds, it is our generation. Our world since September 11, 2001, is more fearful, more anxious, and more uncertain than ever. It is my sincere hope and prayer that through this story many will see that the same God who spoke creation out of chaos, who parted the Red Sea, and who raised Jesus from the dead has overwhelmingly declared His power and His presence once again.

> "The LORD has made bare His holy arm in the eyes of all the nations. And all the ends of the earth shall see the Salvation of our God.
>
> —ISAIAH 52:10

—CHAPLAIN CAREY H. CASH
Marine Corps Base
Camp Pendleton, California
Summer 2003

1

An Unexpected Feast

WAKE UP!"

As the lights to our squad tent flickered to life, I struggled to wipe the sand and grit out of my eyes and to sit up in the sleeping bag that for the last six weeks had been home. I only needed to take one look at the face of my executive officer, Major Cal Worth, to realize what was happening. His eyes were like steel; his face, expressionless. My heart raced.

"You have five hours to get your gear packed and yourselves into your vehicles. We're moving north!"

You could have heard a pin drop in the tent. It was an announcement we had been expecting for weeks, yet his words hit us like a train.

"Any questions? No? Good! Then be advised there will be a mandatory staff meeting in thirty minutes. You'll get more info then. Get moving!" With that he turned and walked out.

For the next few moments, no one moved a muscle. We sat on the tops of our sleeping bags in shock, wrestling with the magnitude of what we'd just heard. We looked at one another, but no one said a thing. We didn't have to. The words still lingered in the stale air of the tent. Then finally, as if we were responding to a choreographed script, every one of us jumped up and started packing our gear.

Within minutes, I could tell that the message was permeating the entire camp. Senior Marines were barking out orders. Trucks, tanks, and High Mobility Multipurpose Wheeled Vehicles (HMMWVs or Humvees) were being moved into place. More than one thousand infantrymen, living in a space no bigger than a parking lot, starting packing their personal supplies, filling their canteens, doublechecking the status of their ammunition, writing last-minute letters, and saying prayers.

A young officer grabbed my arm. "Hey Chaplain, if something should happen to me, will you give this letter to my girl?"

Hey, wait a minute, I thought. *That's just for the movies.*

The man who handed me the letter was a decorated combat veteran. He had been among the first to land deep in enemy territory in Afghanistan. He'd been through this before, and his face was quite serious. I took the letter.

"It's going to be OK," I reassured him.

Was I sure about that? I tucked his letter deep within my pack, quietly hoping that I would never have to pull it out.

Meanwhile, the frenzy of activity intensified. I could see the camps next to ours springing to life as well. Flashlights from every tent shot beams across the clear desert sky. Engines rumbled to life. The sound of men's voices, some laughing and joking, some urgent and tense, were echoing from camp to camp. This was it! We were all heading out. Would we ever see this place again?

It was the evening of March 17, 2003. We had already been in the desert for forty days. Tired and restless, we were quite honestly wondering if the war was ever going to get kicked off. Two or three weeks were all that we'd expected to wait before the official word came to invade Iraq, yet there we were, approaching a month and a half. By now the days were growing longer, and the sun was getting ever hotter. The hope of a hot shower had all but evaporated, and shaving was merciless. The cold water had dulled the last of our razors, producing a wide variety of facial grimaces each morning as we pulled and tugged on our beards.

And then there were the sandstorms. Before arriving in Kuwait, we had all been told about the intense desert winds. But there was no way we could ever have anticipated how violent the storms would get. The weather pattern that brought them about was no mystery. When the wind blew in from the north, we enjoyed clear skies. But when the wind shifted directions and started blowing from the south, the sky would turn a deep dark blue, then brown; and then, like a thundering horde rolling indiscriminately over man and beast, the stinging sand would consume us. There was no escaping its relentless barrage. At times it would beat its implacable drum against our tents for hours. Our romantic notions were fading fast as every new sandstorm further eroded the grandeur of "going off to war."

During those forty days, when we weren't rehearsing our attack, we spent much of our time laboring to piece together any fragments of news we could get our hands on. What was happening in the White House? In Baghdad? Had diplomacy run its course? What of the inspectors searching for weapons of mass destruction? How were Americans viewing the war? How were they viewing us? How real was the threat of chemical weapons? Would the enemy surrender quickly? Or would he fight to the death?

We were all asking the same questions. We were all looking for something, anything, to cling to; any precious bit of news that might provide us with some sense of certainty either way. In the end we would have to settle for outdated newspapers and garbled radio transmissions that relayed as much static as commentary. Phone calls were precious but rare; the mail was slow. After forty days in a vast and often unforgiving desert, urgency had faded into monotony.

Marines and soldiers, however, have solutions for dealing with monotony. In fact, every Marine who is qualified enough to rise to the rank of corporal is expected by his command to be able to accurately diagnose the morale of his men and to come up with some clever antidote for the ailment, like a doctor who writes out prescriptions for sick patients. Of course the antidotes are as diverse as the men who think them up—a forced march, a grueling run. Or, if the men are lucky and their leader happens to be in particularly amiable spirits, the prescription might be a Humvee pull, a tire-throw, or a tug-of-war match.

On that particular Tuesday night in mid-March, it was obvious that no half-measures would do. The frustration of waiting had finally worked itself, like a thorn, into the skin of most of us. Faces were growing long. Arguments were becoming a daily ritual. Friendships were strained. Something had to be done, so the decision was unanimous. The antidote to our desert malaise would be a talent show.

As word leaked out about the night's main event, I could sense growing excitement. At least I know I was looking forward to it. For six weeks, everything had been business: chemical weapons drills, battalion hikes, live-fire ranges, late-night staff meetings, intelligence updates. We knew we were there on a mission, and from day one, we did nothing but prepare ourselves for it. So when the decision was made to host a battalion-wide talent show, it was as if a breath of fresh air blew throughout the entire camp, enlivening even the most dispirited man.

I had just finished off the last of my broiled chicken and rice and was enjoying the sweet taste of my warm soda when I first began to hear laughter. It wasn't the roaring kind of laughter you might expect to come from the lungs of grown men or warriors. This was more like snickering and giggling, the kind of laughter you'd hear behind a child's door at a slumber party. I was amused but also intrigued. The sound of the voices began to lighten my spirit, and like a magnet, it pulled me outside into the cool desert night to investigate. As I walked from tent to tent, I could see groups of Marines and sailors huddled together, feverishly planning out their appearances for the night's coming festivities. They were rehearsing every type of act imaginable: singing, skits, stand-up comedy, classical guitar, and just as I expected, those always-feared, never-avoided impersonations.

Young infantrymen—also known as "grunts"—can't get away with much when it comes to challenging authority; and few ever try. However, impersonations are different. Impersonating a senior-ranking Marine is, to my knowledge, the one and only time a grunt can take a stab at his superiors and still come out alive. It's almost sacrosanct; an understood realm of asylum, of immunity from reprisal. Overhearing some of the skits and impersonations that a few brave men were planning that night, I knew that some of them were sure to get a rise from the crowd that was already beginning to gather around the seven-ton truck that now doubled as our stage.

By 8:00 p.m., the judges were in place, the performers were ready, and the audience was stirring. Under dim flickering lights, and armed with a substandard sound system, the men of First Battalion, Fifth Marine Regiment hosted what must have been the finest talent show the northern Kuwaiti desert had ever witnessed.

Of course I had seen grown men laugh hysterically before. Having attended a military college where I played varsity football, I'd known my own share of rowdy evenings out with the guys. But this was altogether different. More than a good time, this was a release. This was six weeks of pent-up tension and anxiety erupting into the night sky in the form of laughter and cheering. There was no doubt that every person out there needed that night to chase away the stress and frustration of the last six weeks of waiting. We needed it to drive away the feelings of loneliness that grew stronger with every passing night. We needed it to deal with our fear.

Yet therapeutic as the evening was, I couldn't shake the feeling that something was about to happen. There we were in a hostile land, only miles from a border where enemy soldiers patrolled continuously. We all knew that an order might come down at any moment, leading us into mortal combat. Shadowing our exuberance and elation was the very real and imminent prospect of danger and death. One thousand of us were laughing, singing, and cheering; yet we were also poised to enter a different world, where such festivities would be impossible. Was this, quite literally, the last hoorah?

I didn't share my uneasiness with anyone else, but I am certain others felt the same way. Nevertheless, inebriated by laughter and camaraderie, all one thousand of us went to sleep that night in peace about 11:00 p.m. Three hours later, we learned that our lives were about to change forever.

IN THOSE SILENT SECONDS following Major Worth's middle-of-the-night announcement, my thoughts turned toward my fellow chaplains. The four of us had ministered together for six weeks in the desert. We each represented different Christian faith groups: Chaplain Frank Holley, a Methodist; Chaplain Erik Lee, a Nazarene; Chaplain Mark Tanis, a Lutheran; and I, a Baptist. In the course of those weeks, we had all become close friends, even brothers. We conducted services together, assisted each other in baptisms and counseling, and offered one another a listening ear when we needed to vent. When would I ever see them again?

My mind snapped to at the sound of a familiar voice.

"Sir, do you need any help loading your supplies?"

It was a voice I recognized well, even in the dark. Second Class Petty Officer Redor Rufo was my personal assistant—a religious program specialist (RP), who assists me in the administrative tasks required to conduct ministry. That is not, however, his only job. In war, the RP is a chaplain's bodyguard. Geneva Convention and navy regulations do not permit chaplains to serve as combatants. In fact, a chaplain is the only member of the entire military who is not permitted to brandish a weapon. Chaplains sometimes speculate about what they would do if their men were overrun, if they had the choice to defend themselves with a rifle or pistol. It's a tough call, but I always thought that if the life of a fellow Marine or sailor was at stake, I'd use the weapon.

Nevertheless, I knew Rufo would not hesitate to use his rifle if we ever found ourselves in real danger. He had the heart of a giant and the tenacity of a street fighter. A 5'4" Filipino-American with a stout build and cackling laugh, Redor Rufo had come to the States when he was in high school, following in the footsteps of two older brothers who had joined the navy before him. Always the generous peacemaker, Rufo overwhelmingly won the affection of the senior men in the battalion just two days after he arrived. He managed to do this by cooking up some of his famous *panzet* and *lumpia,* and serving them out of our office space.

Rufo's spirited generosity was no passing fancy. He's the only man I've ever heard kidding about having his own island one day; he would call his island Rufo Island, and he would be its benevolent dictator. The truth is, although farfetched, anyone who knew Rufo could easily see him doing just that: granting favors, pardons, gifts, and loving every minute of it. Still, kind and peaceable as he was, Rufo knew how to scrap. It didn't take me long to learn that despite his small frame, he could hold his own with anybody.

The two of us had served together since April 2002, when he joined the battalion. Every day had been an opportunity for us to grow in our mutual trust and respect for one another. Everywhere I went, Rufo was with me. If it meant walking the line together for hours on end, talking to young warriors in fighting holes, he walked beside me. If it meant setting up and taking down for eight worship services in one day, he was there, never flagging in zeal, always an encouragement to the other men in the battalion.

As the two of us loaded supplies into our Humvee, I sensed a note of pain in his voice. "I got to talk to my wife last night, sir. I waited in line for the phone for hours, but I finally got through. I'm so glad I did."

Calling home from Kuwait was definitely a rarity. There was only one phone for more than a thousand men, and more often than not, the phone wasn't working. When the phone actually functioned, you had to be prepared to speak to your loved one through a three-second delay.

"Hello . . . can you hear me?"

Three to four seconds would pass, and then the voice on the other end would inevitably answer, "Yes . . . I can hear you . . ."

On and on this would go, until "good-bye."

Calls home had the effect of producing both joy and pain. We were elated anytime we had the opportunity to call our wives or parents. Yet with each phone call came the quiet realization that this call might be the last one before we went into battle. Every word spoken was precious; every moment, dear. As good as it felt to hear your loved one's voice, many of our men said that it caused more pain than anything else. I know it did for me. It reminded me of home.

And there were more than a few in our battalion who deliberately chose not to call. I could understand why. It just hurt too much.

Clearly, Rufo was glad he'd been able to talk to his wife. But I could tell there was an ache in his heart. There was one in mine too.

It had been more than a month since I had spoken to my wife, Charity, and that conversation had lasted only a few minutes. When the phone rang in our Southern California home, it was 4:00 in the morning.

Charity's voice, suddenly stirred out of sleep, quietly answered, "Hello."

Overjoyed to hear her voice, it was all I could do not to shout to her, "It's me—Carey!"

Immediately, I could tell that she had begun to cry. We both started crying as a flood of emotions swept over us.

"I don't know when I'll be able to talk to you again, but just know that I am doing well. God is taking care of me."

For security purposes, I was not able to tell her exactly where I was, when we thought we might be moving north, or how long our stay might be. But that didn't matter. More than anything else, I wanted her to know that I was okay, that the men were doing well, that we were relying on the Lord, that her prayers for us were being answered daily in our lives, and, most of all, that I loved her and the children. Every minute of the conversation was filled with meaning, every word heavy with emotion. We were eight thousand miles away from one another, and we were separated not only by geography, but by the naked truth that war and death loomed, and that I might never return.

And yet, never in all my life had I felt as connected to Charity as I did in that conversation. With only minutes to speak, we shared with one another only those things that mattered most.

"Honey, I love you."

"I love you too," she said.

"Tell the kids that Daddy is safe, that he is right where God wants him to be. Remember that every night when you look at the moon and the stars, they are the same stars that I saw just a few hours earlier."

I wanted to remind Charity that the same God who had brought us together eleven years before was walking with each of us. He was walking with me in a hostile desert, upholding me as I ministered to Marines on the threshold of battle. And He was walking with her within our busy home, sustaining her as she raised our five children, strengthening her as she encouraged other military wives. When we said good-bye to one another, tears streamed down our faces.

I ached that night as I'd never ached before. And now Rufo was feeling much the same way.

Finished with loading supplies in my Humvee, I asked him to doublecheck the status of his rifle and ammunition. By 0500 that morning, we could see the faint hue of the Middle Eastern sun beginning to cast an orange glow across the desert floor. As vast and desolate as the northern Kuwaiti desert was, a calm beauty spread across it when the sun rose each morning. I often saw Marines standing outside their tents sipping instant coffee in the early hours of the morning for no other reason than to watch the rising sun and enjoy those brief moments of tranquility. Today would be different. Now, as the sun began to bathe the tops of our tents with light and warmth, the results of the night's activity became visible.

The assembly of our vehicles was formidable. Amphibious Assault Vehicles (AAVs) equipped with heavy machine-guns were lined up as far as the eye could see.

These massive troop transports were originally designed to make the grueling ship-to-shore invasions that made the Marine Corps famous in World War II, Korea, and Vietnam. We had come to see that they also made for excellent troop carriers in the desert, capable of carrying twenty-five Marines armed with 50-caliber machine-guns, Mark-19 grenade launchers, and able to move at well over 30 mph on the loose desert floor.

Other vehicles found their way into the convoy. Seven-ton trucks loaded with supplies vibrated back and forth, their engines idling, their drivers ready for the word to go. Combat ambulances, marked with the familiar Red Cross, sat positioned behind the protective shield of tanks and armored ("hardback") Humvees. Communications antennas sprang up from the tops of the command and control vehicles, each antenna serving as a potential lifeline should our troops somehow become separated from the others.

One by one the drivers of each vehicle gave a thumbs-up sign, indicating in no uncertain terms that they and the men for whom they were accountable, were ready. A staff sergeant walked the line of the convoy, making a last-minute check with each crew.

"Got everything you need?"

"Are all your people accounted for?"

"Gas? Chow? Water?"

All he needed to hear from the driver was a "Good to go, Staff Sergeant!" At that, he pounded the side of the vehicle, as if to say, "This one's ready!" And on he would go to the next vehicle.

Rufo and I sat there awaiting the moment when the wheels on the vehicle in front of us began to roll. The sun was completely visible now, and the dust stirred up by all the movement had shaded it into a dull burnt orange. For just a moment, it reminded me how the sunrise over Camp Pendleton, California, slowly burned away the early morning fog.

Rufo and I had driven together countless times in California. We had spent an entire month in the desert at Marine Corps Air-Ground Combat Center, Twentynine Palms, driving from one unit to another, conducting services and offering on-the-spot counseling. We were well prepared for today, but no amount of experience or training could have readied us for the adrenaline that surged through our veins as we waited to move toward the border of Iraq. The sound of the engines running in the convoy was like a powerful symphony, alerting anyone who stood in our path that trouble was coming.

"Make Peace or Die!" was the official motto of our battalion. As we finally pulled out into the vast Kuwaiti desert, the sight of our convoy moving must have proclaimed that motto loud and clear.

For approximately eight hours we drove. We inched slowly

along, stopping routinely for situational reports and double-checking the maintenance of the vehicles. Twenty miles later, the landscape had barely changed; desert looks like desert wherever you are. But by afternoon, we knew we weren't in the same place. We had arrived at a position not far from the Iraqi border, well within range of Iraqi artillery shells.

Once we turned off our engines, we had a chance to reflect on the day's events and ponder what lay ahead. The desert was quiet. There was a gentle breeze blowing from the southwest. As I opened a Meal Ready to Eat (MRE), I looked at the men who were about to step across the threshold into battle. They were milling around their AAVs, each one carrying a rifle and a knife; all of them fitted with flak jackets and helmets to protect them from enemy bullets or razor-sharp shrapnel. As I watched them, it occurred to me that technology has done much to change the face of war, but not the face of the warrior.

For some reason, I thought about Joshua in the Old Testament. He knew what war was all about. He had seen its deadly effects—the bloodshed, the burning villages, the charred remains of resisters. Yet he knew that the real battle lay not in the brandishing of swords or in the shooting of arrows, but in the realm of faith.

In those few quiet moments, I pondered where we were in the world and what our president was about to call us to do. I began to see that for us, as for Joshua, the real battle would be won or lost before we even crossed the line of departure into Iraq. Each of us had to find courage, faith, and quiet resolve, and to experience a peace that surpasses understanding—these were the real victories that had to be won in each of our lives.

As the sun began to give way to the deep blue haze of dusk, I hoped I understood the task that lay before me. I prayed for God's help and strength:

Lord God, prepare me for these last hours before the battle begins. Help me to faithfully offer to these men the same strength and courage that You have given to me so many times before when I have been faced with trial. Help us all to remember the promise of Your Word, which tells us not to fear or be dismayed, but to be strong and courageous, believing that You, Lord, will be with us wherever we go.

19 March 2003

SITUATION UPDATE: ENEMY SURFACE-TO-SURFACE MISSILES LIKELY WITHIN NEXT 24–48 HOURS. CHEMICAL WEAPONS POSSIBLE.

The warning spread rapidly though our particular section of the battalion's convoy. I was in the section called the "combat train." We were fifteen vehicles strong and consisted of the battalion's surgeon, medical corpsmen, ammunition and food resupply personnel, vehicle maintenance personnel, nuclear/biological/ chemical experts (NBC folks for short), and the battalion's chaplain and RP. The combat train's job was simple: follow directly behind the lead combat elements of our battalion with ready re-supply materials. It was the perfect place for me to be. I was almost always within sight and sound of our front-line troops, yet back far enough to monitor the situation on the communication channels and able to drive immediately to any platoon or augmenting unit that needed me.

Normally, a Marine Corps battalion consists of about nine hundred men, all assimilated within a certain company, platoon, and section. However, in times of war, a typical infantry battalion grows to more than twelve hundred men, as special units augment or attach to the battalion. Because these units become a part of us, in essence I become their chaplain as well.

And we definitely had our share of attachments. There were the military police (MPs), who were there to help us process potential enemy prisoners of war (EPWs). There were combat engineers who, despite their name, did a lot more demolition than construction. There was the human intelligence exploitation team (HUMET), which was always moving in and out of the periphery of our battalion, talking among themselves in corners, giving closed-door briefings to our battalion commander, dealing quietly with other unrecognizable operatives in our regiment, and even working at times with the CIA. We never knew exactly what the HUMET was up to, and that's exactly how they wanted it.

Working alongside the HUMET were the ever-flamboyant army special forces. While not officially attached to our battalion (although they were assigned to our regiment), these warriors brandished mustaches and long hair, wore civilian clothes, and drove SUVs. They made their appearance known in our ranks on more than one occasion, especially in the last days before we received official word to move from Kuwait to the border. Wearing jeans and toting .50-caliber machine-guns, they never had to explain themselves. In fact, in our eyes, they were just plain cool, having all the firepower of a Marine infantry platoon, minus the desert camoflage (cammies) and grooming standards. Although we didn't have many dealings with these outlaw soldiers before the war, their presence would dramatically save the lives of many of our Marines one unforgettable day in Baghdad.

And then of course, there were the workhorse attachments: AAVs, or "Tracks," who provided us with armored transportation from beginning to end; Second Tanks, with their heavy gun security; explosive ordinance demolition (EOD), whose singular job was to detonate weapons or ordinance caches found in Iraq; and finally artillery, or as affectionately known, "Arty." In our case, the artillery attachment would be Fox Battery, Second Battalion, Eleventh Marine Regiment. Fox 2/11 consisted of a half-dozen huge two-wheeled Howitzer cannons, whose job was to shadow our every movement in the war. On command, they fired their 100-pound high-explosive shells on enemy positions as far as eighteen miles away.

By the time we had moved into position from the northern Kuwaiti desert to just south of the Iraqi border, all of these attachments had officially become part of the First Battalion, making us now what's referred to as a "battalion reinforced." Twelve hundred

Marines, sailors, soldiers, and even a few British troops, we were all part of an enormous armada of vehicles and men, spread out over five square miles, awaiting the word to unleash and unbridle against the enemy every bit of firepower and expertise we could muster.

As the warnings of possible enemy missiles made their way through our section, I could sense the mood shift from excitement and anticipation to sobriety and reflection. We knew that President George W. Bush's forty-eight-hour time limit had come to a close. We knew the eyes of the world were on us. We knew this war was no longer a prospect or possibility, but a fast-approaching reality, beating like an ever-loudening drum on the horizon. For me, the mission was clear. These next few hours would, in all likelihood, be the final hours of peace before the storm. If ever there was to be a time for prayer and communion with the men, it would have to be now.

As Rufo and I fired up the engine of our Humvee, I looked out at the vast expanse of men, vehicles, and tents that covered the several thousand yards of our battalion's slice of the desert floor. I loved these men. They were my brothers. For the last year and a half, we had hiked together on the mountains of Camp Pendleton, sweated together in the desert of Twentynine Palms, shivered together in the ocean waters off Coronado Beach, and worshiped together in the tents of northern Kuwait. Now we were about to face death together.

As Rufo and I headed out, our wheels kicked up enough dust and sand to forewarn our units that a vehicle was approaching. And if anyone doubted who was driving toward them, a quick glance at either side of our vehicle made it clear—a large white cross was painted on each door. There were those who laughed and said the cross would make for an easy target (looking back, maybe there was some truth to that), but I wanted the men to be able to immediately see a sign of hope and strength in the midst of battle. Thus, several weeks earlier, when asked what kind of identification marking I wanted painted on the side of my vehicle, without hesitation I chose the cross.

The first unit we visited was the 81-mm mortarmen (81s). "Death from a Distance" was their motto. When Marines or soldiers are charging an enemy position, it is the mortarmen who provide the protective covering for them to do their job. Hiding in cliffs, embedded in mountains, positioned thousands of yards behind the advancing troops, the mortarmen lob high-explosive shells over the backs of their advancing comrades to rain down destruction on the heads of the enemy. Even if they don't directly hit their target, the sheer volume of the barrage alone creates such havoc that the enemy's ability to fire back is almost wiped out.

Their leader was First Lieutenant Patrick Henry. A salty Marine veteran, Lieutenant Henry had a toughness about him that made his guys both fear and love him. He was hard on them physically and mentally, but having been a young grunt himself years before, he understood the challenges they faced. He nurtured a carefully concealed concern for them that governed the way he led them. He had come to me on more than one occasion to solicit advice about how to help a couple of his boys who were in trouble. Henry saw potential in his men that others might never have noticed. And in the long run, the guys knew this and deeply respected him.

When Rufo and I arrived at their position, most of the 81s were hunkered down in fighting holes only big enough for two or three men. They, like us, were wondering what the next hours would bring. Most of them had that quiet, determined look about them that has characterized the faces of fighting men for generations. And yet, as I looked into their eyes, I could tell they knew why I was there. They were hungry for assurance. We all were.

"Hey guys! Chaplain's here to pray with us!"

Private First Class (PFC) Rojalio Rosales passed the word to the others. A slight-framed Hispanic-American with eager eyes and a disarmingly kind nature, Rosales was known in his section as someone of a spiritual fiber. His upbringing was both Roman Catholic and Protestant, and his personal ecumenism was evident, even though he was completely unaware of it. For Rosales, whatever background a man came from, the only important thing was whether or not he loved Jesus.

As PFC Rosales started spreading the word down the line that prayer was being offered, men began to quietly stream toward me. I had visited these men many times in training environments back in the States, but this was different. My presence suggested something final about our time of preparation. In every generation that has seen war, men have gathered on the eve of battle to pray for courage, protection, and the will to endure. We were no different. Faced with the terrors of battle, we cried out to God.

We were only hours from crossing the line of departure into Iraq, and as I met with them, I could not help but be encouraged by the story of another army, in another time and place. I began to speak to them about the biblical story of Joshua and the children of Israel. The Israelites, like us, had found themselves spread out along the border of a hostile and dangerous land. They, like us, knew there would be difficult days ahead. They, like us, knew the battles they faced would be fiercely fought. They, like us, knew they were fighting for a just and noble cause. And there was one more thing the children of Israel knew—something God wanted us to know too: We would not be alone in battle. I shared with the men these words: "Have I not commanded you? Be strong and of good courage; do not be afraid, nor be dismayed, for the LORD your God is with you wherever you go" (Joshua 1:9).

I had quoted these words to myself a thousand times in Kuwait. I could still hear my five-year-old daughter, Phoebe, singing them in her neighborhood children's choir. She had learned the verse in song complete with hand motions, and I could still picture her now, her little arms indicating strength, her finger pointing upward to God. As adorable as she was, in truth, I had always thought her rendition strangely profound, even triumphant. They were just children, but she and her friends had sung words of power and promise, words that have for thousands of years offered courage and strength not only to children, but to grown men and warriors as they have prepared themselves for battle and even for death.

The power of that ancient Hebrew scripture washed over us like a flash flood in the desert. Every man there knew he had his rifle, his ammunition, his food and water; but those things seemed to pale in comparison to his need for God. We needed to know that we would not be alone as we rushed headlong into the teeth of battle. Every unit I visited that afternoon expressed the same craving for assurance; every man needed to believe in God's promised presence with us.

This was especially the case when I visited with the British troops at the end of the day. Several weeks into our stay in northern Kuwait, our battalion had been tasked as the parent command for a few British and Royal Irish Coalition forces. Getting to know these men was easy. They were always upbeat, always laughing, always intrigued by the unique mannerisms and customs of the U.S. Marines. We enjoyed watching them as well. They are still the only army I've ever heard of that actually receives a ration of heat tabs every day, just so they can have hot tea or coffee wherever they might be. Of course, my love for coffee endeared me to them, and I spent more than one windy desert afternoon standing under the shelter of their armored vehicles or sitting with them at the long tables of our makeshift mess hall, sipping cups of hot brew.

The Brits knew I was the battalion's chaplain, but our opportunities for discussing matters of faith were rare because they often trained on different schedules than ours. However, when I visited them during those final hours before the war began, the happy-go-lucky spirit that we all had enjoyed together seemed transfigured into one of shared need. One British soldier, who had always been the life of the party, lifted his head after our prayer with tears in his eyes. Another told me about his struggling marriage and his love for his children. Together we placed our hopes and fears into the hands of God.

In the days that had led us up to this point, I had observed the many different ways men dealt with fear. For some of them, humor was the tonic that calmed their nerves. For others, it was the mind-set, "Nothing's going to touch me." Still others chalked it up to fate: "If it's my time to go, there ain't nothing gonna stop it from happening." Now, as I stood with each squad or platoon reading the words of Joshua, praying earnestly for the protective covering of the Lord, it was as if all of our robust mechanisms for dealing with fear (mine included) seemed to melt away. What was revealed was the seriousness of the moment, but also the bright hope that God was offering each of us. As my father-in-law always used to say, "Every crisis is a combination of danger and opportunity." Here was a profound opportunity to look to God and to commit our lives to Him.

That day I closed each service by laying my hands upon every man present. The Bible talks about the "laying on of hands" as a symbol of conferring God's blessing, anointing, or healing on others, but it was not a practice with which I was familiar. However when I concluded those final services of prayer that day, I felt compelled to lay my hands upon each warrior as a symbol of God's presence, as a reminder of God's love and power, and as an encouragement to go forth in the courage of His Son, Jesus.

At the end of the day, Rufo and I made our way back to our assigned position in the convoy. The hours had passed quickly and the sun was already bleeding its last rays of light into the distant horizon. It had been a long day, but a good one.

"It's all in your hands now, Lord," I prayed.

I pulled out my sleeping bag and placed it in the shallow hole that I had dug next to our Humvee. Lying back against the hard packed sand of the desert floor, I drifted off to sleep. Whatever lay ahead, I felt confident that the men were ready.

20 March 2003

LIGHTING, LIGHTING, LIGHTING! SCUD MISSILES INBOUND!

THE ALARM BY OUR OPERATIONS OFFICER blasted over the radio the next morning, igniting our worst fears. "Lighting" was code, and it only meant one thing—enemy missiles had been fired. We knew it must have been retaliation for Coalition strikes.

It was midmorning. I threw myself out of the door to see if everyone else had heard the news. Sure enough, within seconds, every Marine and sailor in sight was fumbling through his chemical protective gear—gas mask, boots, and gloves. We had no reason to believe Saddam would not use chemical weapons on us; he had, after all, used them on his own people. I could feel my hands trembling as I positioned my gas mask over my face. Seconds were ticking away. We had no way of knowing where the missiles were going to impact or how close we were to a catastrophic explosion. We had trained in putting on protective gear in Kuwait, but there was no way to simulate the real thing. It took me about ninety seconds to get everything on before I joined the others, sprinting for the bunkers that had been dug out a day earlier by the bulldozers of the First Combat Engineer Battalion.

Jumping in deep sand holes, we sat low and waited. The blowing of the desert wind reverberated off the sides of our rubber masks. I could hear the Marines next to me breathing through filters. I knew we were all asking ourselves the same question: was the silence of this moment about to be shattered by the sound of a deafening explosion? But seconds turned into minutes, and the minutes dragged on. Voices over the radio crackled back and forth, trying to assess the situation, but most of them were muffled and barely recognizable. Gas masks are not very good conduits for sound.

Longer and longer we sat, hunkered down below the surface of the desert floor. Although there had not yet been an explosion, it didn't matter. We all knew that a Scud missile had been fired, and that someone, somewhere was on the receiving end of the deadly attack.

After twenty minutes of waiting, the all-clear signal was issued. Still, I couldn't stop wondering about where the missile had landed. Again I thought of my fellow chaplains and their units. What was happening to them? And what about innocent Kuwaiti civilians? Of course there was no way to get those kinds of answers. Only one thing was clear to all of us: now that the air war had begun, we had passed the point of no return. The Coalition forces had committed, and Saddam was fighting back. Indeed, during the next several hours, we would be subjected to four more Scud missile warnings. Saddam, witnessing the horrendous bombing of his capital city, was unleashing all he had.

By noon that day, the commanding general of First Marine Division, Major General J. N. Mattis, had directed all units to be ready to cross into Iraq within the next twenty-four to forty-eight hours. As the division's commanding general, Mattis was responsible for planning and executing an attack that would involve more than twenty thousand Marines and sailors, British forces, and U.S. Army attachments. In an effort to prepare us for the impending attack, General Mattis had written a letter that was to be mass-copied and sent out by trucks to every single battalion about to cross the border into harm's way. I received my copy at about noon on March 20. Mattis wrote the following:

For decades, Saddam Hussein has tortured, imprisoned, raped, and murdered the Iraqi people; invaded neighboring countries without provocation; and threatened the world with weapons of mass destruction. The time has come to end his reign of terror.

On your young shoulders rest the hopes of mankind. When I give the word, together we will cross the Line of Departure, close with those forces that choose to fight, and destroy them. Our fight is not with the Iraqi people, nor is it with members of the Iraqi army who choose to surrender. While we will move swiftly and aggressively against those who resist, we will treat all others with decency, demonstrating chivalry and soldierly compassion for people who have endured a lifetime under Saddam's oppression.

Chemical attack, treachery, and the use of the innocent as human shields can be expected, as can other unethical tactics. Take it all in stride. Be the hunter, not the hunted; never allow your unit to be caught with its guard down. Use good judgment and act in the best interests of our Nation. You are part of the world's most feared and trusted force. Engage your brain before you engage your weapon. Share your courage with each other as we enter the uncertain terrain north of the Line of Departure. Keep faith in your comrades on your left and right and in the Marine Air overhead.

Fight with a happy heart and a strong spirit. For the mission's sake, our country's sake, and the sake of the men who carried the Division's colors in past battles (who fought for life and never lost their nerve) carry out your mission and keep your honor clean. Demonstrate to the world that there is "No Better Friend, No Worse Enemy" than a U.S. Marine.[1]

—J.N. Mattis,
Major General, U.S. Marines

Mattis was a legend among the ranks of infantrymen. He had been the commanding officer of the first American troops to step foot in Afghanistan, immediately following the September 11 attacks on the Twin Towers of the World Trade Center. Under Mattis's leadership, a handful of nineteen- and twenty-year-old riflemen had loaded the decks of U.S. Marine CH-46 helicopters and flown four hundred miles, under the cover of darkness, to insert themselves deep into enemy territory controlled by the Taliban.

In fact, there was a rumor that every unit Mattis had ever led had fought somewhere in a real-world contingency. Hearing him speak about war, and seeing the way he inspired Marines through his own life experiences, made the legends about him seem true enough. He was a certainly a warrior, and one who understood the importance of reaching into the deepest reservoirs of a soldier's strength. In a directive sent out to chaplains, doctors, and other caregivers before the war, Mattis quoted the late Army General George C. Marshall, who himself was oft noted for emphasizing the soul of the American GI: "The soldier's heart, the soldier's spirit, the soldier's soul are everything. Unless the soldier's soul sustains him, he cannot be relied upon and will fail himself and his country in the end." There was no other leader who we would rather be fighting under than General Mattis.

Early that evening, before the sun had completely disappeared, our battalion commander, Lieutenant Colonel Fred Padilla, called a command and staff meeting to discuss the scheme and maneuver for what we all expected to be a predawn attack the next morning, March 21. The desert camouflage tent was full of all those who had key leadership roles in the battalion. Communications, intelligence, operations, air-cover, artillery: all critical aspects of the battalion were represented by Marine officers who knew their job better than anyone. It was a team of professionals, but all eyes were on Padilla.

Having assumed command of our battalion just a few months before the attacks on the World Trade Center Towers, Padilla had led us fearlessly for the last year and a half through the ups and downs of a unit that always seemed to be on stand-by to go somewhere dangerous. If ever there was an infantry officer who was destined to lead men into combat, it was him. Exuding a subtle leadership that we all loved and thrived under, Padilla was always offering us timely tuidance and profound insight gleaned from over twenty years of military service, several of which had seen the harsh realities of combat.

However, the most compelling aspect about him was the way he trusted us. He led in such a way that communicated to all of us that he trusted us to do our jobs. Under his leadership, we were empowered to step out of our comfort zones, take risks, exceed our own expectations and be the best military officers we could be.

Now, as Padilla paced back and forth, reviewing the invasion plan, the atmosphere in the command tent was both serious and jovial. We were dead serious about making sure we heard every detail correctly; every green notebook was flipped open; notes were frantically scribbled including grid coordinates, passwords, distances, and the latest intelligence information provided. And yet, behind it all, there was a jocularity, a lightheartedness that was irrepressible. Not that the men had no fear, but these were men who had been training for combat all of their careers. They were infantrymen. It's not at all uncommon for a Marine or soldier to train his whole life for a real-world contingency and never have the opportunity to put his training to the test. Wars don't come around all the time, thank God. Midway through the meeting, as Padilla was in the middle of walking through the next day's scheme, a runner burst in with an urgent message from higher headquarters.

"Sir," the runner said, "phone call from higher."

"Take down the information," Padilla told him. "Tell them I'll call them back after the meeting."

The runner nodded and rushed back to the adjoining tent. But no more than a minute later, he came bursting in again, and this time he would not be turned away. In his hand he held a "yellow canary," a yellow slip of message paper that he immediately handed to Padilla, without asking permission.

I will never forget the moments that followed.

I was standing directly behind Padilla, and as I haphazardly peered over his shoulder, I could see amidst all the writing on the yellow note, one word set apart from all the others, written in all capital letters: IMMEDIATE.

Padilla read the note, took a deep breath, looked at all of us, and said, "It's now. We're crossing the breach now."

The response was complete silence.

Intelligence reports had confirmed that Iraqi soldiers, at the bidding of Saddam Hussein, were beginning to pour into southern Rumeilah with orders to blow up the oil fields, destroying the raw petroleum that would be the life-blood for the Iraqi people in the coming months and years. Our regiment, the Fighting Fifth, was the only unit in a position to be able to stop them. And time was of the essence.

Instead of attacking early on the morning of March 21, General Mattis's orders were for our regiment to invade immediately and stop the Iraqis' destructive mission. We were to head out at 7:30 p.m., nine hours before any other ground combat forces would cross the border. I glanced down at my watch. It was already fast approaching 5:00 p.m.

In what would be the last time our command staff would gather under one tent before the ground war started, and the last time all of our officers would still be alive, the battalion commander turned to me and said, "Chaplain, before we go, would you lead us in a word of prayer?"

After all the training, all the physical conditioning hikes, all the strategy sessions, all the intelligence briefs, all the live-fire rifle ranges, it had come to this—a decisive moment and a sincere prayer. We stood together in a circle, asking God for help, for strength, and for courage. As we bowed together on that afternoon, the ancient words of a familiar psalm came flooding into my mind:

> Even though I walk
>   through the valley of the shadow of death,
> I will fear no evil,
>   for you are with me;
> your rod and your staff,
>   they comfort me.
> You prepare a table before me
>   in the presence of my enemies.
> You anoint my head with oil;
>   my cup overflows.
> Surely goodness and love will follow me
>   all the days of my life,
> and I will dwell in the house of the LORD
>   forever.
>
> —PSALM 23:4–6

The "table" that David spoke about, the "table" that David longed for in the presence of his enemies, was the table of God's presence. It amounted to a feast of spiritual strength and friendship that no degree of danger and no amount of evil could infringe upon. C. H. Spurgeon said it best a hundred and fifty years ago:

When a soldier is in the presence of his enemies, if he eats at all, he snatches a hasty meal, and away he hastens to the fight. But observe: "Thou preparest a table," just as a servant does when she unfolds the . . . cloth and displays the ornaments of a feast on an ordinary peaceful occasion. Nothing is hurried; there is no confusion, no disturbance, the enemy is at the door, and yet God prepares a table.

In the quiet moments that followed our prayer together, I was reminded, by a voice too deep for words, that we were not alone. Even though we were facing great danger, even though we were about to face our enemies head-on, even though there would be desperate and agonizing hours ahead for all of us, God would be there with us.

The irony, the paradox, the bright contradiction was obvious to all of us. We'd been given a mission to tear down and destroy, to go into the teeth of enemy territory and wage war. And yet in those quiet moments of silence and prayer, we had also been given a blessing. We had been invited to a table hosted by God's empowering presence, to taste of the miraculous power that only He could offer. Indeed, it was a most unexpected feast.

Once the meeting was adjourned, we all dashed from the command tent into our vehicles to announce the order. When Rufo and I made it back to the combat train, the men were busy doing last-minute odd jobs, still unaware of the change of plans.

"Guys, it's now!" I shouted. "We've got under an hour to get our vehicles ready and staged in the lineup. The Iraqis are getting set to blow the oil plants. We're going *tonight*."

The mission was finally upon us. Only hours separated us from the battlefield in Iraq. We worked frantically but methodically to check our supplies and ammunition, to ready our vehicles for the long hours ahead. It was twilight; the sun was already beginning to give way to darkness, and the chill of night was slowly creeping in. The enemy was at the door.

2

For Such a Time As This

W e're moving in thirty mikes!" The voice on the radio was crystal-clear and audible to every vehicle in our battalion. "Mikes" means minutes, and thirty mikes was no time at all. As Rufo and I made our last-minute checks, Battalion Surgeon Lieutenant Manan Trivedi and his team of medical corpsmen began working furiously, handing out special medications to all of us.

Dr. Trivedi was one of about fifty U.S. Navy personnel permanently assigned to the battalion including the RP, another medical officer (MO) Erik Koppang, roughly forty-five corpsmen (or "docs" for short), and me. For more than two centuries, the presence of naval personnel within Marine units and vice versa has forged a venerable tradition of teamwork between the two armed services. This tradition is best exemplified in what is probably the most famous war photograph ever taken—the raising of the American flag on Iwo Jima. Of the six men immortalized in the picture, five are U.S. Marines—Ira Hayes, Franklin Sousley, Harlon Block, Mike Strank, and Rene Gagnon—and one is Navy Medical Corpsman John Bradley. It was Bradley's son James who wrote the *New York Times* bestseller *Flags of Our Fathers*.

Dr. Trivedi and I had arrived at First Battalion, Fifth Marines about the same time, during late summer/early fall 2001. Being one of just a handful of navy guys, together we tried as best we could to navigate the unfamiliar world of a Marine infantry battalion. We quickly realized that there were certain customs that could only be learned by trial and error; for example, the way we were supposed to address the battalion commander and staff at the weekly meetings.

Such meetings were always formal and all the men were called to attention when the commander walked into the room. When it was your turn to speak or share any pertinent information from your respective section, it wasn't just a matter of rambling on in any old way.

There was a strict formula: "Good morning (or afternoon), sir . . . Good morning, gentlemen," . . . and then you stated your business.

When you were finished speaking: "Nothing more to pass, sir."

I never stopped poking fun at Trivedi for one of his debut entrances at a command and staff meeting in early fall 2001. He walked in late and a bit flustered, but just in time for Colonel Padilla to ask him if he had any important matters to share from the medical department. Everyone at the conference table waited for his report. We waited and waited.

Problem was, Trivedi had forgotten what time of the day it was, and he was visibly flustered. "Good morning, sir . . . uh . . . I mean afternoon . . . uh . . . How ya doing, sir?"

"How *ya* doing, sir?"

It was a classic outburst of sophomoric nervousness colliding with 226 years of military regimen. Fortunately for Trivedi, the often stonefaced Padilla could not hold back the grin that swept across his face. In reality, the only reason I could poke fun at Trivedi for his foul-up was that I had done the same thing myself a few weeks earlier. Life as a naval officer in a world of Marines was always providing comic relief.

I had joked to a couple of Marines that the Marine Corps was just a department of the U.S. Navy. Their answer fired back like an artillery shell: "That's right, sir . . . the *men's* department." How could I compete with that?

Now the U.S. Marines and U.S. Navy were set to launch yet another attack. We had hoped for a daylight strike, but time seemed to be flying by and the sun was no longer visible. As the last of the medications were being handed out, our convoy began staging in line, ready to follow the trucks and Humvees in front of us. The radio in my vehicle was tuned to the battalion-wide channel, making it possible for me to monitor everything that was going on.

Finally at 6:30 p.m., the word was given: "We're moving!"

The vehicles slowly began to inch ahead. By now the sky was almost totally dark, and because of the dust the massive convoy was kicking up, we could only see the vehicle directly in front of us. Rufo was wearing night-vision goggles (NVGs), which made the landscape in his view an eerie green.

In the meantime, I kept my eyes wide open, looking to the front and right side. With every second that passed, we were that much closer to the Iraqi border, where potential enemy forces were waiting. The dampness in the cool night air deadened the atmosphere. It was almost too quiet. All we could hear was static-punctuated voices on the radio, the low hum of our motor, and the grinding of the wheels against the rocks and sediment of the earth beneath us.

Sitting in my Humvee looking out the window north toward the blackness of Iraq, I began to reflect on the people and providential events that had brought me to this time and place.

BECAUSE OF MY FATHER, I grew up with a deep respect for the military. Roy Cash Jr. was always a towering figure of strength and seriousness. Standing 6'4," he commanded respect from everyone who knew him. He was not a domineering man, but one who made everyone around him feel safe. He was born on December 31, 1939, just an hour and a half from the decade that ushered in World War II. He grew up the only boy in a household of four sisters, all of whom were younger than he. He found his niche in reading and music, and he entered Memphis State University in 1957 as an English and theater major.

There he met my mother, Billie Hall. After seeing her rehearse for a campus play in the fall of 1962, he remarked to his friends standing in the auditorium, "I'm going to marry that woman!"

My mother was a true southern girl who had spent the majority of her life moving from town to town throughout the southern United States. Her father, a construction worker, had relocated the family from Tennessee to Arkansas to Louisiana to Mississippi to Texas and back to Tennessee again, always looking for a job. By tenth grade my mother had been enrolled in thirty-three different schools.

Ever the "new girl" in the class, Mom's ability to make lasting friendships was always cut short by the next move. Understandably, her plan was to settle down for four years of college life. However, less than a year after her matriculation, and after my father's grand proclamation to his friends, the two were married. In the end, my mother admitted that all the moving and relocating had prepared her well for the often transient life of being a navy spouse.

My father's decision to enter the navy in 1963 came at a time when America was growing more and more conflicted about the role and calling of the military. On campuses across the nation, activists disdained the very existence of the armed forces, not to mention their mission. It was this controversy, Dad later said, that fueled within him a patriotic defiance toward the spirit of the age. My father believed deeply in service to country; he believed it in a way that only a few from each generation ever perceive within their hearts.

By 1968, as a navy pilot, he had already deployed three times, including an eleven-month combat tour to Vietnam. On July 10 that year, he got into a dog-fight with a couple of Soviet-made Vietnamese MIG fighter jets. At the age of twenty-eight, he became the first F-4J Phantom pilot to shoot down a Vietnamese enemy fighter.

Four years later, the enemy returned the favor.

On June 19, Father's Day 1972, flying his F-4J Phantom over the Gulf of Tonkin, he was shot down by North Vietnamese anti-aircraft fire. Both he and the other officer in his jet lived through it, but barely. A search-and-rescue sailor, having jumped out of a helicopter that was hovering just over the site of the crash, managed to cut my father away from the parachute lines that were beginning to drag him to the bottom of the ocean. Trying to save my dad, in the thrashing and churning of the rescue, the sailor nearly sliced off his own finger. The ocean water ran red with blood, and as he saw it all around him, my father was certain he was dying or in shock. He didn't talk about that event very often, but when he did, it was clear that something about it had changed him; that experience had defined him forever.

Images of Dad wearing his military uniform made a deep impression upon my sister, Kellye, and me. The bright ribbons that covered his chest made us proud to walk next to him. In our eyes, he was the biggest and strongest man in the whole world. I even fought a boy once in front of a large crowd to prove that my dad was tougher than his. Now that I'm a father of sons, I realize that such fights, although usually broken up by frustrated mothers, are a matter of honor for boys. I thought the world of Dad and was never in any doubt about what he thought of me.

When I was ten years old, I had the opportunity, along with about two hundred other boys, to fly to Malaga, Spain, and meet the aircraft carrier *U.S.S. Saratoga*, on which our fathers were stationed. The ship had been deployed for almost six months and was enjoying its last port call before making the twelve-day voyage across the Atlantic Ocean to the States. As I waited to pull myself up the ladder from a small boat onto the stairwell of the giant carrier, my eyes scanned to and fro across the crowd of men decked out in their uniforms, gathered along the rails. I watched as one by one the boys in front of me climbed the ladder and found their fathers.

There were firm handshakes, pats on the backs, even some guarded hugs. But when I found Dad, he scooped me up as tight as he could and kissed me right on the lips for all to see. I couldn't have pried myself from his grasp if I wanted to. There he was, the commanding officer of a naval fighter squadron, respected by all, yet he was not the least bit afraid to show his emotion and his love for his son. It never mattered to him what others thought. The only thing that mattered was that my sister and I knew how much he loved us.

If my father was the star of the family, my mother was without a doubt the quiet hero. She demonstrated a love for Dad that always made his absences bearable. In thirty years of naval service, his deployments added up to almost fourteen years. It would have been easy for her to grow bitter and to project a negative image in front of us impressionable kids. But she never did. She learned early on to take her hurts and worries to God in prayer.

And she prayed for us.

Each morning before heading out the door for school, I would tear off a calendar Scripture verse for the day, wad it up in my pocket, and whenever needed, pull it out and read it. Every year, before the first day of school, Mom would sit down for hours and write a little one sentence note under each day's Scripture verse for the coming year. It was usually something simple, like "Praying for you today, son," or "Don't forget He's right with you, wherever you go."

My mother prayed for Dad, Kellye, and me every single day of our lives. It was not uncommon for me to find her awake before the sun came up, pouring out her heart and soul to heaven. I'm sure there were many nights when my mother's heart broke in loneliness. But because of her love for Dad and her confidence that he was where God needed him to be, my life as a military son was full of peace, security, and pride.

For me, this amounted to an understanding of being called to something greater than myself. My father was called by God to serve his nation. My mother was called by God to raise Kellye and me, and to support Dad's mission in life. There was no competition between the two callings. It was a seamless union of respect, love, and mutual support, making any sacrifice we experienced as children bearable and worthy of our best behavior. Our family life wasn't always easy, but deep within my own heart, my parents were my heroes.

It wasn't surprising then, that upon graduating from high school, when the Citadel in South Carolina offered me a full scholarship to play football, I didn't hesitate to take it. I was impressed with the first-rate education the school offered, and the opportunity to continue playing football was inviting. But perhaps on a deeper level I was drawn to the military structure of the place—its tradition, its legacy, its history. Alumni from the Citadel had served in every branch of our armed forces and had fought in every major war. There was an instant connection. It was a special moment when I called my dad, who was deployed to Israel at the time, and told him of my decision.

Four years later in November 1991, I walked beneath the giant life-sized ring that every graduating senior at the Citadel passes through in anticipation of his last year at the school. Many of my fellow cadets escorted girlfriends or even fiancés. Some walked through with their mothers. To my left stood my mother, who had prayed me through more tests, exams, and college football games that I could count. To my right stood a beautiful University of Tennessee freshman named Charity Ellis.

Charity was a beam of sunshine who had burst into my life during the summer before my junior year in high school. We met in Virginia Beach in 1986 on a youth-group beach outing. A slender blonde with bright green eyes and a radiant smile, Charity won my heart. Her innocence and wholesomeness shone as brightly as her natural beauty. I remember thinking, *That girl is beautiful, and she doesn't even know it.* Her father was also a naval officer, stationed in the same area where we lived. After two years of puppy-love (she wasn't allowed to formally date until she was sixteen), her father received orders to another duty station, and the Ellis family moved away. I didn't know if I would ever see her again.

Aside from a few rare phone calls, Charity and I didn't communicate for the next four years. I was away in college and she was finishing high school in Tennessee and Hawaii. Then for some reason, during the summer before my senior year at the Citadel, we both decided at roughly the same time to call each other. She was still in Hawaii and about to enter the University of Tennessee in Knoxville as a freshman; I was a rising senior at the Citadel. We hadn't talked to one another in at least two years, and I will never forget one of the first things she wanted to know about me: Was I still walking with God? I was surprised.

There was so much about Charity that I loved. She was beautiful and had a charming personality. She liked to have fun and was wholesome and extremely bright. But by far what was most compelling about her was her love for God and her desire to follow Him. Her question to me revealed so much about her character. This girl's faith was the most important thing in her life. And she wanted to know if my faith was still strong too. From that day forward, she became the standard by which I measured all others.

No one ever compared. In July 1992, two months after I had graduated from college, we were married by her father, a navy chaplain, in the hallowed halls of the Citadel's Summeral Chapel. Our first act of visible union together as a married couple was receiving Holy Communion. We knelt and prayed, and we asked God to forever bind our hearts as one under the guidance of the Lord Jesus Christ. Our first year together was filled with bliss and all the joys newlyweds experience in their first season of forever.

Then in August 1993, little more than a year after our wedding, the proverbial rug was ripped out from under our feet. Sliding a scan of my brain into a lighted glass window, a radiologist pointed out the clear outline of a brain tumor. Charity and I stared at the image in shocked silence. The news was catastrophic. Just months after graduating from college and getting married, I had begun to experience blurred vision and mild headaches. After getting a clean bill of health from more than one eye doctor, I was finally directed to see a radiologist, just to make sure there was nothing more serious causing the problem. We felt certain nothing would show up on the MRI. Our life together had just begun. So many good years lay ahead.

When Dr. Lee Norris pointed to the cause of my symptoms, all I could think to myself was, *God, how can this be?* The tumor was located on the base of my brain stem and appeared to be inoperable. The doctor's look was one of deep concern. Even though his bedside manner was sympathetic and full of compassion, I could easily see that he was worried. "We need to do further tests. We just don't know what it is." It was the only thing he could say, and it left us with nothing but uncertainty.

That night as Charity and I lay in bed, we stared up at the ceiling. We wondered. We cried. We struggled with the potential implications of the diagnosis. We knew God had called us to be married, but for how long? Was this the beginning of the end of our hopes and dreams? For the first time in our lives, we were truly afraid.

In the months that followed, we visited with several doctors and neurosurgeons who all offered the same prognosis: not good. The tumor was not cancerous, but it was located in a very dangerous place on the brain stem. Any growth could become a terminal situation. And surgery was too dangerous.

My confusion deepened. All my life, I had found my identity in my physicality. I prided myself on being a disciplined athlete. I had always been physically strong, someone who could take care of himself. Now the very attribute that had defined me throughout high school and college was being threatened, maybe even stripped away. I experienced a vulnerability I had never known. As a football player, I made it a habit of studying my opponent and trying to overpower him. In this new game, I could not have been more powerless. What was God trying to do?

Then something quite unexpected happened, something that became the beginning of God's answer. My father-in-law, an ordained Baptist minister and active-duty naval chaplain, had given me an unusual Christmas gift in 1992. It was a set of books explaining the New Testament, chapter by chapter. I had read the Bible growing up and had even been involved in a few Bible studies in college. A baptized Christian, my faith had always been important to me, and Charity and I made certain that once we were married, we would join a local church. The books had sat collecting dust for a few months, but now in the fall of 1993, something began prodding me to start reading them. And when I did, I soon realized there was something different about these books. Or maybe to be more exact, now that I was facing the prospect of terminal illness, there was something different about me.

Putting to use the books my father-in-law had given me, I studied the Bible with a hunger and intensity I had never known before. One by one, I searched the words of Jesus, and of the apostles Paul, Peter, and James. In their words, I found what none of the neurosurgeons could ever give me. I found certainty.

At a time in my life when my future seemed the most dismal, hope began to burn in my heart, brighter than any hope I'd known before. My symptoms continued every day, sometimes every minute—that same blurred vision, those same headaches. Yet each new day brought me a new promise from God's Word, stifling my fears and turning my eyes toward the Great Physician, for whom no medical crisis is ever out of control.

The doctors kept saying, "We just don't know . . . we just can't say what will happen." The Spirit of God kept saying, "Take courage, be not dismayed, for the Lord your God is with you wherever you go." And, "I know the plans I have for you . . . plans not to harm you, but to prosper you . . . to give you a future and a hope." Paul's words in Romans 4 seemed to crystallize exactly what was going on in my life and what God was asking me to do:

> And not being weak in faith, he [Abraham] did not consider his own body, already dead (since he was about a hundred years old), and the deadness of Sarah's womb. He did not waver at the promise of God through unbelief, but was strengthened in faith, giving glory to God, and being fully convinced that what He had promised He was also able to perform.
>
> —ROMANS 4:19–21

My life may have been as good as over in the eyes of some people. But something deep inside was calling me to turn my eyes away from the situation and to trust God, who knew exactly what He was doing. Whatever His perfect will for my life was, He had promised that He would carry it out for His glory and for my good.

It didn't dawn on me all at once. But slowly, like the momentum of an ocean's tide, after six months of suffering under the cloud of a catastrophic medical diagnosis, only one desire remained in my heart. And that desire gave life to every dark day and strength to every uncertain moment. More than anything else on earth, I wanted to grow in my relationship with God and to share the hope of His Son, Jesus, with anyone and everyone who would hear it.

A phone call to my father-in-law one quiet afternoon in the fall of 1993 made my path even clearer. Since he was an active-duty naval chaplain, and had given me the set of books in the first place, I asked him what he thought I should do next. "Is this a call to the ministry?" I asked him. "Should I think about seminary or church work? Where do I go from here?"

"Carey," he asked, "have you ever thought about the chaplaincy?"

The thought had never occurred to me, yet something about it seemed right. Even though I had been a navy brat for eighteen years, and even though I had attended a military college, for some reason the thought of military chaplaincy had never crossed my mind. Part of this was because the only association I had ever made with the military was being a line officer: a pilot like my father or ship's captain, a submariner. But a chaplain? Something about it made perfect sense. In the weeks that followed, I began to pray that God would specifically direct Charity and me. Although my medical condition was no better, my desire to discover God's plan for my life could not have been stronger.

I don't exactly know when, but sometime soon after my phone conversation with my father-in-law, I recognized that something was happening inside me. It was barely perceptible, yet growing larger every day. That deep respect and admiration I had always had for the military was stirring. A love for God and a love for the military community; a desire to serve the Lord and a desire to serve my country—these realities began intertwining, growing together, flowering within my heart, giving me a clear sense of direction and calling. The men and women of the military had always been my heroes. Was God calling me to go back to them now? With all my heart, I began to believe it.

Of course there was only one minor mitigating circumstance: I had been diagnosed with a brain tumor that might cost me my life. At the very least, it would probably keep me out of the navy. People with brain tumors just don't get into the military very often. So what were we to do? While reading my Bible one day, I came across what I perceived as God's answer to my very real dilemma. It was a passage from the book of Proverbs in the Old Testament: "Trust in the LORD with all your heart and lean not on your own understanding; in all your ways acknowledge him, and he will make your paths straight" (Proverbs 3:5–6 NIV).

What struck me about the passage was that it suggested that in life there are always two understandings at work within us, simultaneously courting our allegiance and vying for our attention. There is our human understanding, which is limited by our mortal frailty and clouded vision. And then there is God's understanding, which is perfect, all-wise, all-knowing, and always trustworthy.

My own understanding said, "Chaplaincy: no way." Yet on a different level, it looked as if the path that God was making straight was leading directly there. God seemed to see something that I didn't, namely, that with Him all things are possible. So with Charity's encouragement and support, I stepped out into unfamiliar waters, submitted my chaplaincy application, and made plans to enroll in seminary.

Meanwhile, my symptoms continued. A family friend, a doctor of internal medicine, suggested that we seek out the opinion of one of the best-known neurosurgeons in the world, Dr. Albert Rhoton out of Shands Teaching Hospital in Gainesville, Florida. Driving in our beat up, old Chevy Blazer from Charleston, South Carolina, to Gainesville, Florida, Charity and I both knew that his would probably be the last opinion we would hear on the subject.

Dr. Rhoton's fine reputation preceded him; every other specialist we had talked to had mentioned his name. When we arrived in his office, we were both scared. I knew that his job often required him to deal with terminally ill patients. He was used to speaking to frightened couples, people like us, who were desperate for a good report, for some grain of hope to hang their dreams upon. Like anyone else in similar circumstances, we wanted most to know what to expect in the coming months and years.

Dr. Rhoton had a gentle manner, and I could sense that he fully understood our concern. After viewing the MRI films prior to our visit, he ran me through some very brief motor skills tests and then asked us sit to down. Charity and I were holding each other's hands very tightly. I cannot remember exactly how he said it, but I fully understood what he meant.

Dr. Rhoton explained that he had seen hundreds of patients with my same type of tumor—patients who had lived completely normal lives. He didn't promise us that my condition would never worsen. He didn't promise that the symptoms would go away. He simply said that I had probably been born with the tumor, and in all likelihood, *it would never change or grow*. What's more, he believed that I was more than fit for active-duty service as a military chaplain. Finally, he said he would write a letter, if necessary, confirming this prognosis to the Bureau of Naval Medicine in Bethesda, Maryland.

It was an experience that Charity and I will never forget. Leaving his office, we felt like the weight of the world had been removed from our young shoulders. "Full steam ahead!" was our course of action. Although I was still experiencing symptoms, I was determined to keep walking the path I believed God had made straight before me. The results were up to Him.

In September 1994, just a month after I entered seminary, I received an official letter of rejection from the Bureau of Naval Medicine on the grounds that I was medically disqualified. Three months later, after Dr. Albert Rhoton wrote a letter affirming my fitness, I received a second letter from the navy. Rhoton's endorsement was all the navy needed. "Congratulations," the second letter said. "Your application for medical waiver for the United States Naval Chaplaincy Program has been approved."

My heart nearly burst with joy. God's promise never fails, but to us it seemed that He had really done the impossible this time. Later that fall, another prayer was answered. My erratic and often painful symptoms completely ceased and never came back.

The miracle bore fruit in August 2001. Believing the time was right, Charity and I, and our five children—Caleb, Justice, Phoebe, Nathanael, and Ella Joy—stepped out in faith and entered active-duty service.

During the preceding five years, I had graduated from seminary, served as a youth pastor to a growing church in South Carolina, and served as the senior pastor of a small congregation in western Tennessee. Those were days of seasoning and preparation that we wouldn't have traded for the world. But now, entering the active-duty chaplaincy, we knew that we were finally doing the one thing to which we had been called.

When asked what kind of assignment I would like to have, without hesitation, I asked to serve with the Marine Corps. Although my father was a navy pilot, he'd had the privilege of serving with the Marines on many occasions. So had my father-in-law, and they both had a great respect for the men who made up their ranks. What's more, Charity's grandfather had served as a Marine for thirty years. He had fought on the beaches of Guadalcanal and Tarawa, and had led an entire regiment in the Korean War.

I still remember my father's advice: "If you serve with the Marines for your first tour, it will impact you for the rest of your life. You'll always expect more of yourself. You'll always wear your uniform a little more pressed. You'll always stand a little taller. You'll come to demand excellence the way they demand it of you."

At last I received my first assignment as an active-duty chaplain in the United States Navy. And when I saw that I would serve within the First Marine Division—First Battalion, Fifth Marine

Regiment, I did not realize that the Fifth Marine Regiment, or "Fighting Fifth," as they call themselves, was the most highly decorated regiment in the history of the Marine Corps. I also had no idea that the Fifth Marine Regiment was the very same regiment that Charity's grandfather had commanded in Korea.

When I told him the news, my father-in-law's words to me over the phone were a comfort. He sensed my excitement, but also my trepidation. "Providence . . . Remember, the providence of God is in all of this."

Providence is the idea that behind all of our decisions, and even in some sense behind the decisions of others, there stands a God who is lovingly directing the course of events in our lives to bring about something good in the end. As a pastor, I had preached on the theme a dozen times, and in my own study I had discovered that while the word *providence* itself never once occurs in the Bible, its truth permeates every page. The providence of God is an unassailable comfort. In essence, it means that no matter what the decisions of others may be—whether good, bad, or indifferent—for those who love God, and His Son Jesus Christ, God will work out all things together for our good. The apostle Paul says it best in Romans 8:28: "And we know that all things work together for good to those who love God, to those who are the called according to His purpose."

There is no secret about what the New Testament means when it mentions people who are "called according to His purpose." It's not talking about a special club to which God invites some and not others. To be called by God is to be one who has heard and answered the call that God makes to everyone: "Look unto My Son, Jesus, and be saved." In the end, not all men respond to that call. But for those who do, nothing, absolutely nothing, can separate them from God's providential plan working out in their lives.

Before leaving for Camp Pendleton, California, I was required to attend chaplain's courses in Newport, Rhode Island. By early September 2001, most of the chaplains in our class had already headed off to their new assignments. However, those of us who were assigned to Marine units still had another course to attend—CREST, or chaplains and religious program specialists, expeditionary skills training. It's a class taught at Camp Lejeune, North Carolina, by Marine instructors for the purpose of thoroughly acquainting chaplains and their assistants (RPs) in the culture of the Marine Corps.

And if there is one thing that stands out about the Marine Corps, it is its culture. Steeped in battlefield histories and brash personalities, the Marine Corps prides itself on its uniqueness. It has its own lore, its own language, and its own standards for success. Marines sleep in holes, hike with gas masks on, and stand to attention to songs with titles like "Waltzing Matilda" and "From the Halls of Montezuma." The instructors at CREST faithfully taught us all these things, and by the second week, we were starting to get the hang of it.

Early the morning of September 11, 2001, my classmates and I boarded buses and made our way to Camp Geiger, a Marine Corps base adjacent to Camp Lejeune. Our training that day was simple—we were to get suited up in chemical protective gear, go into a chamber filled with riot-control gas, and then, at the command of the Marine operating the chamber, take off our masks. The Marines don't necessarily intend for the training to be torturous. But the only way you can be assured you understand how to operate a mask is by taking it off in the midst of acrid fumes and then "donning and clearing it."

The results tell the tale. If after you put your mask back on, you're still coughing and choking, either you didn't clear it properly, or you don't have a tight enough seal. If, however, you're able to attain some semblance of normal breathing after the mask is back on your face, then "Hoorah," as the Marines say, you've passed the test.

By midmorning, all of us had gone through the chamber and were busy sneezing, coughing, and spitting out the lingering taste of the fumes that still burned our eyes and throats. Gathered in a grassy field, we waited for the buses to take us back to the schoolhouse, where a full day of classes awaited us. As the white government buses pulled up, we all started moving toward the doors. We quietly joked about the morning, recalling the few who had really gotten a good dose of the burning fumes into their lungs. Our bus jostled up and down as we drove down the gravel road that led back to the schoolhouse. Amidst all of the bumping around, talking to one another, and laughing about the day's events, we first heard the alarm in the bus driver's voice.

"Something's happened," he said.

He was listening to the radio in the front of the vehicle. His head was cocked forward toward the speaker, and the way he looked made us realize that he was trying to hear every word that was being spoken. His demeanor silenced us.

"There's been a plane crash or an attack. I can't tell."

He kept trying to tune the radio to a clearer station, but it was to no avail. All we could tell was that something had happened in New York City at the World Trade Center involving airliners, and there was the possibility of terrorism.

The conversations on the bus had turned into an incessant buzz. "What is going on?" None of us knew, but as we approached the parking lot, I could already see several of our instructors waiting for us. Their faces were sober; they told us to get into military formation the instant we stepped off the bus.

"Ladies and gentlemen," one of them told us, "from what we can tell, there has been a major attack in New York City. The information that we have is that, just minutes ago, two airliners filled with passengers were flown into the Twin Towers of the World Trade Center in New York. There are unconfirmed reports that other airliners have crashed in Washington, D.C., as well. What I'd like everyone to do as soon as this formation is over, is to report to your classes and await further instructions."

Once we went inside, our worst fears were realized. One television set was surrounded by a crowd of people with their arms folded and their mouths open. No one was talking. From where I stood I could see what looked like buildings engulfed in smoke and flames. The camera then turned to the streets beneath them. People covered in ash and choking in the smoke ran aimlessly looking for help, searching for friends, crying aloud.

By now, it was clear from the news commentary that there had been an orchestrated and malicious attack on the United States. Soon camera crews were feeding live footage from the Pentagon, where more towers of smoke billowed up. There was word of a crash in Pennsylvania as well. No one needed to tell us that innocent people had lost their lives. The sounds of the sirens and screaming pierced us with sorrow. I sank into my class seat and could not hold back the tears. An incurable wound had been inflicted upon our nation, upon all of us.

I had to call Charity. The first thing she said was, "Carey, are you seeing this?"

"Yes. I can't believe it."

"But what does this mean for *us?*"

Her question struck deep. We both knew I had orders in hand to report to a combat unit of infantry Marines. Watching those towers fall, hearing the reports confirming that it was an act of terrorism, could only mean one thing: Marines and soldiers, like the ones I would soon be joining, would be going into harm's way. And I would probably be going with them.

Before long, our class began to discuss what all this meant in the immediate future. Chaplain Orr, our lead instructor, decided that the class schedule should go as planned. We still had two weeks left, and there was no better place for us to be. What could be more important than learning how to minister to the very ones who would soon be called to confront the evil that had assaulted our way of life?

That's when I began to sense it again—my father-in-law's words—providence. Here we were, new chaplains heading straight for units that would be on the tip of the spear in defense of our country. True, we were heading into potential danger and harm, but more than that awaited us. We were also stepping into a sacred stewardship. We were heading into a defining moment in our nation's history.

Entrusted to our care would be men and women asking the timeless questions of faith and spirit. They would be wrestling with the prospect of death and sacrifice, witnessing the terrible casualties of war, and needing someone to point them to God. A deep and abiding peace began to flood my mind as I suddenly remembered a passage of Scripture that I had learned years earlier: "Yet who knows whether you have come to the kingdom for such a time as this?"(Esther 4:14). The sorrow of September 11 was beginning to give way to an urgent sense of responsibility and the recognition that perhaps God was preparing all of us for this dark but difficult hour.

September came and went, and so did our course of training. When Charity and I and the kids pulled out of her parents' driveway in Pinehurst, North Carolina, and headed for California, we knew we were heading toward the very place God wanted us. Despite the prospect of war looming on the horizon, we believed with all our hearts that we were walking in God's perfect will. It brought us peace, and a deep assurance that God would take care of us, no matter how terrifying the events of the world would become.

The next year and a half would only confirm what I felt that day as I watched the twin towers fall. Troops began to pour into Afghanistan. Our battalion of nine hundred continued to train for battle and ready itself for deployment. The rumors of war in Iraq soon became reality, as more and more troops based at army, navy, marine Corps, and air force installations across the country began making their way to the deserts of northern Kuwait. The build-up had begun.

On December 20, 2002, five days before Christmas, our battalion was given the order to go. This wasn't just a scheduled six-month deployment. The White House was still trying to solve the crisis with diplomacy, but every indicator seemed to point to one conclusion—war. The mood at Marine Corps Base Camp Pendleton was one of quiet intensity.

One by one, the First Marine Division and its supporting units were deployed. Neighbors of mine, serving with other units, would be mowing their front lawns one day and gone the next. Wives walked alone to bus stops in the morning. Wives stood in circles speculating about what the next months would bring. My unit began making all the preparations needed for saying our good-byes: there were family readiness meetings, wives' get-togethers, and the signing of wills and powers of attorney. The day was fast approaching.

On a cold Tuesday morning in February, with my gear resting near my feet, I said good-bye to the woman who had been my life partner through all the joys and sorrows of ten years of marriage. Our five children were crying, yet I knew that they couldn't understand the full weight of what was happening. Charity did. This was war. Men would die, and our battalion would be right in the middle of it. There was nothing I could say to assure either one of us that I would come back. All we could do was pray and trust in God's divine purpose. It was He, after all, who had brought us to this point in our lives.

MY EYES TRIED TO FOCUS in the midst of the thick darkness of the northern Kuwaiti desert. I could barely see my hand in front of my face. The air was even colder and damper than when our convoy had started rolling. The enemy border was getting closer and closer, and the only sound I could hear was the hum of the motor and the crunch of our wheels on the desert floor.

And that's when I saw it: a flash, momentary but blinding. Looking out of the window of my vehicle, I sat in shocked silence. The ground war . . . had finally begun.

3
Fiery Furnace

20 March 2003

IN THE MOMENTS BEFORE I saw that first flash of fire on the horizon, unexpected message traffic had rasped through the battalion command vehicle's radio. It would mark our unit's entry into combat.

"You can't be serious!" First Lieutenant Jay Lappe stared at the map that was pasted to the interior steel walls of the command and control AAV. Although the message had come through his radio broken and barely readable, he had figured out enough of its contents to make him cringe. The voice on the other end of the transmission came to life again, and this time it was clear:

> Geronimo, Geronimo, this is Grizzly. I repeat. All divisional artillery fires have been cancelled. All fires have been cancelled. How do you copy?

Within seconds of the transmission from Grizzly, the cramped compartment of the command AAV began to stir with activity. The smell of fuel wafted throughout the small space as the big engine roared to life, causing the red interior lights to dim momentarily and all communication to go static. The tracks underneath the hull churned the hardened desert floor into loose sediment and created the effect of being swayed side to side like a ship in a mild storm. The men strained against the seat harnesses that were wrapped tightly around their waists. One by one, they began preparing themselves for what might lie ahead.

For a while no one said anything. They just rocked up and down and swayed side to side as their AAV pressed on in the darkness toward the Iraqi border. But their eyes said it all. As barely intelligible voices continued to break through over the radio, reality was setting in. No divisional prep fires? In short, the message could translate into the horrific scene of nineteen-year-old Marines rushing headlong into Iraqi troops who were well dug-in and lying in wait.

From the initial planning stages of the U.S. invasion of Iraq, a preliminary artillery bombardment had been considered crucial, entailing eight hours of firing on known enemy tanks, troop transports, artillery batteries, and rocket launchers. A successful series of these fires would devastate any Iraqi effort to employ heavy guns against our troops. Even at a minimum, eight hours of "prepping" the area would cause such ear-bursting chaos and confusion among the enemy soldiers that, in all likelihood, they wouldn't be able to concentrate on our advance. With any luck they would be reduced to panic, running from bunker to bunker, keeping their heads down.

But now the eight-hour barrage had been called off. Instead it would be up to Lieutenant Lappe alone to order the first shots fired of the ground invasion into Iraq, paving the way for our advancing troops. We all had our own private thoughts as our convoy continued to lurch toward the border. But for twenty-nine-year-old Lieutenant Lappe, only one thought predominated: *at my order, the enemy's first blood will be drawn.*

Jay Lappe had only been in the Marine Corps for six years, but he was one of those rare individuals who carried himself like a well-seasoned veteran. He did so for good reason. Both of his grandfathers had served in the navy during World War II, and both had been aboard ships that were sunk by the Japanese in the South Pacific. His father, a former sergeant in the Marine Corps, was himself no stranger to war. Having endured nine firefights in Vietnam, the last of which saw a North Vietnamese mortar round explode right on top of him, he had spent almost an entire year convalescing in a veteran's hospital in Bremerton, Washington.

Yes, war was in Lappe's veins.

I met Jay Lappe not long after I first reported to the battalion. We were at a change-of-command ceremony where he was turning over a rifle company of one hundred-plus Marines to an incoming captain. He had only served for a few short months as the interim officer in charge, but to this brand-new chaplain, Lappe's way of addressing the Marines communicated the utmost in confidence and capability.

He had been one of a handful of officers selected from the battalion to attend the mountain warfare leadership course in Bridgeport, California, one of the Marine Corps' most physically arduous tests of endurance and mental toughness. When he returned from the six-week-long course, I asked him how it went. "Oh, you know . . . no big deal," he responded. Nothing ever seemed to faze Lappe except perhaps the inconvenience of having a low stock of chewing tobacco.

One of five siblings in a devout Catholic family, Lappe's oldest brother had become a priest after attending St. Thomas Aquinas College. Jay and I often talked about his family's religious heritage. He was proud of his brother, and deeply respectful of his choice to enter the ministry. Jay was also exceptionally thoughtful about not only the tactics of war, but about its morality.

A quote from an unknown source, printed in the Marine Corps training manual, says, "The nation that makes too great a distinction between its scholars and its warriors will have scholars who are cowards and warriors who are fools." Lappe was neither a coward nor a fool. On more than one occasion, he and I handed back and forth articles from popular religious or political journals discussing the moral and ethical underpinnings of just war. Perhaps this quieter intellectual side of him that gave him such an air of confidence. He seemed to understand the "why" of the Marine Corps' mission, as well as *what* we were about to do in Iraq. He was thus able to fully invest himself in the cause.

When the orders came down canceling the preliminary artillery bombardment, Assistant Intelligence Officer, Gunnery Sergeant Douglas, who sat three consoles down from Lappe, knew exactly what to do. With his finger on his map for reference, he began methodically writing down the ten-digit grid coordinates where, the day before, intelligence sources had observed known enemy threats. One by one he prioritized them according to the degree of danger they posed to our advancing companies. The Iraqis had their share of weaponry, including artillery pieces that could outrange our own— rocket launchers that could fire multiple warheads, surface-to-air missile sites, tanks, and mortar tubes. Douglas quickly handed the bulleted piece of paper to the waiting Lappe, who immediately began citing specific targets to the artillery officer at Kilo Battery 3/12.

Kilo 3/12 was acting in place of Fox 2/11 on the night we crossed into Iraq. With each grid coordinate Lappe passed on, an "affirmative" was repeated on the other end of the radio, ensuring that Kilo 3/12 had a solid transmission of Lappe's message traffic.

"Time on target?"

It was the last bit of information Kilo Battery needed to know before their guns let loose and the maelstrom began. All the trajectory paths had been established; all the guns were loaded. Only one question remained: when?

Lappe paused as the first AAVs of our battalion's convoy positioned themselves to enter the black desert of Iraq. He was about to commit the first mortal act of war. He had called for artillery fire hundreds of times before on practice ranges at Camp Pendleton and Twentynine Palms, but this was real. Real, flesh-and-blood men would be on the receiving end of his barrage. Enemy troops would surely die. Nevertheless, he couldn't wait any longer. Our battalion was about to cross, and U.S. military lives were depending on him.

"Now! Time on target . . . now!"

Once Lappe gave the word, the radio went silent. Somewhere in the night six young men holding the trigger lanyards of their mighty guns pulled with all their strength.

It was in that instant that I looked out the passenger side widow, scanning the northeast sky for any signs of fighting, and saw that first flash.

After a moment's silence I said, "Rufo, did you see that?"

"See what, sir?" His eyes were still focused on the blurry-green night-vision landscape in front of him.

With my heart pounding, I locked my eyes toward the direction of the flash, scanning for another, unsure of what I had seen. I waited. The scene reminded me of an image from an old war movie where advancing soldiers survey a field they are about to cross. All seems quiet. The field appears deserted. But the soldiers know better. They know that out there in the dark, enemy forces are poised, waiting to fire at them.

Just then, a second flash of blinding light came from the same direction as before, momentarily illuminating the entire horizon like heat lightning on a summer night. I stared in disbelief at what followed.

Brilliant as diamonds, a cluster of four dazzling lights hurled themselves upward into the desert sky, leaving glowing contrails streaking like shooting stars behind them. Within seconds they disappeared, only to be followed by four more. Then eight. Then ten. One after another, in single bursts, or in clusters, supersonic artillery shells imprinted their after-burn streaks on the night sky, exploding like fireworks upward and outward over the horizon. It was breathtaking. Back at Camp Pendleton and Twentynine Palms I had seen artillery firing too many times to count. Our home sat only miles from the range where most of our big guns roared and quaked. But this was like nothing I had ever seen before.

The sky lit up from end to end as the men of Kilo Battery worked furiously to reload their smoking artillery guns, pouring water over the red-hot chambers to cool down the metal. Jay Lappe was drawing first blood. And he had to. There was no other way to provide safety for our advancing Marines. Even then, there was never a guarantee.

Though the blasts were distant, I could still feel their thump in my chest and gut. Round after round of high-explosive steel projectiles were shredding the landscape of distant oil fields. The ground quaked underneath our vehicles as each hundred-pound artillery round crashed into the desert floor. The targets were enemy bunkers and troop transports, but more importantly, tanks, artillery pieces, and rocket launchers that could be used to obliterate our slow-moving AAVs—vehicles that were filled to the brim with nineteen- and twenty-year-old Marines.

Of course men were dying on the receiving side of those artillery rounds. They were enemy soldiers, yet men nonetheless, men with wives and children, families and friends. My heart was in my throat.

"Rufo, are you seeing this? This is for real. Are you seeing this?"

Rufo kept plowing ahead, laboring to keep his focus on the shadowy vehicle in front of us. But he was clearly as shaken as I. It was hard to believe that just months ago, he and I were working out of the comforts of a Camp Pendleton office space, eating lunch together at the chow hall, manning responsibilities at the chapel. We both had wives, and he was expecting his first child. And now here we were riding through the gates of what had just become one of the most dangerous places on earth.

The distant fires of the Iraqi oil fields that had haunted us for six weeks in Kuwait were clearly visible now. Their towering flames billowed up toward the sky. I was already wondering where our men were—the ones in our most forward-reaching companies. I could almost see the faces of guys I had spent the last six weeks with.

Private Robert Harriott, a small-framed New Englander, who wanted more than anything to act in movies one day.

Sergeant David Roza, whom I had come to know under the stars of the Mojave Desert as we prayed together for a particular need in his life.

Private First Class Rojalio Rosales, whose bright eyes and genuine love for others made his faith come to life.

Second Lieutenant Shane Childers, a fellow Citadel graduate whom I had spent many an hour talking with about how best to help the Marines he loved.

Staff Sergeant Bradley Nerad, a giant of a man who had inspired nearly a whole platoon into baptism by his St. Peter-like enthusiasm for Christ.

Maurice "Doc" Bailey, a young navy corpsman who must have had the brightest smile I've ever seen.

First Sergeant Luke Converse, who had been imprisoned by Saddam's regime in 1991 and rarely let a day go by without asking me how my morale was doing.

Lance Corporal Jeff Guthrie, who was still searching for answers.

What was going on inside those men right now? What were they seeing and feeling? How many enemy forces were lying in wait for them, hoping to take their lives? With my eyes locked on the northeastern sky, I prayed with all my heart that God would protect our Marines. I prayed that He would make them aware of His awesome presence, even in the midst of danger and fear.

I remembered how many letters I had received in Kuwait from churches and schools across the United States, telling me that people everywhere were praying specifically for God to grant our men faith and courage as we crossed the border into harm's way. My thoughts turned to a verse in Psalm 18, a scripture Charity had quoted for me in a letter she had sent just days earlier:

> He rescued me from my powerful enemy,
> from my foes, who were too strong for me.
> They confronted me in the day of my disaster,
> but the LORD was my support . . .
> You, O LORD , keep my lamp burning;
> my God turns my darkness into light.
> With your help I can advance against a troop;
> with my God I can scale a wall.
> As for God, his way is perfect;

the word of the LORD is flawless.

He is a shield for all who take refuge in him.

—PSALM 18:17–18, 28–30 NIV

During the long weeks in the Kuwaiti desert, we had often talked about God's protection and had prayed for it in every service. We had asked God for courage and quiet resolve in the face of the enemy. We had quoted the Psalms, the words of Joshua, and the letters of the apostle Paul, all of which encouraged us not to fear but to be strong and courageous, remembering that God has not given us a spirit of timidity, but one of power. We had sung the great hymns of the faith, had spoken the time-honored confessions and creeds, and had been strengthened by one another's fellowship.

We had spent forty days of spiritual preparation, soul-searching and personal inventory in that Kuwaiti desert. New decisions had been made, new steps had been taken, and new life in the Spirit had been received. For six weeks, many of us had looked to God for grace and help in our time of need, and God had graciously responded. He had calmed our fears, breathed hope and confidence into our souls, and readied us for the fight. So many men had made life-changing decisions. They had stepped out for the first time into the realm of faith, entrusting their lives to God. Would their new faith sustain them through the brutal reality of war? Would my faith sustain me?

My thoughts turned back to the day we had arrived in Kuwait six weeks earlier. I remembered it like it was yesterday.

THE WHEELS OF OUR BOEING 777 touched down on the darkened runway of Kuwait City International Airport, and the banter of 250 voices making small talk across the aisles came to an immediate halt. Our plane was the first to land, but after eighteen hours of flight including a refueling stop, a series of 777 aircraft had brought our entire battalion of more than nine hundred infantry Marines and sailors to the same destination.

As we rolled to a stop, the flight attendants, who had been unfailingly upbeat and gracious, suddenly seemed to be at a loss for words. Their smiles looked frozen as they said, "Good luck." "God bless you." See you soon." "We'll be here to take you back home."

Their uneasy farewells betrayed what we all felt. We were going to war. Some of us probably would not return.

Before long, we were led to a fleet of buses, side windows obscured by curtains, parked just a few feet from where the jet had stopped. Immediately, gunnery sergeants started barking out orders. "Load your magazines and set your weapons for condition three!"

Every Marine was being directed to load live rounds into his rifle and to prepare his weapon so it could be fired at a moment's notice. One simple charge of the bolt handle, one thumb-click off the "safe" mode, and the barrel could be blazing lead. It isn't often that Marines are given the authority to load magazines of live rounds into their weapons. Most of the time, rounds are only given out on practice ranges under the direct supervision of a senior instructor or safety officer. But now all that was behind us. We had entered a different world—a hostile world. The rounds were real because the threat was real.

It was late when the long line of buses finally arrived at a non-descript plot of desert soil. Looking out of my window, I could see nothing more than a single generator-powered spotlight, standing alone, set up to give us some sort of orientation and visibility while we off-loaded all our sea bags and equipment. The wind was whipping so loudly that we had to shout to hear each other. And it was cold—the temperature that night had plummeted below freezing, making our fingers ache as we labored to off-load the heavy containers. I saw more than a few young Marines looking around, their faces reflecting the same question that was on my mind. *This is going to be our home?*

There was no sign of civilization anywhere—no tents, no trucks, no buildings, nothing. In every direction, there were only hard-packed desert floor and the immense blackness of the desert sky. We found our sleeping bags, zipped ourselves up to stay as warm as we could, and did our best to sleep under the stars.

Over the next few days the other units in our regiment arrived just the way we did. Little by little, the vast, empty wilderness was becoming a tent city. Two-man "hootches," as we called them, lined the desert floor in columns, each one home to two fully-loaded combat Marines and every bit of gear that would sustain them for the months to come. Water "bulls" dotted the landscape, providing potable water for drinking and hygiene.

By the end of the first week, the trucks and the heavy equipment started to arrive as well. Tanks, Light Armored Vehicles (LAVs), AAVs, seven-ton trucks: our new neighborhood continued to grow every day. Each morning we would awaken to more activity. By now troops and gear had transfigured the barren Kuwaiti desert into a thriving metropolis of men and machinery. And in the midst of the off-loading, the setting up, and the arrival of more troops, we all shared an acute awareness. We weren't "in Kansas" anymore.

Within the first two weeks, several suspicious men were found walking though our camp for no good reason. For example, one night a Middle Eastern stranger was apprehended near our water container. When asked what he was doing there, he explained in broken English that he was checking the status of our water, to see if it needed refilling. Marines, of course, fill their own water containers. Locals were hired to do other things, but maintaining the water supply was not one of them. Thankfully, we never saw him again.

Nor did we ever again see the two characters who wandered uninvited into one of the nearby regimental kitchens. They were discovered near huge vats of food—"chow" that was being prepared for thousands of Marines and sailors. When spotted, they ran off and vanished into the desert darkness.

The next day the threat condition (THREATCON) for our forces was heightened in the wake of two mysterious explosions in the area, not to mention an intercepted communiqué wishing known Al-Qaeda operatives, "Good luck in your upcoming attacks."

And then there was that eerie light on the distant horizon. Every cloudless, star-strewn night, the northern horizon was aglow with fires burning in the oil fields of southern Iraq. We were less than twenty miles from the Iraqi border, close enough to see the orange hue of those immense flames. Standing outside the tent I shared with the battalion surgeon, I often found myself staring at the fires. There was something unsettling about seeing them burning so brightly, so close to us.

I knew what kind of power our unit could bring to the fight. But I also realized that the Iraqis knew very well where we were. You can't hide the deployment of thousands of troops from an enemy who is less than twenty miles away. Sometimes, I saw young Marines and sailors silently smoking their cigarettes, staring at those oil fires flaring in the night. Like me, I'm sure they had a sense of foreboding in their hearts. Danger was in the air.

But danger distills the vital, and it was the vital matters of life and death, mortality and eternity that began weighing on all our hearts and minds. As focused as our battalion was on the mission ahead, countless warriors began to discover a new focus: their own lives.

"Chaplain, are there certain sins that God can never forgive?" The question came out of nowhere as I talked to a couple of Marines after a worship service. The young corporal who asked me had wandered into a service I was giving in one of the more remote areas of our desert encampment, near a stockpile of ammunition. He was well-known for his toughness and tenacity—the kind of guy you pray you'll be next to if you're ever in a dark alley all alone. Or in a war, for that matter.

I could tell by the look on his face that his question was not based on detached theoretical inquiry. I was careful with my answer. "God's love never changes," I replied. "If we're willing to open up our lives to His healing power, there is no sin He won't forgive."

"But you don't understand, Chaplain. How could God ever forgive me when He and I both know what I've done?"

As I began to explain God's unfailing love for us through His Son, Jesus, the Marine's eyes welled up with tears. I could see that something inside him was changing. In the moments that followed, the young Marine shared with me some regrets about his life that he had carried for years. He told me that the memory of his misdeeds had kept him from taking so much as a single step into a church building, and that he had never known real joy in his life. At the end of our conversation, he and I bowed our heads in prayer, and together we asked God to give him new life, new joy, and the peace that can only come through God's forgiveness.

Day and night, similar conversations with young Marines and sailors continued. In tents, lying in fighting holes, sitting together over MREs, warming ourselves by the fire, questions abounded, coming from men who were searching for answers. Life, death, salvation, heaven, hell, forgiveness, broken relationships, learning to trust again: these were the issues first and foremost on their minds. Sweeping through the camp were a hunger for God and a hunger for spiritual resolution.

As we gathered in a large white tent one afternoon, I immediately noticed that our Bible study group had landed more takers than I had expected. We had been talking about forgiving others, and toward the end of our session, I asked if there was anyone who had questions. There were more hands in the air than I could count. I tried my best to provide answers, or to at least point them toward relevant biblical passages.

"Chaplain, what if someone in your life has truly hurt you . . . deeply? How do you ever forgive them? You're always talking about forgiveness. You don't understand what . . . what they did to me."

The young lance corporal made no effort to disguise his pain. After sitting through the Bible study with thirty fellow Marines, he could no longer hold back his emotions. I silently prayed that I'd say the right words. "Forgiveness is not easy," I began. "And sometimes, forgiving is more for our good than for the sake of those who have hurt us. Do you want to talk about what happened to you?"

He did. And as he did, Marines all over the room began to resonate with similar experiences. They talked about broken homes, betrayals, failures and disappointments, dying marriages, expectations not met, and debilitating fears. One by one, they opened their lives up to the possibility of God's healing and restoration. They shared with one another deeply personal stories that they'd kept to themselves all their lives.

What had started out as a couple of minutes of questions turned into two hours of intense soul-searching. We lost track of time, and none of us wanted to leave. God was speaking to our hearts.

A couple of nights later, I walked into the communications tent looking for a Marine who had asked for counseling earlier in the day. I was immediately greeted by Master Sergeant Flowers, the "comm. chief."

"Chaplain, you've got to see this!" he said. "Look at them, all of them."

I found myself staring at the sixty or seventy Marines who made their home in that tent. At first, I didn't know what I was seeing. But then I realized that small groups of five or six were spread out all over the room, huddled together, engaged in intense conversation.

"Chaplain, they're studying the Bible."

"They're doing what?" I replied.

Master Sergeant Flowers was smiling from ear to ear. "I've never seen anything like it," he said. Sergeant Flowers had served in the Marine Corps for almost two decades, had watched innumerable Marines come and go, and had witnessed many real-world contingencies and their accompanying deployments. Now here he was, bearing witness to something completely new.

For forty days the men of First Battalion, Fifth Marine Regiment, camped in the desert of northern Kuwait and prepared themselves for war. Forty days in the wilderness—a duration of biblical proportions. The days were long, and the wind was merciless. The nights were cold, and the sky was always alight with the glow of distant fires burning in a dangerous land. And yet, in that vast, desolate and inhospitable setting, the ache of loneliness, and uncertainty became the blessing of solitude and spiritual hunger.

It has always been in places of barrenness and isolation, where the heart of man begins to perceive that which, in the midst of his

fast-paced life, he never could. Removed from the subtle pleas-
antries and distractions of his work-a-day world, his needs become
simplified and yet more urgent; his ears become more sensitive and
able to hear those gentle songs of heaven beginning to resonate in
his soul. He looks out on the vast but beautiful night sky filled with
thousands of brilliant stars, and he is reminded of a Creator, who
has set the seasons and times and boundaries above for all to marvel
over. He listens as the whipping wind beats against his ears. And in
the all-consuming quiet, he is confronted with his own emptiness,
his own spiritual poverty. He is forced to confront those inner
recesses of the soul that craved the bread of heaven and the water
of life; but until now have only known the emptiness of a fast-food,
image-driven world.

Indeed, whenever God has desired to bring His people into a
deeper understanding of Himself, it has more often than not, been the
wilderness, the desert, the barren places of the world, where He has
chosen to do so. The Old Testament book of Hosea reminds us of this;
when speaking on behalf of the Lord Himself, the prophet foresees:

> Behold, I will allure her, I will call her out into the desert,
> And there I will speak kindly unto her . . .
> —HOSEA 2:14

On the bright afternoon of March 3, only days before we would
witness the terrors of war, forty-nine Marines and sailors gathered
together before the eyes of the entire camp. Professing their newfound faith, they were baptized into the kingdom of God as new
Christians.

MANY DAYS LATER, on March 20, we were twenty miles north, and
Captain Blair Sokol and the men of Alpha Company had just
crossed into Iraq. Twelve AAVs and three M-1 Abrams tanks crept
slowly along, each driver's eyes constantly checking his forward,

flanks, and rear for any sign of the enemy. Our own artillery fire was still lighting up the sky as steel Marine Corps beasts churned through the sand and sediment of the desert. The evening was cool and damp, but the inside of each swaying AAV was stifling hot, crammed with twenty-five Marines in combat gear, who were squeezed into a space no bigger than a dentist's office lobby. Sweat dripped down their foreheads. They shifted continually, adjusting themselves, checking and rechecking their gear, making sure they had everything they needed: ammo magazines, grenades, water, night-vision goggles, crosses, prayer cards. They gripped their fully loaded rifles, and more than a few of them prayed. There was no turning back.

Retired Marines and soldiers, who have served in past conflicts, talk about landing on enemy beaches, and most of them report the same ambiguous feelings that Captain Sokol and Alpha Company felt as they crossed over the Iraq border—unsure whether they were walking into a deathtrap or taking a stroll in an abandoned park.

Captain Blair Sokol had arrived at the battalion shortly before September 11, 2001. Since then, he and Alpha Company had earned the reputation of being one of the toughest, most tenacious companies in the First Marine Division. Alpha hiked faster, stayed out in the field longer, and slept less than any other unit around.

But of course, Sokol was only requiring of his men what he required of himself. At 6'7" he was a former Naval Academy starting offensive lineman, who not only towered over his contemporaries, but also exuded an aura of strength. His personal discipline manifested itself in a near-perfect military persona, complete with high-polished boots, heavy-starched cammies, and a rigorously maintained shaved head. Yet as daunting as he was, his demeanor was rather quiet, even studious. Never the social type, Captain Sokol would much rather prefer to bury himself in a good book on military history or the psyche of the soldier than exchange late-night glory stories with the guys. Of course his stoic personality only made him more intimidating. But once I got to know him, I discovered that he was more than a paragon of machismo. He was also a man possessing a thoroughly engaging Christian faith.

Blair Sokol had a Roman Catholic background, and I believe with all my heart that his spiritual leadership as Alpha Company's commanding officer resulted in the awesome religious awakening that occurred in that company during the war. He even asked me to come to his command tent one day and deliver a sermon. Of course attendance was optional, but there was no doubt in my mind that Sokol wanted to give his troops every opportunity to make their peace with God.

On this night, March 20, 2003, Alpha Company's mission was simple. They were to secure an abandoned rock quarry so the battalion commander could set up a hasty command post. From there, Sokol and his staff could direct the companies in their attacks. Riding in a vehicle near the center of the company's column, Sokol called to each of his platoon commanders— McCully, Shull, Horton, Childers, and Broaddus—to check whether they were seeing anything suspicious. They had all trained together for months, each one charged with leading forty-five riflemen into whatever situation the mission demanded. All of them scanned the sea of blackness to their left and right, looking for anything that could provide cover for enemy forces to fire from: a structure, a vehicle, a suspicious outline. They saw nothing but desert. Perhaps the first ten kilometers really was what the intelligence reports had predicted it to be—empty.

But at 8:30 p.m., when Alpha Company had just logged two kilometers inside Iraq, First Lieutenant Adam McCully spotted something to his right that made him nervous. It was at least one thousand meters away, but it was definitely a man-made structure. He quickly adjusted his night-vision goggles to gain a sharper focus. He hadn't even noticed that the flashes from the exploding artillery shells had momentarily ceased. Now with a south wind blowing, the night gave off a strange quietness. Lieutenant McCully squinted and tried to focus on the object.

It was two tanks, and immediately he recognized that they weren't ours.

McCully's stomach sank and his fingers fumbled to key the

handset on the side of his helmet. "Apache 6, Apache 6. This is Apache 1. We've got contact. Two enemy tanks to my east; maybe a thousand yards . . . I think they're T-52s."

"Contact!"

The word reverberated throughout the headsets of every platoon commander. It meant just one thing—the enemy was in sight. Within seconds the Marines in each one of Alpha's AAVs had heard the report as well. Clustered together, they once again attempted to prepare themselves, rechecking the condition of their weapons, swallowing hard. Each AAV had a steel ramp in the back that could swing open in seconds, allowing two squads of men to rush out, guns blaring if necessary. Were they ready?

Meanwhile, the driver of Lieutenant McCully's AAV was turning the barrel of his .50-caliber machine-gun toward the two tanks. And by now their enemy clearly wasn't just tanks. Scurrying to and fro around the vehicles were Iraqi soldiers brandishing weapons and calling out orders. The driver couldn't see what the Iraqis were doing, and he didn't really care to find out. He let out a short burst from his machine-gun then waited for a moment to see how close to target he had come. The red-hot tracer rounds actually made it easier to see one's degree of accuracy at night. His rounds must have fallen close to the enemy troops because the Iraqis suddenly hit the dirt.

Everyone knew that it would take just only one enemy tank round to impact one of our AAVs, and in the blink of an eye, twenty-five men would be obliterated. Captain Sokol worked fast to direct fire on the two tanks, even though they still had not fired back. And all the while he was painfully aware that for some reason, intelligence had not known about them. The next obvious question had to be, "What else is out there that we don't know about?" Lieutenant Colonel Fred Padilla, who had been listening in on the engagement the entire time, was asking himself the same thing. Padilla, who was not far from the rock quarry himself, didn't like the looks of things.

No matter what army you're talking about, the formula is pretty consistent when it comes to tank warfare: two tanks rarely ever venture out alone. Padilla and the rest of the battle planners had to square with the possibility that there might well be more enemy tanks and infantry units closing in toward the border, taking advantage of the thick cover of darkness and dust. Padilla radioed back to Sokol concerning the enemy.

"Roger that, Apache 6. Use whatever means necessary to engage and destroy them. I'm sending Bravo Company to reinforce."

Captain Sokol immediately dispatched a javelin team to fire a vehicle-mounted rocket at the second tank, which now appeared to be in mass confusion due to the machine-guns firing from McCully's AAV. And that's when he first heard another sound snapping over his head, like a whip being cracked. It was unmistakable—incoming bullets. But where were they coming from?

As far as Sokol could tell, the two tanks to the east were being effectively engaged, and so far they weren't firing back. Major Steve Armes, riding not far behind in another AAV, heard the bullets too; so did Chief Warrant Officer Phil Ross, the battalion's NBC officer. Someone else was firing at the Marines. The enemy tanks weren't alone.

By now, Corporals Spears and Lee, the javelin team attached to McCully's First Platoon, had their sights set on the enemy tanks, praying for a direct hit. There wasn't a man in the entire company who didn't realize what they were up against. When the all-clear was given to fire, Lee, sitting atop his armored Humvee, held his breath and pulled the trigger of his weapon. Nothing. He pulled the trigger again and again. Still nothing. His weapon system had failed, and time was running out.

The Iraqis could now clearly see where our men were hunkered down, and each second gave them more time to turn their turrets on our men and level deadly blows. A second javelin was already being primed and charged for the shot.

"Dear God, help us," Spears cried out under his breath as his hands frantically worked over Lee's weapon to check which part of the system was not engaging.

The two got set for another try. The second missile was now leveled and good to go. "Sight on target . . . all clear . . . fire!"

Again nothing. A *second* weapon system failure. The electrical circuit responsible for transmitting the charge to the fuse had misfired. More to the point, the turret of the Iraqi tank began to slowly pivot in the direction of the Marines.

The AAV gunner was still blasting away at the first tank, and it looked like his rounds were finally on the mark. The Iraqis who had not been hit had either begun to run away or to climb back inside the tank for cover. McCully felt that he had at least made a mobility kill, and the tank was now rendered dead. He called in the results to Captain Sokol, who had made positive visual contact with the source of the mysterious rounds that had been cracking overhead for the last couple of minutes.

The shots were coming from an Iraqi troop carrier (BMP) positioned less than a thousand meters to his west. There was no way of knowing how many enemy troops had already dismounted the vehicle or had moved unnoticed under the thick cover of darkness.

"All clear?" Spears had his javelin team up and ready. He had looked over the system and could find no reason to believe it wouldn't fire this time. Lee, seated on the top of his vehicle, braced his feet against the inner ring of the circular turret and placed the red cross hairs of his sight directly in the middle of the opposing enemy tank.

The all-clear was given. Lee pulled the trigger.

With a blast that could be heard in every sealed vehicle in the forward convoy, the armor-piercing rocket launched out of the tube and filled the night sky with a back-blast of stunning light and noise, accompanied by the sensation of having the wind literally sucked out of your lungs.

Lee, who fired the shot, slowly began to count, "One one-thousand, two one-thousand, three one thousand, four . . ."

The explosion was too distant to be especially loud. But after watching the flames and debris leap up and outward from the tank's hull, both Lee and Spears knew it was a direct hit.

Soon the Iraqi BMP off to the west suffered a similar fate. While Spears and Lee were busy engaging the tank to the east, Sokol had managed to contact a section of our own M-1 Abrams tank that was now in position to help. Ask any infantry officer, and he will tell you that the best weapon against a tank is a better tank. The M-1 Abrams is certainly the best. Moving in on the scene like an angry avenger, the Abrams closed the distance with the BMP, acquired its coordinate, and fired. Seconds later, the enemy hull was barely recognizable.

So began the first ground engagement in the war with Iraq, and although it was a victory for our Marines, it still raised questions. Most notably, the presence of the enemy, undetected and so close to the border, was most disturbing to the men in charge of the battle. If reconnaissance flights had not discovered these enemy forces, what else might be lurking in the shadows of the southern Rumeilah oil fields?

That wasn't the only question. For Captain Sokol, the most striking aspect of the encounter lay in the fact that for some unknown reason, the Iraqi tanks had never fired their main guns. The firepower of an Iraq T-52 tank alone, can, if on the mark, decimate an American AAV and kill every man inside. One round and the Iraqis would have plunged our battalion into catastrophe. They'd had every opportunity, yet it never happened. Why?

As our forward companies penetrated more deeply into the southern Iraqi oil fields, our combat train paused on the side of a dirt road, just inside the Iraq border. After getting separated from our convoy three times in the blackest night we had ever seen, Rufo and I, our hands still trembling, had thankfully joined the others.

I stepped out of my vehicle, leaned against the hood, and took a deep breath, scanning the field to my east. Marines were being dispatched to search the dark wasteland for enemy movement. Like so many shadowy dots up and down the dirt road, lying in a prone position, I could see them peering through their night-vision goggles, searching for even the slightest hint of trouble.

The dampness and chill of the air mixed with the sweat on my neck and forehead, forcing a shiver down my flak jacket and into my bones. It was quiet, disturbingly quiet. The distant sound of artillery was unceasing but low enough that I could hear the wind on the sides of my helmet. Every once in a while I recognized the hot glow of distant tracer fire as it volleyed from some soldier's rifle. Iraqi or Coalition? I couldn't say. The effect was a sickening feeling in my stomach.

And still the oil wells captivated me. Although they were more than a thousand yards away, their towering flames licked up the dark sky around them with such volatility that I could hear a deep rumbling sound mingled with the percussive snap of exploding fuel. Even if it sounded a little like a crackling hearth, I wasn't exactly feeling the good cheer of a cozy fireside. The scene reminded me more of a scene from Dante's *Inferno*.

The flames from the oil fields were actually nothing more than exhaust, typical of any gas-oil separation plant—I'd seen many of them driving across Texas. But on that pitch-black night, March 20, 2003, they served as a hallmark of the fear, desolation, and ruination that inevitably follows when humans oppress one another. The scene was nightmarish. Raging flames blazed against a backdrop of utter darkness. The night seethed with danger and smelled of death. The sense of hostility in the air was palpable.

Yet God was with us.

In the early morning hours of the next day, I learned not only that the enemy tanks had failed to fire their main guns, but that a brigade of three thousand Iraqi soldiers, armed with enough rifles, rockets, and mortars to inflict awful losses upon our battalion, was surrendering en masse. If even half those Iraqi soldiers had fought as they had been ordered to, the first hours of our invasion would have been a deadly confrontation, costing many lives on both sides of the conflict.

During our last three weeks in Kuwait, intelligence had confirmed that the nearly empty Rumeilah oil fields were becoming a veritable hornet's nest of enemy activity. As many as three thousand Iraqi soldiers had begun to mass around the oil plants and pumping stations, equipped with all the trappings of modern war—artillery, rocket-launchers, tanks, antiaircraft guns. Yet in what almost seemed like an orchestrated collapse, hundreds of Iraqi soldiers had simply raised their arms and begged for surrender.

Admittedly, most of them were conscripts who had been forced by the Republican Guard to enlist in the Regular Army and fight to the death. Still, they had their orders, and enough vitriolic rhetoric behind those orders made it very clear what their generals wanted of them. Indeed, we would go on to find out that many enemy troops were commanded to do no more than pull a pre-sighted trigger lanyard, a single act that would have sent a barrage of artillery and rocket fire raining down upon us. But instead of pulling those lanyards, instead of taking up arms and fighting, instead of making the most of their overwhelming three-to-one odds, nearly all the Iraqis, to the man, either vanished altogether or begged for mercy.

Of course reasonable explanations for the behavior of the Iraqi soldiers abounded: bad equipment, no will to fight, lack of internal communications, poor night vision, and the element of surprise. And all of these surely played some part in their sudden collapse. But perhaps even more compelling were the letters I had received days before our attack, from people all across America who promised that they were praying. More specifically, they were praying that once we had crossed into harm's way, God would restrain and confuse the enemy. A letter from a grandmother from Mississippi captures the spirit of thousands, maybe millions of prayer warriors who went before us into battle:

We are asking God for three things concerning this war:
1. Confusion among the generals of Saddam's army; chaos—causing them to lay down their arms.
2. Salvation for many!
3. Legions of warring angels with drawn swords going before you as you make your approach.
We know God is able![1]

Could the results of those prayers have been any clearer? We saw confusion, chaos, mass surrender, and the laying down of arms. Many of the Iraqi soldiers that our forward companies encountered during the night ran right out of their boots, pleading for capture rather than having to face the onslaught of approaching American troops. Several Marines confided in me after the night's crossing, that they could actually *hear* the enemy before they could see them. Wailing in Arabic and begging for pardon, hundreds of them fled toward the approaching AAVs in the dark, their arms raised high in surrender, their forms silhouetted against the flaming oil fields.

One young Marine told me about seeing an enemy soldier cautiously approaching the rolling convoy then stop dead in his tracks. The Iraqi looked up as if to the heavens, mumbled something in Arabic, then fell on his face seconds later in abject surrender. It looked to us as if the enemy was collapsing right before our eyes. Armed with enough weaponry and sheer numbers to have brought great loss of life upon our battalion, the enemy forces instead turned away from the conflict.

We had stormed across the border nine hours before any other unit could provide flank support to our east or west, leaving us vulnerable on both sides. We had no forward air protection from hidden enemy targets, leaving us wide open to the enemy's heavy guns and tanks. And because the preliminary eight-hour artillery bombardment was called off, we were attacking a waiting enemy force that had not been sufficiently disoriented by the "shock and awe" caused by a full-blown artillery strike. In the words of one officer, "We were walking into a potential lion's den."

Perhaps a more apt description might have been a "fiery furnace."

I couldn't help but think of another group of men who once found themselves surrounded by death and destruction. More than two thousand years ago, those three men refused to bow down and worship an idol, and they were therefore thrust into a fiery oven by a wicked king who expected them to be consumed alive by the oven's flames. Knowing their cause was right, Shadrach, Meshach, and Abednego, three faithful followers of God, chose of their own accord to be thrown into the furnace rather than to pay homage to the king's idol. In what might have been their last words, they said,

> If that is the case, our God whom we serve is able to deliver us from the burning fiery furnace, and He will deliver us from your hand, O king. But if not, let it be known to you, O king, that we do not serve your gods, nor will we worship the gold image which you have set up.
>
> —Daniel 3:17–18

"Our God whom we serve is able to deliver us . . ." The three courageous souls had no idea just how able He was.

> Then King Nebuchadnezzar was astonished; and he rose in haste and spoke, saying to his counselors, "Did we not cast three men bound into the midst of the fire?" They answered and said to the king, "True, O king."
>
> "Look!" he answered, "I see four men loose, walking in the midst of the fire; and they are not hurt, and the form of the fourth is like the Son of God.
>
> —Daniel 3:25

The men of First Battalion, Fifth Marines, like Shadrach, Meshach, and Abednego, had walked into a fiery furnace. And like the three ancient followers of the true God, the U.S. Marines had not experienced the death and destruction that might have been. Instead, God had shown us His peace, empowerment, and divine protection.

God had been with us, and as I looked out upon the towering fires of Iraq's oil fields, for a brief moment I didn't see a symbol of death and ruination. I didn't feel the hand of oppression and desolation. No, what I experienced was a sense of assurance that promised me I was not alone; a sense of assurance that I would later discover was sensed by many in our battalion that night—from the youngest privates to our battalion commander himself.

I suppose there will never be a way to ask the Iraqi soldiers what they saw when we stormed through the breach and into their land that first dark night on March 20—what made them surrender so quickly, laying down their arms at once, what made them decide not to fire their guns. But there can be no doubt in any of our minds about the "Fourth"—the One who was loosed and walking among us, providing for our every need, delivering us from the hand of evil, empowering us to be faithful.

4
K.I.A.

SECOND LIEUTENANT Therrel "Shane" Childers was the eldest son of Joe and Judy Childers, born on June 19, 1972, in West Hamlin, West Virginia. Shane, as he came to be affectionately known, grew up doing all the things little boys love to do—hunting, fishing, terrorizing his siblings, and pretending to be a soldier. His father, Joe, had served an entire career in the navy as a member of the famous Seabees Construction Battalion. In 1990, Shane followed in his father's steps and, fulfilling one of his boyhood dreams, joined the military. But for Shane it would be the Marines.

Having had the opportunity to travel with his father to the American embassy in Tehran when he was a little boy, Shane spotted something that would forever alter the course of his life. He saw two stone-faced Marine infantrymen guarding the gates. From that point on he knew, whatever those guys were, he wanted to be one of them. Only a few months after joining the Corps, Shane got his wish and found himself driving Light Armored Vehicles over the sands of Saudi Arabia and Kuwait. By the end of 1991, he was only nineteen and already a war veteran.

With a combat tour already under his belt, Shane was accepted to the highly competitive Marine Security Guard Program. Only those who have an outstanding record and excellent physical fitness, and who can produce extremely high scores on a rigorous aptitude test are accepted. The reward is a prize military job—serving as a special guard detachment to a foreign embassy or consulate. Childers's first assignment was to the American consulate in Geneva, Switzerland, where he not only guarded the compound but broadened his mind. Shane was deeply inquisitive, and not in a trivial way. His bent was definitely philosophical and religious. This leaning was no doubt strengthened at his next tour of duty, guarding the American embassy in Nairobi, Kenya.

In 1998, Shane Childers entered the Citadel in Charleston, South Carolina, where he graduated in 2001 as a commissioned Second Lieutenant. Since we were both alumni, the Citadel became common ground between Shane and me, a subject of many of our discussions. It was one of those bonds based on common experience that can never be erased.

Shane was wiry and athletic, and when I first met him he was doing what he loved to do the most—leading riflemen. He arrived at Camp Pendleton in the summer of 2002 as one of our "Lieutenants of Destiny"—brand-new infantry officers who came to First Battalion as we were readying ourselves for our impending deployment to Iraq. As a chaplain, I had begun to notice the way Marines, even senior Marines, offer respect and deference to young new-joins (whether they be enlisted fresh out of recruit training or officers straight out of Quantico) who enter a unit at a time of impending war.

One example of this was Staff Sergeant Betancourt of Charlie Company. Even though he had been in the Marine Corps for more than twelve years, his men still talked about his first tour of duty. Only days after graduating from the school of infantry (1991), he was sitting on a military transport flying to the Persian Gulf where he was soon fighting as a rifleman against the fleeing Iraqi Army. This story gave Sergeant Betancourt something akin to military sainthood.

Shane Childers, like the other new second lieutenants, wore the same halo.

By the time Shane and I met, he had already established himself as a leader, and over the course of the next months, I couldn't keep track of the many times he was in my office, asking advice about how he could help out his young grunts. Whether it was their finances, marriages, or family lives, it didn't matter. Because of this, his men loved him, and he loved them. He loved them to the end.

MARCH 20, 2003, never quite ended; it just blurred into the following day. After our initial engagement with the enemy, we traveled all night, and as the last vestiges of darkness finally drained away, we saw the dull orange Middle Eastern sun rising above the now war-scarred Rumeilah oil fields. The distant booming of artillery and air strikes thundered like drums. Occasionally an explosion felt closer than the rest, causing my stomach to tense and my eyes to dart wildly in both directions, searching for danger.

By daybreak March 21, 2003, our convoy had traveled no more than eight to ten miles into Rumeilah, and now we found ourselves on a wide-open gravel road where we sat awaiting further orders. To our north stood three burning oil plants, belching huge flames of fire upward into the pale-blue sky. To the south, an enormous herd of camels wandered about aimlessly, their expanse almost neverending in sight. Even they were suspect—our security platoon continued to watch them, in case they were somehow serving as a shield for enemy troops. On my immediate left, no more than a couple of football fields away, was a small oil facility. I could see two civilians standing in the front of the structure waving white flags furiously and hoping to get our attention. I could only imagine what they had been through in the past hours.

It was barely 6:00 a.m. The air was still chilly, and all of us needed a good shave. I pulled out my journal and began to write. I wanted to record exactly what I was experiencing, not so much because it was remarkable, but because I had the feeling of being on another planet. Our location was not just geographically far away from my family and friends, but it was truly another world where different values shaped the society, different dangers abounded, and different customs and norms governed behavior, some of which were antithetical to ours. After writing for a while, I stepped out of my Humvee and made my way to the front of the column. Rufo followed closely. Sometimes I forgot that I was unarmed and that anytime I got up to go anywhere, it meant Rufo had to go along since his rifle was the only protection for the two of us.

First Lieutenant Chad Roberts and Gunnery Sergeant James Kirkham sat in the lead vehicle of our combat train, monitoring the radio, keeping an eye on one of the burning oil plants. In the year and a half that I had served as the battalion's chaplain, I had not gotten to know either of them very well. But now, having driven with them for the last three days, I felt like I had known them for years. The bond that develops between those who have shared experiences in war is hard to explain. One or two good fire-fights, or dangerous breach crossings, and we felt our friendships extended way, way back. Perhaps that bond is one of the few "graces" of war.

Bond or no bond, however, there was no question who was in charge. Lieutenant Chad Roberts was hands-down one of the most authoritarian Marine officers I had ever met. A former enlisted Marine from Ohio City, Ohio, Roberts stood about 5'9" and had the build of a college wrestler. He had already served in the Marine Corps before becoming an officer, so at twenty-eight he was older than most lieutenants. He rarely smiled during the entire war and I'm not sure I wanted him to. His job was critical and demanded nothing short of constant vigilance and security awareness.

Lieutenant Roberts was responsible for ensuring that our forward rifle companies, who were bearing the brunt of the fighting, had enough fuel, ammunition, food, water, and mechanical parts. Moreover, he was responsible for seeing that every vehicle in our train stayed up to speed, which at times had to be lightning fast. And unlike a forward rifle company where heavy machine-guns and mortars abound, our security consisted only of rifles and one heavy machine-gun. All of it rested on Robert's young, but admittedly stern, shoulders.

Thankfully, his chief assistant, Gunnery Sergeant Kirkham, had served as a Marine sniper earlier in his career. He, like Roberts, didn't smile much, but the two of them gave our train such a sense of security and wherewithal, that we all would have literally followed them through the gates of hell. Indeed, come to think of it, in just a few short days, we just about did.

Like the rest of the men in our company, as their chaplain, I had a responsibility to the two of them as well. But that morning, as Rufo and I walked to their vehicle, I had no agenda but to say hello, and make my presence known. It was then that an urgent call came in over the battalion radio net.

"Casualty! Casualty! Two Marines down at Pumping Station 2. Request chaplain."

The voice was that of Captain Wil Dickens, the headquarters company commander. The message was short and choppy and provided no more information. I turned toward Roberts.

"Isn't Pumping Station 2 Alpha Company?"

He nodded his head.

Immediately, I began searching my mind, wondering who in Alpha could have been injured. I could see so many of their faces right now—Guthrie, Cecil, Sandell, Talley. What had happened? Who was it? Silently I prayed that the situation wasn't even more serious, but I knew what the possibilities were. Despite reports that large numbers of the enemy had surrendered without much of a fight, it would take only one stubborn Iraqi soldier to change everything. In any case, since a chaplain had been requested, I would soon find out for myself.

Rufo and I ran back to our vehicle and waited for the security team to come for us and to escort us to the site.

Before the war had started, intelligence had reported that enemy resistance could be fiercer at the oil pumping stations than anywhere else. These sprawling complexes were built to pump the huge volumes of petroleum being produced in Rumeilah's gas/oil separation plants. Because they were so critical to Iraq's revenue, if we wanted to be able to help the people of Iraq, we would seize these complexes first.

Within minutes the dust of a speeding Humvee signaled the approach of Captain Dickens, whose vehicle was mounted with a Mark-19 grenade launcher on the top. It would be something I would have to get used to in the weeks ahead—traveling anywhere meant going with security. The landscape was just too dangerous for Rufo and me to drive alone, especially in a nonarmored vehicle like ours.

Driving away from the combat train into open desert gave us a definite feeling of vulnerability. We were out of sight of everyone, and I knew in the back of my mind that there was no way every pocket of Iraqi soldiers had been rooted out. That would have been impossible in such a vast and desolate region.

As we drove on, I saw more and more signs of the previous night's artillery bombardment. There was wreckage everywhere—burned-out hulls of tanks, troop carriers, bunkers, smoke rising in large plumes. Here and there a waft of smoke leaked out of a bunker that had, in all likelihood, become an instant tomb.

When we finally arrived at our destination, I quickly stepped outside my vehicle and tightened my door shut (it was always coming loose). Looking over my shoulder to the right, I stared at what looked like an outdoor amphitheater. Marines were walking around its perimeter, rifles held tightly against their bodies. As I approached the site, I realized what it was—a makeshift enemy prisoner of war (EPW) holding facility. There must have been two hundred Iraqi soldiers inside. Most of them were sitting Indian-style, some smoking cigarettes, several with no boots on their feet, all carefully watching the Bravo Company Marines who were guarding them.

Just then Captain Dickens updated me about the two Alpha Company casualties. There was no way I, or anyone standing with us, could have been prepared for his words.

"KIA. One of them was killed in action."

My heart sank. My impulse was to grab Dickens and shout, "No! It's not true. Nobody's dead!"

Instead I quietly asked, "Dear God, who was it?"

"It was Shane."

In the hours that followed, as I talked to the men who had been with him, I was able to piece together the last hours of Lieutenant Shane Childers's life.

Alpha Company had already come through the gauntlet of the first night's breach crossing, and they had done so with no casualties. The Iraqi tanks that had materialized just across the border had capitulated, and the cacophony of voices coming across the radio from other companies indicated a massive enemy surrender in the area. Whether the supposed surrender was genuine or not, Captain Sokol and the men from Alpha assumed nothing.

As their staggered column of AAVs roared north toward Pumping Station 2, Captain Sokol keyed his company's radio frequency. Every platoon commander could hear his voice. "This is Apache 6. Be advised, significant enemy still expected at or around the southwest and southeast corners of the Pumping Station. Assume nothing. How copy?"

One by one the young platoon commanders answered, "Solid copy . . . solid copy. . . ."

The early light of the sun was only beginning to brighten the eastern horizon when Captain Sokol called his column to a halt no more than one thousand meters from the southwest corner of the plant. Intelligence had reported that well-entrenched bunkers, artillery pieces, and antiaircraft guns were skirting the southern flank of the compound. From where he was sitting in his AAV, Sokol felt sure they were there. It was too quiet, and Marines had reported seeing shadowy figures darting around the area.

Before the first real light of day revealed his position, Sokol relayed a call that eventually got to the "cannon cockers" of Fox 2/11. He requested Fox to let loose fifteen minutes of artillery fire on the suspected enemy positions surrounding Pumping Station 2.

This would allow the company to push around the western flank of the compound and, while utter chaos was raining down upon the Iraqis, envelop it from the north.

Within ninety seconds the young artillerymen, located eight or nine miles away, began pulling the trigger lanyards on their Howitzers and firing the round of choice: DP-ICM. That particularly deadly shell explodes while still in the air, directly over the target, showering the enemy with multiple bomblets that are deadly enough to render him incapable of repelling an advancing attack.

When the rain of explosives began, the percussion of the impacting rounds was almost too much for the unsuspecting Iraqis to tolerate. As the blasts sent shock waves throughout their intricate underground bunkers and caves, Captain Sokol and his men methodically moved west in a giant semicircle. After fifteen minutes of bombardment, the entire company was situated on the northern end of the compound. The Iraqis, still reeling over the artillery attack, were oriented south, certain that a Coalition attack would come from the direction of the border. Many of them never saw what hit them. As one hundred sixty Marines systematically began to sweep down from the north, most of the Iraqis simply dropped their guns and ran. A few others hunkered down and fought in last-ditch desperation.

What followed was a skirmish, which although relatively small in scale, was right out of an infantryman's training manual.

Interestingly enough, although war has drastically changed in technology in the past sixty years, the method for clearing a "hot trench" or bunker is still the same as it was for the men who did it on Okinawa or Normandy. A grenade is tossed in. There is a brief wait, followed by an explosion. Then a team of riflemen burst in, each positioned to fire at different angles, each man holding his rifle in order to guard the man next to him, every gun poised to erupt at a trigger's pull. Alpha had practiced this age-old method of doing battle for weeks and weeks. They proved their mettle on the morning of 21 March 2003.

The few Iraqi soldiers who did decide to fight were no match for our well-disciplined men. Almost as a last resort, some enemy soldiers did attempt to swing the massive turrets of an antiaircraft gun down at face level and use it as a heavy machine-gun. If they had been successful, the results might have been gruesome. However, one of our M-1 Abrams tanks discovered the attempt before the enemy pulled it off. One round from the Abrams, and the gun and its gunners were no more. One of our Marines did, however, manage to set off a "toe-popper" land mine.

When the explosion occurred, Corporal Brent Gross didn't know what hit him. He had been sweeping through the compound, rifle raised at eye level, ready to fire at any unexpected threat. He had no way of knowing that among the rubbish-strewn field, the Iraqis had buried dozens of those "nasty little doohickies," as some Marines called them. Mine explosions are not necessarily intended to kill, but are surely meant to maim. Why? Because a maimed soldier takes more out of a unit than a dead one. He will need at least one, probably two buddies to carry him, burdening them with extra responsibilities.

Fortunately, when Corporal Gross set off this land mine, it barely even did that. Blowing his outer chemical protective boot to shreds, the shock sprained his ankle and slightly cut his foot. That was it—he was into a safe area to await a medevac helicopter. Corporal Gross was the first of the two casualties that morning.

The fighting went on sporadically for the next thirty minutes to an hour, and Alpha Company became more emboldened with each inch of ground they gained. By the time they had reached the southern flank, every Iraqi who was not running for his life had thrown his hands into the air in surrender, pleading for mercy.

Still at high alert, a couple of Alpha's platoons began processing the captured Iraqi soldiers. From across the southern most road the weary soldiers began to pour, hands lifted high, frightened looks on their faces. Many of them were bleeding from their ears and noses because of the previous night's artillery bombardment. Occasionally a stray round would be heard flying overhead as a few holdout Iraqi soldiers clung to their orders: "Fight until the bitter end." But most had some sense, and seeing they were being overwhelmed from every direction, they simply gave up and collapsed.

We later learned from our intelligence sources that the overwhelming majority of these men were forced at gunpoint to conscript into the Iraqi Army in the first place. The Republican Guard knew that the densest concentration of U.S. forces would be in the Rumeilah oil fields. Thus, using threats and intimidation, they bused most of these forced conscripts into the area weeks prior to our invasion. They provided them with aging weapons and a cache of ammunition. Many were told that if they didn't cooperate, they would have no wives or children to return to. One Iraqi soldier confided in an intelligence officer after the fight that the only direction he was given by the Republican guard officer who had conscripted him was, "You'd better not leave this bunker when the Americans come."

By 7:00 a.m. it looked as if most the shooting had ceased. Iraqi soldiers from across the road, where the majority of the bunkers and fighting holes were, flooded the compound with their hands in the air. Marines from Alpha methodically processed them as best they could. Still, it was a bit confusing. Sokol knew that every bunker had not yet been cleared. He was well aware that the appearance of a complete surrender was just that—only an appearance.

By now the sun was well above the horizon, shedding light on every dark corner that the Marines had swept through in the hours before dawn. Daylight brought both the comfort of being able to see and the mild alarm of being seen yourself. If there is one thing U.S. forces do better than anyone else in the world, it is fighting at night. I'm amazed at the kind of high-tech night combat gear issued to the newest of new-joins in an infantry battalion. In fact, one of the quickest ways to get your name known to the command leadership is to lose a pair of night-vision goggles. A thorough investigation usually follows.

Nevertheless, daylight did bring good feelings for most of the men of Alpha. The sheer size of their AAVs and tanks, which were now visible to all the Iraqis, had to be intimidating. Nothing wrong with that. So, as the men from Second Lieutenant Nick Horton's Third Platoon kept watch on the southwestern flank, Childers's men readied themselves to reboard their AAVs. There were still a few bunkers that had not been cleared, and Sokol had tasked Shane's platoon to saddle up and move into the uncovered areas.

The warmth of the sun was finally causing beads of sweat to form on the Marines' foreheads and upper lips. Even though the distant sound of artillery was unceasing, the occasional chirp of a sparrow seemed to lighten everyone's spirits, reminding them that even in the carnage of war, life goes on. The sporadic gunfire had now completely stopped, and it looked as if the remainder of the morning would consist of little more than tightening up the area and holding EPWs for the support battalions who were on their way.

Then the hidden enemy made its move.

Lance Corporal Jeff Guthrie saw the strange vehicle first. It was a light brown pickup truck, and by the time he saw it coming, it was already moving at more than 50 mph. It had been hidden behind a concrete wall several hundred yards down the road. Its occupants, seven Iraqi gunmen, had been waiting for just the right time to speed by and fire their high-powered assault rifles into the crowd of unsuspecting Marines. As the truck began to accelerate, Lieutenant Childers was continuing to corral his men into the back of the AAV, each man stepping up onto the steel door dubbed as a gang-plank. Seeing the group of Marines huddled together boarding the AAV, the driver slammed his foot down on the accelerator and began a suicidal course that would both send our Marines reeling and seal his own fate.

Within milliseconds of seeing the speeding vehicle, Guthrie rightly assumed the worst. The crazed driver, swerving deliberately from the right side of the road to the left, headed directly toward Guthrie, who along with several others had to literally dive off the shoulder of the road into the brush. It was then that the deadly salvo began.

Just as Childers and the others realized that something was wrong, the brown truck reached its top speed of 70 mph, and the firing started. Holding their assault rifles over the railing of the truck and parallel to the ground, the five gunmen lying in the bed of the vehicle began spraying a stream of lead toward Shane Childers and his men.

The crack of Iraqi rounds exploded over the heads of the Marines, slamming into the sides of the armored vehicles, kicking up geysers of dirt next to their feet. Almost instantly, Corporal Odom and Lance Corporal Lamb, who were standing near Childers, hit the deck and began firing back into the side paneling and window of the passing truck. Within moments of the initial volley, the rifle barrels of thirty infantrymen were blazing back, the impact of their rounds nearly lifting the vehicle off its wheels.

Still, the Iraqis had managed to squeeze off four or five stray shots into the small cluster of Marines at the back of the AAV. All the shots missed save one. It struck Shane Childers in the lower abdomen, just beneath his protective flak jacket. For a moment, he staggered back, clinching at his clothes, unsure of what had happened.

Childers's platoon, not aware that their leader had been struck, sought immediate revenge for the unprovoked "drive-by." As the truck continued to speed past, every rifleman within sight opened up, shredding the sides of the truck, disintegrating metal, tires, and whatever was left. The truck careened off the road, finally stopping at the bottom of a shallow embankment. By then its fuselage was all but gone, its windows were shattered, and it was covered in blood.

Meanwhile, Childers was lying on his back grasping at his clothes, searching for his wound, a blank stare of shock and confusion on his face. The lone bullet had passed completely through him, and he was quickly losing both blood and strength. Odom started yelling wildly for the corpsman.

"Doc, Doc! Lieutenant's been hit! Lieutenant's down! We need a doc!"

At the same time, Staff Sergeant Nerad, Childers's second in command, reached down and picked up the wounded officer, slung him over his shoulders, and carried him to the lowered AAV ramp.

Nerad kept talking to Childers: "It's gonna be all right, sir, hang in there. We'll get you fixed up in no time. You're doing just fine."

Talk as he might, however, Nerad could feel that Childers half-conscious body was already beginning to go limp.

In response to Odom's urgent plea, three navy medical corpsmen arrived and frantically peeled off Childers's clothing. Docs Tapley, Calzado, and Glanville worked as one, dressing both the entry and exit wounds, administering disinfectant, trying to keep Childers awake. Stripping his vest off his body, they also tried to talk him through, tried keeping him conscious. Their arms were covered in blood up to their elbows.

"Come on, sir! Come on, sir! Hang in there; medevac's on its way. Stay with me, sir!"

The bullet had passed through Shane's liver, and the internal bleeding couldn't be stopped. Corporal Odom cradled Lietenant Childers in his arms, jostling his naked upper body from side to side, trying helplessly to keep him awake, alive.

As the medevac helicopter made its way to Pumping Station 2, Sokol called in the casualty to Lieutenant Colonel Padilla. "Hondo, Hondo, this is Apache 6. Be advised, we have an 'urgent' down with a gunshot wound to the abdomen. Have requested medevac immediately. How copy?"

Padilla, along with the sergeant major, was already en route from his makeshift command post to Alpha's position. "Roger that, Apache 6. I'm on my way now. Be there in ten mikes. Hondo out."

The three "docs" continued to work furiously to keep Childers conscious, their medical bags by their sides, the contents strewn all over the sage brush. "Come on, sir! We're right with you. Hang in there. Medevac's on its way . . . medevac's on its way . . ."

In the end, it was all to no avail. His internal hemorrhaging was fatal, and Second Lieutenant Shane Childers drifted away, with an unexpected look of peace upon his handsome face.

He was the first combat casualty in Operation Iraqi Freedom.

Once the word was passed, despair descended over Alpha

Company. They had lost one of their leaders, and it was only the first day of the war. Even though we were all fully aware of the potential for death and injury that war brings, there was no way any of us could have been prepared for the feelings that swept through our hearts and minds when he died. Childers's platoon was devastated as they watched the lifeless body of their lieutenant being loaded onto the helicopter medevac.

For some, Childers was the one Marine officer who seemed to care about their personal lives—not just as Marines, but as husbands, estranged sons, fathers. For others, he was the one who gave them the opportunity to try again after they failed. Still others saw him as the one who, even if it meant holding them after hours in training, made them mentally tougher than they ever would have believed they could become.

Jeff Guthrie, a Marine who'd seen his fair share of personal setbacks, told me later about Childers's influence on his life. "I always admired him. He loved the Corps, but more than that, he cared about us. Several times, he came over to my house after hours to check and see how me and my wife were doing (we'd had some problems). He didn't have to do that, but that was him. I personally know that he spent well over a thousand dollars of his own money to buy those of us in his platoon some needed equipment that the Marine Corps wouldn't pay for. He was always calling us together and saying, 'Hey guys, look what I got for you,' and then handing out some new piece of gear just so that we would be outfitted with the best stuff. He cared for us all. I remember once when he took me aside after I'd screwed something up, and said, 'Guthrie, you know if I wasn't an officer and these were different circumstances, we could probably be friends . . . you and I. But you know we have to keep the chain-of-command relationship in the platoon, and I need for you to pull yourself together.'" Guthrie would to on to say that losing Lieutenant Childers "was like losing our coach."

First Sergeant James Green, who had driven up just moments before Shane died, called in the update to Captain Sokol, who at this time was still trying to manage the clearing of bunkers that had not yet been secured. "Apache 6, Apache 6, this is Apache 8. Be advised that our 'urgent' is now a 'routine.' Apache 2 Actual is down. How copy?"

The Marine Corps, under advisement from its doctors and corpsmen, must label each casualty with a specific code or nomenclature. "Routine" refers to one of two situations. Either the injury is minor and can be treated effectively by the attending corpsman, or "routine" means the injury is no longer considered an injury because the injured man has died. For a casualty to go from "urgent" to "routine," usually means just one thing.

Still, Sokol couldn't quite believe what Green was relaying to him. Surely the docs had just misdiagnosed Childers's injury the first time as "urgent," and were now downgrading it. But the tone in Green's voice pierced through Sokol's mind—he knew what had happened.

He immediately notified Lieutenant Colonel Padilla, who was now only a minute from the compound. Lieutenant Colonel Padilla told me later that when he heard Sokol's voice he also knew that the worst had happened. One look on the faces of the Alpha Marines, as he stepped out of his command vehicle, confirmed his grief. His diary for that day, 21 March 2003, read,

We lost Second Lieutenant Shane Childers, 2nd Platoon, Alpha Company. He sustained an abdominal gunshot wound during the fight for Pumping Station 2 . . . the Marines and Sailors of Alpha Company and the rest of this battalion are saddened by this terrible loss. It underscores, this isn't a game. These fine young men put it on the line for God and country. . . . I'm very proud of my men. They performed tremendously well in the midst of the fog and friction that is combat. I arrived on the scene at Pumping Station 2 shortly after Second Lieutenant Childers was wounded. When en route, I heard the cas-evac being called in—it was urgent. I then heard, as I was arriving, that the cas-evac was downgraded to routine . . . this is not a good sign and I knew it. The faces of the Marines told the story.

A platoon lost its commander; lieutenants lost a friend, and a company commander lost one of his boys . . . so did the battalion commander. The two corpsmen who tried to save Shane were emotionally and physically exhausted. I spoke with them as they had tears streaming down their cheeks and blood up to their elbows. They tried so hard to save him . . . they simply couldn't. Both Blair Sokol and Spanky Lawler also couldn't fight back the tears as the dust settled . . . nor could I . . . I pray I don't lose another. I can't help thinking that his folks are being paid a terrible visit right around now. I so much wanted to bring all my boys home alive. But that's not my call.

By the time Rufo and I, escorted by Dickens's security team, arrived at Pumping Station 2, Shane's body had already been flown out by the helicopter. Flies buzzed around the heads of the Marines as they sat with their backs resting against the knobby sides of the AAVs' tracks. They were exhausted and made no effort to shoo away the irritating insects. The charred remains of Iraqi bunkers, tanks, and even body parts were strewn across the adjacent fields of the compound, littering the landscape like an unkempt graveyard. Shane's platoon sat huddled around their AAVs, drinking from their canteens, trying to eat (for many it had been almost twenty-four hours since having had any food), or staring off into space. The looks on their faces told the story. No one could believe he was gone.

In the infantry, when a man falls in battle, the most senior man beneath him must step up and assume the place of the fallen leader. That man was Staff Sergeant Bradley Nerad, a big, brawny Marine with a deep New England accent and a large, intimidating jaw. I had just baptized Nerad as a new Christian about two weeks earlier, and it was Nerad's baptism that had inspired more than half of his platoon—Shane's platoon—to follow.

Now, as I met with Nerad and his men, there wasn't much to say. And words were not what we needed right then. God Himself was beginning to confirm in all of our hearts something we hadn't really thought about before. Of the forty-nine Marines who had been baptized in northern Kuwait, thirty-seven were from Alpha Company. And of those thirty-seven, almost three-fourths were from Shane Childers's platoon. These very men who had, moments earlier, experienced the sting of death, just days before had experienced the hope of heaven's greatest victory.

It was as if, in the midst of terrible loss, dark curtains began to pull away momentarily, revealing a deeper story, an unseen script that had been in the making for months. It was a story not of death and tragedy, but of a sovereign God who, knowing the trials we will face, providentially prepares us to face them.

As I stood there in silence, I remembered how God had begun His new work.

IT WAS OCTOBER 2002, and in light of the ever-loudening drumbeat of war, we were training for conventional desert operations. We still weren't positive we were going to Iraq, but every indicator was pointing us in that direction.

"Chaplain! Has anyone seen the chaplain?"

I immediately recognized the voice. It was First Lieutenant Nate Shull, Alpha Company's executive officer.

"I'm right here!"

I tried to raise the level of my whisper as loud as I could to get his attention, but I could tell he still didn't know where the voice was coming from. So in a stroke of bravery (some would argue it was rule breaking and not bravery at all), I turned on my red-lens pocket flashlight and started waving it back and forth, making clucking noises as I did.

It worked. Nate had come to inform me that the entire company was waiting for me to conduct a worship service on a hill about a mile south. If I was ready, all I needed to do was hop in my Humvee and follow his AAV to where they were.

Our battalion was in the middle of the desert at Marine Corps Air Ground Combat Center, Twentynine Palms, California. In fact, when Nate Shull came to find me, it was the final night before our last big exercise, and the desert stars couldn't have been more brilliant. Immediately Rufo and I jumped in our vehicle and off we went in search of Alpha Company.

When we arrived at the hill, one hundred sixty Marines and sailors were huddled together. Some were eating their chow, some were laughing, all of them were waiting patiently for me to arrive and lead them in worship under those breathtaking stars.

I had more or less decided that I would try to conduct services that afternoon, but only if I could beat the sunset. Since our battalion had arrived at our position later than expected, the last rays of sun had disappeared before I could make it to the companies, so I adjusted my plan to conduct services the next day. Alpha Company hadn't adjusted anything. They wanted services that night. And what a night it became.

There in the Mojave Desert night we worshiped God, sang hymns of faith, shared prayer requests, and allowed the Lord to speak to us from His Word. My sermon was brief, but considering the ominous state of the world and where we might find ourselves in the months to come, I thought its theme was fitting: Fear Not. My text was 2 Timothy 1:7: "For God has not given us a spirit of fear, but of power and love and of a sound mind."

With the prospect of war looming, I wanted more than anything for the men to know that despite the fears that assailed us all, God would give us the bravery we needed to do whatever our country might call us to do. I recalled for them a helpful quote: "Courage is not the absence of fear, but the determination to do what is right in spite of our fear."[1] I wasn't sure at the time who had said it, but I knew it was true. Marines and soldiers of every generation had demonstrated it to be so in every war our nation has faced. That night we prayed together that God would grant us the same reckless faith Jesus had demonstrated when, looking death and the Cross right in the face, He said to His Father in heaven, "Thy will be done" (Matthew 26:42).

In the months following, I came to see that evening service as emblematic of what God was doing among the men of Alpha Company. Indeed, in the months leading up to our deployment, a silent revival had begun among them. It was an awakening that came to its fullest fruition in the deserts of northern Kuwait, and amidst the billowing flames in southern Iraq.

During a 2002 meeting with all the battalion commanders in First Marine Division, Major General J. N. Mattis had remarked that in light of a potential war, it would be wise for commanders to encourage their men to prepare themselves not only mentally and physically, but spiritually. To paraphrase him, "Ensure that each one of your men has made peace with his God and is ready, if called upon, to face the dangers of battle, and his own mortality."

Blair Sokol hadn't been at the meeting, but a passing attendee had relayed to him the gist of the general's remarks. It was all Sokol needed to hear. As far as he was concerned, it was a directive from his commanding general that had to be followed. He was to make sure that his men have every opportunity to seek God, to wrestle with matters of faith, and to develop their religious life. Sokol approached it with essentially the same enthusiasm as he did any other aspect of the Marines' vital training.

Thus began an ever-deepening relationship between the two of us. Whenever possible, whether in training or in garrison (back at camp), Sokol would allow me every opportunity to be with his men. I valued his trust, cherished his friendship, and was humbled by the freedom he gave me to conduct services, teach, or just be with his guys.

But if it was Sokol's leadership that paved the way for the new faith of so many in the company, it was without a doubt First Sergeant James Green's enthusiasm that set the example. Green, a wiry African-American, breathed integrity, and walked with a strut of confidence that never failed to inspire me.

In chaplains' school, I remember being told that if we wanted to be wise Marine chaplains, we should get to know and follow the examples of our first sergeants. Why? Because a first sergeant has been in the Marine Corps for at least fifteen years and has witnessed every possible "knuckleheaded" mistake a young Marine can make. He is without a doubt in excellent physical fitness and wears one of the most striking uniforms in the battalion.

All of this was easily true of James Green, as well as of the other four first sergeants in the battalion. A thirty-eight-year-old husband and father of two, Green had arrived in Beirut in 1983, two days after the Marine barracks were bombed. Two hundred Marines died that day, and Green was in the midst of all of the rubble, helping clean the site and process remains. It was an experience that changed his life, marking him forever as a man who understood the value of sacrifice, and making him an ideal leader of young Marines as they wrestled with the prospect of war and perhaps even death.

He was known for leaning forward a bit, his arms crossed, and asking, "How ya doing, Devil-Dawg?" Green owned the respect of his men, which opened the door for them to appreciate his lifestyle and faith. Whenever I had the privilege of conducting services for his men, he always prayed as a lay leader and assisted me in serving communion. It's one thing for a chaplain to administer communion. It is quite another to receive it from your first sergeant.

Green's visible faith helped nurture spiritual growth in the lives of his men that came to fruition in the barren wasteland of northern Kuwait. This awakening in the lives of the men of Alpha had begun in the States, but it took on a whole new dimension when the company was on the threshold of war.

February 19, 2003, during a worship service off of the back of an AAV ramp in Kuwait, twenty men from Alpha responded to an invitation I had extended to anyone who wanted to talk about becoming a Christian and/or Christian baptism. The men who responded came from all walks of life, from every racial and socio-economic background, from every educational level. But they shared one thing in common—a desire to know the peace and assurance of a personal relationship with God.

BY THE END OF SIX WEEKS in the Kuwaiti desert the numbers spoke for themselves:

- • 120 involved in Bible Studies / 56 from Alpha Company
- • 49 baptized as new Christians / 37 from Alpha Company

Some of my personal journal entries:

26 February 2003

"Classes, counseling, prayer, and ministry . . . At my big Alpha Company class, we decided to do 'question time' instead of the lesson . . . They would have stayed there for two hours . . . Thank You, Lord, for the work You are doing in their lives."

27 February 2003

"Another incredible day! From 1300–1700 straight preaching, teaching, counseling, and prayer. Many souls are entering the kingdom of God."

09 March 2003

"Powerful movement of the Holy Spirit in the service. Marines shared what God has been doing in their lives . . . many shared. The Marines are spiritually ready."

11–15 March 2003

"What a week! Baptized two more. Classes are growing at an incredible rate. Souls being born into the kingdom."

THAT LAST ENTRY was made just a week before I stood staring at the saddened faces of Alpha Company after they'd lost their lieutenant. I knew they loved him. I loved him too. Yet despite the sadness I felt, I couldn't help but reflect upon the providence of God in it all. From the beginning, He had known this hour was coming—a dark and difficult hour, an hour of almost unbearable sadness for some of us. Yet as a Good Shepherd cares for His sheep,

God had provided for these men everything they would need to sustain and strengthen them.

God had given them a company commander who saw it as one of his highest priorities to ensure their spiritual lives were attended to.

God had given them a first sergeant whose winsome life was a living embodiment of Jesus.

And God had given them a tough staff sergeant whose public step of faith had shown them that a U.S. Marine can be a rugged man and a warrior and still follow Christ with the faith of a child.

The spiritual awakening in the lives of the men of Alpha Company was no mere coincidence, but it was the gracious gift of God given to those men who would one day need that gift as never before. Behind the grief of those moments at Pumping Station 2, I think many of us could sense it . . . the Author of faith, the Giver of life, our Refuge and Strength in times of trouble, "Him who makes all things work together for good for those who love God and who are called according to His purposes." He was with us that dark day on the morning of March 21.

The words of Ezekiel 34:12 summed up what we all felt despite our tears:

> As a shepherd cares for his herd in the day when he is among his scattered sheep, so I will care for My sheep and will deliver them from all the places to which they were scattered on a cloudy and gloomy day.

Gathering the men together around the AAV where their lieutenant had been lying just hours earlier, we observed a brief service of committal and entrusted the soul of our fallen brother to the all-merciful hands of our Father in heaven. And we knew we were not alone.

5

A Sign in the Storm

Early sunday morning, March 23, just two days after Shane Childers was killed, I opened my eyes to a gray-orange sky. We were somewhere in the middle of the vast void that separates the Rumeilah oil fields from Baghdad, and although our convoy had traveled most of the night, we had managed to get a few hours of sleep before daybreak. We had burrowed deep inside our insulated black sleeping bags, bedded down in the shallow pits we slept in— pits we dug as close as possible to the side doors of our vehicles. It was always much safer to "snucker" yourself up next to your vehicle. That way you wouldn't be run over in the middle of the night by a truck or tank operator who failed to see your black bag lying alone in a field or on a patch of dark earth.

The sounds of men's voices and of engines roaring to life offered a certain sense of comfort. The morning before, we had awakened on the side of what we thought was an abandoned road, only to discover at first light that we had slept no more than fifteen feet away from a row of Iraqi machine-gun bunkers. Thank God, they were unmanned. But we were horrified—we'd had no idea they were there. Now, with so much noise and movement around, I didn't foresee a similar surprise.

As I pulled myself out of my bag and rubbed my hands over my two-day-old stubble, I searched around for my desert boots, which I had taken off in the middle of the night. We often slept with our boots on, but it had been five days since I'd removed mine. Like most of the men, by then my feet had been more than ready for a good "airing out."

As I located the boots, a silvery metal identification tag caught my eye. It was woven through the thick black laces of my left boot. Each of us was ordered to have two "dog tags"; one hung around our neck, and the other was laced to the outside of our left boot. Dog tags are well-known items in military life, bearing each man or woman's vital information on a thin metal strip—name, rank, Social Security number, blood type, and religious preference. If we were injured or captured, the dog tag around our neck could be quickly identified by a corpsman, doctor, chaplain, or anyone else who might need to know who we were. However, the boot dog tag served a more sobering purpose—it was a means of identifying our bodies should we be killed and disfigured beyond recognition. Of course seeing the glint of metal in the laces of my left boot that morning immediately reminded me of Shane and the prospect of death that we all faced.

I breathed a quick prayer for Charity. She and the children seemed so far away, and I knew very well that she was anxious for me, for us all. In a way, wartime separation is harder on wives than on warriors. Wives never really know their husbands' whereabouts, and they are left to watch ambiguous news reports, stifling the fear of that sickening knock on the door by men in dark dress uniforms.

It occurred to me that anybody who said, "The perfect will of God is the safest place to be" had never crossed the border into Iraq. God's will may be the *best* place to be, but it isn't necessarily the safest. Following Him sometimes means that we are led into the shadow of death, where valiant and faithful men will give their all. There was no escaping the harsh truth about where I was that Sunday morning. Nonetheless, with the sound of artillery already booming over the distant morning horizon, I collected myself, took a deep breath, and placed all my hopes, dreams, and fears into His hands.

Judging by the numbers of trucks, Humvees, and AAVs that were slowly migrating toward the refueling tanker, I knew I would have ample time to conduct Sunday worship services for our men before our battalion headed north. I grabbed my Bible, portable altar, notebook with a few notes I had scribbled the day before, and headed out. Because our battalion was so spread out, rather than gathering large numbers of worshipers together for one or two services as I'd done in Kuwait, I simply moved from one AAV to another and brought worship to the men right where they were.

The services were brief that morning, consisting of prayer, Bible reading, and Holy Communion. Realizing the intensity of emotion and soul-searching that was going on in the hearts of all of us, I decided to say as little as possible, instead allowing God to communicate His presence in His own way. In fact, during our time in Kuwait, I had come across a passage in Isaiah that reminded me of something that Protestants (and especially Baptist preachers like me) too easily forget: Sometimes our greatest ministry to others is simply to speak the Word of God into a situation where it has not been spoken before and without frantically explaining and expounding, to allow God, in His own way, to meet those deep and often imperceptible needs that lie in the inner reaches of every human heart. Isaiah wrote,

"For My thoughts are not your thoughts,
Nor are your ways My ways," says the LORD.
"For as the heavens are higher than the earth,
So are My ways higher than your ways,
And My thoughts than your thoughts.
For as the rain comes down, and the snow from heaven,
And do not return there,
But water the earth,
And make it bring forth and bud,
That it may give seed to the sower
And bread to the eater,
So shall My word be that goes forth from My mouth;

It shall not return to Me void,
But it shall accomplish what I please,
And it shall prosper in the thing for which I sent it."

—ISAIAH 55:8–11

I spent the bulk of the morning going from vehicle to vehicle praying with the men and conducting informal services. Before long, a chorus of engines began to roar to life, telling me that our convoy was about to head out again. Looking over a sea of green and tan vehicles toward the direction of my own, I could see the men in my lineup waving me down from a distance, letting me know in no uncertain terms that I'd better get back.

Sergeant Kevin White was my new driver. Now that we were facing combat, Rufo, who had the only weapon between us, couldn't drive and provide adequate security at the same time. It was just too dangerous. Everywhere we went, we encountered Iraqi prisoners of war (some incarcerated, others walking of their own accord waving white handkerchiefs, presumably surrendering themselves to the nearest Coalition unit) and civilians, freely roaming around the oil fields. I'm sure that most of them were legitimately harmless. Just two days earlier, however, a harmless-looking civilian pickup truck had done its worst, taking the life of Shane Childers.

For several very good reasons, the day after crossing into Iraq, Lieutenant Roberts and I had decided to place Rufo in charge of our vehicle's security and to commandeer another Marine to focus on the singular task of driving. Sergeant White was only twenty years old, relatively young to be a sergeant. This could only mean that he had done an outstanding job in his section (motor transport—vehicle operator), and had therefore been recommended for early promotion. Usually it takes a Marine at least four to five years to put on the sergeant chevrons. White had done it in three.

Perhaps this was because of White's keen intellect and passion for doing the right thing. I soon realized that this lanky vehicle operator had a mind for philosophy and politics. He had grown up in a devoutly Christian home with several other siblings, and he had to learn early on how to make his voice heard at the dinner table. And when he spoke, he always had something to say.

White knew the issues of politics, not merely for popular reasons, but insofar as they touched the moral pillars of his life and faith. I think that's what made him such an anomaly to his friends. He came across as very cool, very smooth, and yet there was far more to him than met the eye. And a recent experience in Iraq had further deepened him—a frightening episode that took place the night before our first meeting.

In the midst of the breach crossing between Kuwait and Iraq, White's vehicle had somehow been wrecked. Having no radio and only one rifle between him and his assistant driver, the two had spent the night together hunkered down in the floorboard of their seven-ton truck, wearing their gas masks in case of an enemy chemical attack. That long night had made a profound difference in White's young life. Now he was convinced that being assigned to the chaplain's vehicle was nothing short of a confirmation from God that he'd better get back on track and get his life together. That sounded good to me.

As our convoy began to thunder to life and inch forward, we received word that our mission was to move north one hundred sixty kilometers and "root out" known enemy tanks and foot soldiers along Route 1, a major artery that ran southeast of the city of Ad Diwaniyah, a city that had harbored known terrorist training camps and guerilla warfare tactics schools for years. We knew Ad Diwaniyah wouldn't fall without a fight. We piled into our vehicles and headed out.

The ride north that afternoon was relatively uneventful, although we were constantly faced with a culture unlike anything we had seen before. Along the roadsides we saw ancient-looking adobe dwellings, stone wells, sheep herded by men in long black tunics, women whose eyes were barely visible through the narrow slits of their veils, and children with no shoes, smiling from ear to ear, pointing, and waving.

Meanwhile, I can only imagine how other-worldly we must have looked to the Iraqis as we surged through the desert landscape in our colossal armored vehicles, wearing helmets with goggles, staring through binoculars, carrying automatic weapons, talking on high-tech radios, and guarded by helicopters, fighter jets, and missiles. I often wondered what the Iraqis thought about it all. Did they even know why we were there? We couldn't help but suspect that they were not only divorced from most of the civilized world, but probably from their own government too.

Our military convoy stretched as far as the eye could see—tanks, trucks, AAVs, LAVs—bending back and forth for miles in both directions like a green and tan snake. Considering our size, we were moving fast. Orders from the top—probably from the president himself—were to move northward in-country as rapidly as possible, at times bypassing some enemy forces and moving in position to "cut the head off the snake" in Baghdad. The idea was to fragment the enemy into small and ineffective outfits that would, upon seeing their leadership topple, throw down their arms and surrender.

Looking back, this strategy worked well, and history will probably confirm its success. However, what this meant in practical terms was that the enemy (even if small in number and generally ineffective) was everywhere, able to move toward us from every direction. The classic battlefield, where the proverbial frontlines are "way up there," and the rear area is secured for miles and miles behind, just wasn't the case in Iraq. Once the war started, there really wasn't a "rear" area. Small, unconventional enemy forces were everywhere.

It is true that many Iraqi troops threw down their weapons and vanished into thin air. But there were those that didn't, and they presented what military analysts call an "asymmetrical" threat—their forces were considerably smaller than ours, yet they possessed enough small arms and chameleonlike capabilities to inflict significant harm. Indeed, our battalion would go on to experience what many believe was the single worst battle in all the war, fought against such asymmetrical forces in Baghdad on April 10.

A nagging sense of uncertainty lurked in our minds as we rolled to a stop the night of March 23. Our battalion had been halted short of our ultimate destination due to an "increased enemy threat" along our route. The combat train, of which I was part, found itself on the shoulder of an abandoned road southeast of the Euphrates River. And as the night sky rapidly turned from dark blue to black, the voices over the radio in our convoy reported that a lone Iraqi antiaircraft battery had been spotted no more than two hundred meters to our southeast. We quickly dispatched a squad of riflemen armed with armor-piercing missiles, who discovered the vehicle to be abandoned. Even so, the sense of danger in the air was palpable. The darkness carried with it an oppressiveness that I had never known, a fear that left me feeling exposed, defenseless, watched.

Psalm 74:20 puts the feeling to words: "For the dark places of the land are full of the habitations of violence." Indeed, we were in a "habitation of violence" (NASB). And then, during those eerily quiet moments as we sat on the side of the road in the pitch dark, we first heard the report that American prisoners had been taken hostage.

Initially, it seemed to be a rumor, but within minutes it was confirmed by one of our own embedded media journalists, whose satellite phone picked up the story. It's hard to explain the effect that report about American POWs had on us, but it was deeply psychological. We were in the pitch dark of a moonless desert night; the unceasing sound of artillery boomed in the distance. We were several hundred kilometers inside a country where days before, Saddam Hussein had promised to spill our blood in his streets. Now he might get his chance. Somewhere, somehow, Iraqi soldiers had captured American soldiers. Not one of us felt safe.

Looking back, I believe it was that moment, when we heard the unconfirmed reports of the first American POWs, that I first understood one of the chief differences between watching a war on cable news from the comfort of a living room and actually being in the war zone, feeling like an infinitesimal speck on the field of a constantly changing threat. Beyond the obvious issue of safety, the other difference that I never would have been able to understand or appreciate, had I not been in the thick of a front-line infantry unit, is that of *information*.

When the first Persian Gulf War kicked off, I was a junior at the Citadel, and like most Americans, I watched in real time as bombs and missiles impacted buildings and compounds in Baghdad. I listened to the strategists explain over and over the sweeping tactics of the U.S. Armed Forces. I had a good grasp of where our men were, where the enemy was, and what degree of success we were achieving. But now, in the heart of the conflict, the news about the American POWs underscored the unsettling reality that we would have to come to accept throughout the entire war: we had little or no idea what was going on with the other units around us.

Historians and military leaders call this phenomenon "the fog of war." I had read about it countless times before in military history books, and had even taught on the subject when giving a course on combat stress. But this fog doesn't merely refer to the confusion brought on by a chaotic battlefield, as I had first thought. It is a vaporous cloud that seeps into the mind as well, creating an indefinable uneasiness. This uneasiness eventually rises to the conscious level, causing you to feel alone and afraid, uncertain where you are in relationship to the enemy, and wondering if your unit is the last one standing.

The news about the POWs was more than enough to distress us. Then the desert wind really began to blow.

Journal Entry—25 March

"Woke up this morning and punched out at 8:30 a.m. Stopped right now, due to zero visibility—sandstorm. More to come . . . Winds must be 50–60 miles per hour . . . the worst storm I've ever been in . . . sand, wind, rain blowing sideways . . . cannot see vehicle fifteen feet in front of us."

There would be few experiences in all the war that would compare to the hours between 9:00 a.m., March 25 and 2:00 a.m., March 26.

When it first began, the storm looked like nothing more than a routine temporary desert gust. We'd experienced dozens of them in Kuwait; and while they could be irritating, they usually evaporated fairly soon and without incident. But this storm was altogether different. It descended with such fury that one of our Marines half-jokingly commented, "Maybe the air force nuked Baghdad and forgot to tell us about it."

When the first blasts hit us at around 9:00 a.m., we almost immediately lost sight of the vehicle in front of us. The radios in our convoy crackled to life. "Easy, easy, just stay on my rear and we'll get through this."

The first person we heard on the radio was Staff Sergeant Apodaca or "Lugnut," who was in the vehicle in front of ours. He called back to each driver one by one, checking on both their status and their sanity, and assuring them that no one was going to be left behind.

Already the wind was blowing so hard sideways that any crack or seam in the lining of our Humvee's doors or "floppy-back" cab became an instant funnel for sand and dirt. The air in the vehicle was thick with floating orange silt. Our convoy continued to push north along the route in hopes that the storm would blow over and that we could get to our objective by the early afternoon.

Between 10:00 and 10:30 in the morning, the storm seemed to be dying out. Visibility improved, and our convoy picked up its pace. The respite, unfortunately, was brief. Moments later, like a fierce dragon, the Middle Eastern desert unleashed its blinding red breath with such a fury that we could only watch in amazement. The sky went red, and in the course of a few seconds, visibility was reduced to zero. All movement ground to a halt, and the convoy was ordered to "wait it out."

The wind blew so furiously that we wondered if our Humvee would roll over onto its side. To make matters worse, breathing was growing increasingly difficult. The inside of the Humvee's cabin was a soup of noxious dust and dirt, coating every inch of our bodies with a thick residue. I could feel silt literally pouring into my lungs, tickling and scratching my airway with each breath I drew. The order came across the radio to don our respirators. Even then, there was no way to keep the dust out of our mouths.

Over the course of the next two hours, the sky grew redder and the wind increased in velocity. By midafternoon, it might as well have been night. I could barely make out the silhouette of Sergeant White, who sat only four feet away from me, and any attempt to see anything outside the vehicle was a lost cause. Even though we were all positioned just feet from one another, each of us felt as if we were the only person left alive, cut off from anything and anyone familiar.

Compounding the turmoil that each of us felt during those hours was the realization that a mechanized enemy force, including tanks and armored vehicles, was only a few kilometers to the north, east, and west. The Third Battalion, which was acting as the day's main effort, was already locked in combat with a company-sized enemy force along Route 1 to our direct north. In support of their fight, Fox 2/11 began firing their massive artillery cannons, causing the sand-filled sky to explode in blinding flashes of orange and red heat. All around us we could hear the sounds of guns, each blast confirming that the Iraqis were still fighting, storm or no storm. Of course our greatest fear was that, while we were hunkered down and immobilized, the indigenous Iraqi forces, knowing the weather and terrain far better than we did, would continue to function.

We never stopped searching through the haze, trying to see who or what was out there. We knew that because of the isolating nature of the storm, an infiltrator could easily move in, attack a vehicle, and no one would know until the sandstorm was over. In fact, one crazed Iraqi civilian had already meandered through the convoy, shouting and ranting. Roberts and Kirkham had their rifles pointed at him, safeties clicked off, ready to fire should he make any threatening move or indicate that there were others behind him. His appearance stirred up feelings of panic when we heard about it. We all must have thought the same thing—*Is this the beginning of an ambush?* The intruder eventually vanished into the desert, while the storm raged on and on. For the next several hours, all we could do was wait, take shallow breaths, and pray.

Meanwhile, a few vehicles away from ours, a small drama was unfolding, with repercussions far more meaningful than any of us could have imagined at the time. Captain Wil Dickens, the headquarters company commander, along with Corporals Hardy, Beavers, and Batke, was hunkered down in his vehicle, like the rest of us, listening to his radio. Dickens had a compassionate nature and a moral imagination that frequently gave him unique insights into the everyday problems facing his young men. He looked out for them, recognizing that they were sons or husbands or fathers before seeing them as Marines.

Perhaps this is why Dickens was so adept at his job. Unlike other company commanders, Dickens didn't command a rifle company. His command was over all those in the battalion who provided logistical support to keep the rifle companies moving and alive, including radio, supply, medical, administration, and motor transport. Such a job required a patient leader who, perhaps more than anyone else in the battalion, had to work with people and personalities rather than with maps, missions, and ranges. In Kuwait, Dickens had confided in me that he could envision himself eventually making his way into some government position, but not in grand-scale politics. He was more interested in local, hands-on, town-oriented government. It wasn't hard to imagine him doing a job like that, and doing it well.

During the darkest hours of the storm, Dickens and his crew were keeping themselves busy monitoring the radio, since their task in particular necessitated being ready to move out in a moment's notice. They were also reading by red-lens flashlight and discussing among themselves tough verses from the Bible. Corporal Hardy, a bright young Marine from Alabama, always kept his fellow passengers busy with frequent references to the Bible and Scripture memory quotations. In fact Hardy's green pocket Bible had become something of a symbol in the cabin, a sort of a spiritual fixture.

Days earlier, Hardy had insisted they keep it lying on the center radio mount as a reminder that God was with them, and that He would never leave or forsake them. No one protested, and soon the pocket Bible was being passed around from man to man, read silently or aloud, serving at times a centerpiece of discussion and debate. In truth, they all enjoyed the conversation it was generating—especially Zebulon Batke.

Corporal Zebulon had a deep voice and dark eyes, and was responsible, along with Beavers, for manning the Mark-19 grenade launcher that was mounted on the top of their vehicle. It was a particularly dangerous place to be in a country like Iraq, where the enemy often struck unexpectedly and seemingly out of nowhere. At 6'5" Batke was especially vulnerable. Perhaps this is what generated his newfound interest in Hardy's discussion of the Bible.

From the day they had crossed the line of departure, Hardy had not stopped talking about his faith, and about God's ability to shield and protect them from the enemy. It wasn't that Batke believed everything Hardy said—that was hardly the case. But he was impressed by the way Hardy said it. It was as if Hardy was certain, like he'd seen proof of God's existence.

For Batke, belief in God was a stretch. As a young teenager in his Washington State hometown, Batke had fallen into the trap of doing drugs and making bad decisions. His 1999 decision to enter the Marine Corps was in no small part an effort to get away from the distractions and temptations he'd experienced in high school. Religion had never played a part in Batke's life. He'd been disappointed by many of the adults in his life, and it was hard for him to trust anybody. He wanted proof of God, he explained later on, because he really did want to believe in something.

Batke was a self-proclaimed seeker. So when he came face to face with the dangers of war, it was Hardy's unswerving belief in God that got Batke's attention. Here was a man who spoke of promises and truths as if he absolutely knew they would come to pass. Batke was intrigued, to be sure, but he still hadn't found the proof he needed.

During the course of the day, the storm was so intense and the sand in the air so thick that it was intermittently blocking some of our radio frequencies. Later that evening, Dickens and his crew received a call from the Bravo Command Group with what sounded like information about when the convoy was going to move. The voice, however, was garbled and barely readable. Because the information was important, Dickens asked Hardy to find his way across the road and ask one of the nearby vehicles if they had heard the same message.

Hardy pried open the Humvee's door and stepped out into the storm. The sand stung his face and he struggled to pull his neck warmer up just beneath his eyes. He would have used his goggles, but their green tint made everything look even darker. Fumbling his way across the narrow road, hands outstretched in front if him to feel his way across, Hardy located another vehicle, got the information he needed, and made his way back.

When he'd first jumped up and headed out into the night, Hardy had forgotten that the Bible had been lying in his lap. And it was only after he made it back to his vehicle and out of the stinging wind that he realized the green-covered Bible, which the four of them had come to depend upon as a sign of God's presence, was lost in the sand.

"Sir!" he announced to Dickens, "I . . . I lost the Bible!"

Opening the Humvee door, Hardy climbed outside again and began blindly feeling around in the sand for its coarse, leathery cover.

"It must have fallen out when I stood up."

For several minutes, Hardy and the others searched high and low, inside and outside the vehicle. They closed their eyes and padded up and down the desert floor outside the driver's side door, but to no avail. The night was too dark, and the wind was blowing too hard for them to continue their search.

"We'll just have to find it in the morning," Dickens said, trying to cheer up the frustrated Hardy. The Bible's presence had comforted all of them during the first week of the war. They knew there would be more fighting in the days ahead. For some reason, it had always been a relief to see it sitting there on the radio mount, silently offering its reassuring words. And now it was gone.

Needless to say, Dickens and the others could have easily located another Bible. I carried hundreds of pocket New Testaments in the back of my vehicle for that very reason. But this had been, for them, "our Bible." It had accompanied them ever since they'd crossed the breach. And for those who go to war, such symbols, which are cherished through frightening circumstances, take on an almost sacramental power.

Warriors speak of "my cross," or "my St. Christopher's prayer medallion," or "my scripture card," or "my Bible" with an almost childlike possessiveness. Surely it is a sort of human affection God understands and even smiles upon. How many times had Charity and I tried to replace one of our children's favorite stuffed animals with another that looked just like it? It never worked, at least not at first. Human beings naturally connect to those things that have brought comfort and strength, which is why we often prefer the ragged original to a new replacement.

Dickens and the other three corporals—along with the rest of us in the convoy—sat biding their time for the next several hours, nodding off for a few minutes now and then, until the next gust of ear-splitting wind rocked the vehicle and jarred them awake. The final hours of the storm were unquestionably the worst. Seventy mph gusts of wind drove not only sand, but rain, and then golfball-sized hail screaming at us sideways like a meteor shower.

Just before dawn the violence finally dissipated, and the wind was reduced to a gentle breeze. Not long afterward, Dickens and his crew received an immediate directive to refuel and then push out. Hardy fired up the Humvee's engine and drove away from their position.

One by one, all the vehicles behind Dickens's lurched forward and also headed down the road to be refueled by the massive tanker-trucks that were attached to our unit. The road where Dickens's vehicle had sat idling all night came alive as dozens and dozens of Humvees, trucks, and artillery pieces churned and dug through the muck that the rain had produced. It was a sea of slog and red mud, stamped from end to end by the tread of tracks and the imprint of wheels.

Hardy steered the vehicle into the refueling area and then made his way back into line, moving in something like a big circle back to where he had started. It was still quite dark, before sunrise. The wheels of Dickens's Humvee sloshed and slogged back down the road toward its original place in the convoy's lineup. Just then Hardy, without warning, slammed on his brakes.

Dickens did a doubletake. "Hardy," he blurted out, "what are you . . . what do you think you're doing?"

"Sir, it's . . . it's the Bible!" And with that, oblivious to the string of vehicles behind him that suddenly had to slam on their brakes, Hardy opened his door and jumped out.

Batke and Beavers, seated in the rear, looked at each other and then lurched forward in their seats. "What'd he say?"

"It's the what?" Dickens shook his head in disbelief.

There was no stopping the excited Hardy, who had already flung himself down on his knees in the mud. When he reappeared in the Humvee he was smiling from ear to ear, holding in his hand the lost Bible that had disappeared the night before, right in the middle of the storm.

The four men marveled over Hardy's discovery like happy kids who had found a lost toy, each taking turns to inspect it to make sure that it was indeed theirs. They gripped it in their hands, thumbed through its pages, and reacquainted themselves with the coarse feel of the leather cover.

But the strangest thing of all was its perfect condition. The Bible had been dropped from a vehicle onto a dirt road. It had been assaulted for hours by 70 mph winds carrying stinging sand, rain, and hail. It had been lying on a road that, for the past two hours, had borne the weight of every vehicle in the convoy. Still, the Bible had not moved an inch from where it had first landed. And it was not torn. It wasn't bent. It wasn't even wet.

Hardy looked it over, clutched it to his chest, and while looking at Dickens said with all his heart, "Sir, this is a sign from God."

Batke and Beavers stared.

"This is a sign," he continued. "I know it is. God has put a shield around us, and He's going to protect us from this day forward. And this is His way of proving it to us. We need not fear from this point on. Sir, do you believe?"

"I believe it," Dickens answered, nodding and looking over his shoulder at the smiling faces of the two Marines behind him.

Batke didn't say anything at that moment, although he had to admit to himself that it was uncanny. What were the odds of finding the lost Bible after the convoy had moved out, refueled, and repositioned itself? More to the point, Hardy's Bible was just a flimsy little book. They all knew what had gone on outside for the past twelve hours. Yet as he held it in his hands, Batke could clearly see that the Bible looked like it had just come off the shelf of a cozy fireside library, untouched and totally unharmed.

As they followed the vehicle ahead of them into the dawn, Hardy triumphantly placed the Bible back on the radio mount for all to see. "From that point on," Dickens confided in me later, "we believed we were shielded from the enemy. It was a sign . . . a gift from God. We knew it. And we believed it."

If there is anything the history of God's dealing with men teaches us, it is that God is as much concerned with the little things in our lives as we are. And He is pleased—even delighted—to reveal through seemingly small and insignificant details the enormity and grandeur of His love and presence.

Who of us could ever forget the story of Medal of Honor winner and infantry Marine, Platoon Sergeant Mitchell Paige? He single-handedly drove off platoon after platoon of Japanese soldiers on the island of Guadalcanal. Using the machine-guns of killed or injured Marines, Paige held the critical air-base ridgeline for hours until reinforcements could arrive. And when they did, he fearlessly led a bayonet charge into the teeth of the Japanese stronghold. When the battle was over, Paige, his hands burned and charred from cradling hot machine-guns, rummaged through his pack to find the one thing his mother had said would sustain him throughout the war—his pocket Gideon Bible. Opening it up on that life-changing day, its pages fell open to the very same verse his mother had imprinted upon his memory when she said farewell and sent him off to serve in the Marine Corps six years earlier:

Trust in the Lord with all your heart, and lean not upon your own understanding. In all your ways acknowledge Him and He shall direct your path.

PROVERBS 3:5–6

For Dickens, Hardy, Beavers, and Batke, that path would lead them right back to the same symbol of refuge and strength that had sustained Paige fifty-two years earlier. And they would need that symbol as never before in the harrowing days that would follow. All of them would soon find themselves plunged into the thick of what many believe to have been the fiercest fire-fight in all of the war. It would be a battle that would see over seventy-five of our men become casualties, claiming the life of one. And yet for Hardee, Dickens, Batke, and Beavers, the experience of that battle would be nothing short of a testimony to the presence of Almighty God, a presence that was confirmed by a Bible that refused to be lost. As the psalmist wrote,

Forever, O LORD, Thy Word is settled in heaven . . . it is a lamp unto my feet and a light unto my path . . . Thou art my Hiding place and my Shield . . . I will wait for Thy Word . . . I rejoice at Thy Word as one who finds great spoil.

PSALM 119:105,114,162

6
Filthy Hands, Pure Hearts

Shattered by a huge explosion, I jumped up from my bivy-sack, praying it wasn't what I thought it was. I could still feel the violent percussion and ear-splitting noise resonating throughout my body, reverberating in my gut. Two seconds later, Kirkham, who was monitoring the radio no more than twenty feet away, shouted what we all feared.

"Incoming! That was incoming!"

My stomach sank and sweat began to bead up all over me, making me feel like I was being prodded and poked with tiny needles. I fumbled to get out of my sack and into my chemical protective suit—boots, mask, and gloves. I could hear myself breathing rapidly, and out of the corner of my eye I could see others doing the same things I was doing, frantically donning their chem-gear, jumping into the bottoms of their fighting holes, praying. The Iraqis were firing on us.

Within seconds, the official warning came over every radio net in the battalion, punctuating the sleep of the few Marines who weren't standing watch: "Lightning! Lightning! Lightning! Incoming enemy rounds! Go to MOPP Level 4!"

Instantly one thousand Marines and sailors, spread out over an area of two to three kilometers, began rifling through their packs, eyeing the nearest fighting hole, and tripping over each other to get their into protective gear. In the back of our minds I know we were all thinking the same thing: *Where's the next one going to land?*

Many fears race through a warrior's heart and mind on the field of battle. *What if I get shot? What if I'm ambushed? Will I see terrible suffering? Will I get separated from my unit? Will I live or die?* All of these flitted through our minds from time to time. But without a doubt, the greatest psychological turmoil and intense fear was caused by incoming artillery shells or rockets. The reason was simple—we couldn't see who was firing at us.

Artillery, or indirect fire, is meant to devastate the morale and will of the enemy. By showering him with lethal explosions from a distance too far to see, he never knows what hit him, or where it came from. Compounding this fear is the distinct expectation that if he manages to survive the first salvo, the aggressor, who is no doubt watching his position from a well-hidden looking post, will call in another one within seconds. And this time he may well be on target. What all this amounts to is the disturbing feeling that even before the enemy rounds blasted into your area, you were being watched.

By the time I had found the bottom of my fighting hole, most of this reasoning had gone through my mind. Then came a distant popping noise.

"They're doing it again. Get ready!"

Kirkham was sure, and I believed him, that the popping noise was the sound of the enemy's distant rounds leaving their chambers and hurtling our way. I prayed that whoever had been spying on our position and had called in the first sortie was a terrible mathematician.

Just then, with what must have been the force of a thousand colliding locomotives, the six artillery guns from Fox 2/11 exploded to life, hurling round after round in the enemy's direction. The guns were little more than two hundred meters away, just across the road, and they shook the earth and my bones with such violence that I felt like something inside of me had broken. Fox was firing back.

Rufo and I stared up into the dark night sky and watched the

Talent Show—March 17th, 2003

RP2 Redor Rufo

Last prayer before crossing into Iraq with Bravo Company
First Platoon and Weapons attachments.

Inside of the Command
and Control AAV

Captain Blair Sokol

Mark Avery/Orange County Register

Steven Smith/Family Permission

Second Lieutenant Shane Childers

Worship Service with Alpha Company

The "Top Three." Lt. Col. Fred Padillo (seated) at center,
Executive Officer, Major Cal Worth (left); and
Operations Officer, Major Steven Armes (right).

Lance Corporal Eli Schleuter

The Altar went wherever we went,
and was the center of our worship.

Gunny Bohr speaks to the men.

Sergeant Jesus Hernandez receiving Holy Communion during
a worship service at the Ammunition Re-supply Point.

Captain Van White surrounded by excited Iraqi children.

Captain V. White, USMC

Lance Corporal Jeff Guthrie

Earnie Grafton/San Diego Union Tribune

Baptism of Lance Corporal Sean Lamb

Lt. Colonel Fred Padilla talking to the men after
"major hostilities" were declared over.

afterburners of our high-explosive artillery rounds kick in one after the other, launching the shells even further over the horizon. While the firing was ear-splitting, the sight of the clustered rounds flying up toward the heavens was almost peacefully quiet. They floated up and away and then disappeared in the far sky.

No more than ninety seconds later, the horizon ignited in white-orange flashes. Again and again, we watched as one-hundred-pound fragmentary rounds sought out the perpetrators of our middle-of-the-night attack. And it must have been an effective response. Despite the popping noise we'd heard just a few minutes earlier, there was no more incoming impact that night. Fox 2/11 had apparently silenced the enemy, and soon after the all-clear was given, indicating that we could take off our masks.

It was the night of March 30, more than a week since we lost Lieutenant Childers, and the war in Iraq was in full motion. In the days that followed Childers's death, our battalion had continued to push north through the Euphrates River Valley, across the sparsely populated lands of the Bedouin sheepherders, and finally into the outer rim of the only real civilization we had seen—the eastern side of the city of Ad Diwaniyah. It was, in fact, from Ad Diwaniyah that the enemy rockets had been launched.

The last few days as we pushed north had been anything but uneventful. Just three days earlier, our battalion had been issued orders to move north a few kilometers and seize an enemy airbase at Hantush. Already, Marine Cobra helicopters had encountered fierce fighting there and had recommended that at least an infantry battalion's worth of fire power be brought in to secure the area for good. We were told upon departing to keep our eyes open on both sides of the road, since Iraqi soldiers and Fedayeen gunmen were acting as snipers, attempting to pick off unsuspecting Americans one by one.

The drive to the airbase was quiet. Aside from a few distant helicopter air strikes, we saw no enemy forces, heard no small-arms gunfire. However, our sense of security, if anyone could actually call it that, was shortlived.

A report came over the radio that Second Battalion, Fifth Marines, a sister unit, had successfully cleared the air base of the enemy, and therefore our battalion was cut loose to return to our position for the night. However, on the way back, as we were traveling down the same road on which we had driven north, we watched, mesmerized, as two F-14 Tomcat fighter/bomber jets pounded at enemy forces hiding meters from the same portion of the road we had just driven over. Spellbound by the spectacular display, at first we didn't make the connection. We simply watched as, one after another, the screaming jets unloaded their bombs at low altitude. Then, it gradually hit us—the enemy they were destroying was positioned within a stone's throw of where our convoy had just been. The place was teeming with enemy forces.

Each new morning seemed to arrive with the constant and increasing threat of incoming artillery fire, mortars, and sniper ambushes. Already several men from our battalion's regiment had been killed along Route 1. One particular casualty that was weighing heavily on our hearts and minds was the March 25 death of Hospital Corpsman Michael Johnson. He had been called up at the last minute from Balboa Naval Hospital to support Third Battalion, Fifth Marines, a unit that fought side by side with ours throughout the war.

The afternoon of March 25, as the wicked sandstorm descended on our convoy, we'd heard that Johnson, while attending to one of his injured Marines, had been killed by enemy mortars. Not only was this disconcerting because of our proximity to 3/5 (they were only a few kilometers from us when it happened), but because corpsmen are considered noncombatants. Although they carry a sidearm, corpsmen are never used in an offensive operation against the enemy.

We didn't know Corpsman Johnson, but we grieved as if we did. Reports like that one, coupled with the sight of casualties all around us, and the sporadic reports of brutality toward American hostages, made it abundantly clear to all of us: no one was safe. But then, as chaotic and frightening as the landscape was becoming, God found a way to speak once again into our lives. In the midst of the chaos, confusion, and carnage of those days, I began to notice something happening. Something good. And a young man named Corporal Campbell was one of the first signs of new life.

Leaning against the hard, cold earth of my deep fighting hole, I closed my eyes and listened to the wind whip across the top of my helmet. I had just finished the last morsels of my MRE, which on that occasion consisted of a slab of white chicken, crunchy yellow rice, and a brownie. Not bad when you read about what soldiers used to eat. The chicken certainly wasn't the favorite MRE of choice, and there was a running joke surrounding the fake "grill-marks" embedded on the meat. I guess it was the military's way of making you feel like you were eating a down-home dinner right off the barbecue. Nevertheless, I didn't mind it so much that night, and after half a canteen of warm water to wash it down, I actually felt kind of full.

Even though it was dark, no one was allowed to go to sleep yet. It was the hour of the day called "Stand-To," one of two times each day when our entire battalion assumed a heightened posture of readiness. The first was at dawn, just before sunrise; and the other, just after sunset. Historically, most enemy attacks come during one of those two times, when light is poor and men are in a sluggish state, whether having just awakened, or feeling relaxed and ready to bed down for the night. In any case, I was wide awake when I heard someone say, "Chaplain Cash . . . Chaplain Cash, is that you?"

The whispered voice momentarily startled me. I turned around to see the silhouette of a Marine standing at the upper edge of my fighting hole.

"Is that you, Chaplain?"

"That's me . . . you found the right guy. Who's there?"

"It's Corporal Campbell . . . from Tracks."

I tried to remember who he was. Over the last eight weeks, since arriving in Kuwait and now in Iraq, our battalion had been steadily growing in numbers through the addition of attachments, those augmenting units temporarily assigned to our battalion. These attachments always brought added muscle or enhanced our capabilities to accomplish our mission.

Corporal Campbell was from the Third AAV Battalion, better known as "Tracks." Without those guys we would never have gone anywhere. Our battalion had somewhere in the neighborhood of fifty AAVs, along with their crews and the commands that ran them. Campbell's specialty was AAV mechanic.

As I pulled myself out of my fighting hole, even in the dark I recognized his face; and as in the case of almost every AAV mechanic, it was smeared with oil. He was smiling, and I could tell he wanted to talk.

Walking him to the side of my vehicle (Kirkham was always warning us about standing alone as a silhouette for an enemy to draw a bead on), I leaned against the hood and asked him what was up. "I've been trying to find you for some time now," he said. "I'm attached to the Bravo Command and they said that you were near Alpha Company. So I decided to just come over here and find you for myself."

I started doing the math. "Bravo Command . . . that's a long ways away from here, isn't it?"

He didn't say anything; he just nodded his head in agreement.

"In fact, the Bravo Command is over one thousand meters from here!"

Again, he just nodded.

This young man had walked over one thousand meters, by himself, in the dark, along a road that we had every reason to believe was clearly visible to enemy forces. "Why would you walk so far just to see me?"

I tried not to think what could have happened. I assumed that maybe he had been informed about a crisis in his family and just needed to talk. But the faint smile on his face seemed to rule that possibility out.

"I haven't been to church in a while," he explained. "I'm from a Christian tradition that worships on Saturdays rather than Sundays. Since it's Saturday night, I was wondering if you and me, just the two of us, could do church together?"

What could I say to that? My heart melted.

I quickly grabbed my Bible, pocket devotional, and red-lens flashlight; and the two of us, huddling together in the back of Dr. Trivedi's combat ambulance, worshiped God.

As we bowed in prayer in that darkened and cramped compartment, my soul was flooded with the awareness that we might as well have been in the world's most beautiful cathedral. It didn't matter. There we were, only two of us, filthy—neither of us had taken a shower in at least two weeks. We were turning the torn pages of a mud-stained Bible. The only light we had to guide our reading was the dim red glow of a flashlight the size of a pen. But for us, that ambulance was holy ground because we were in the presence of God. It was a worship service I will never forget.

And Corporal Campbell wasn't the only one reaching out to God. Faced with the ruination, desolation, and despair of war, Marines of every rank and responsibility began hungering and thirsting for lasting peace in their lives. God seemed to be using the very chaos of war to provide a stark contrast with the peace and assurance that He brings through His Son, Jesus. This was especially evident during times of group prayer that I shared with the Marines throughout the war.

I would find an AAV with its engine running, ready to push out on a mission. As loudly as I could, I would pound on the back of its massive hatch. A couple of muffled voices from inside the compartment would yell, "Who is it?"

"It's the chaplain!"

The hatch would swing open like an ancient vault, revealing twenty-five Marines huddled together—sweating, uncomfortable, faces covered in dirt, but good to go—ready, willing and able to execute their mission. I was always amazed at how many burly Marines could fit inside a poorly ventilated space no bigger than a long bathroom, loaded down with weapons, water, and all their other gear. How could they still be smiling when the hatch swung open?

"Hey guys, how about a prayer before you head out?"

It never failed. Just like that, without a moment's hesitation, all twenty-five of them would lower their rifles to their sides, grab one another firmly by the arms, and bow their heads.

Of course our prayers were simple, but they were exactly what we all needed. We prayed for protection, for courage, for victory, for faith in difficult moments, for the assurance that we were not alone, for help in making tough decisions, for grace to endure, and for strength to overcome. We called out to God as children, as men in need, as brothers facing trial. We relied on the power of the Psalms, the will of God, the teachings of Jesus, and the promises of eternal life. We clung to hope, trusted in God's love, and believed in a divine purpose and plan behind it all.

Capturing the passion and simplicity of how we prayed in those significant moments together is a prayer found in the official *Marine Corps Field Devotional Book*. It is called "My Morning Offering."

O God, for another day, for another morning, for another minute, for another chance to live and serve You, I am truly grateful.

Do . . . this day free me:
> from all fear of the future,
> from all anxiety about tomorrow,
> from all bitterness towards anyone,
> from all cowardice in the face of danger,
> from all laziness in the face of work,
> from all failure before opportunity,
> from all weakness when Your power is at hand.

But fill me
> with Love that knows no barrier,
> with Sympathy that reaches all,
> with Courage that cannot be shaken,
> with Faith strong enough for the darkness,
> with Strength sufficient for my tasks,
> with Loyalty to Your Kingdom's goal,

with Wisdom to meet life's complexities,
with Power to lift me to You.
Be with me for another day, and use me as You will. Amen.[1]

———————————

WHEN OUR TIME FOR PRAYER WAS OVER and it was time for the AAV to pull out, I tried, as best I could, to lay my hands on each one of them, on an arm, a shoulder, or a hand. Human touch, I found, became an all-important symbol to them, nearly sacramental in its import.

Sometimes I found myself standing in the dust of a departing AAV, having just prayed with a group of warriors. Staring off into the desert sky, I thought to myself how clear all of it seemed—life, faith, God. We Christians are sometimes the worst at "majoring in the minors," embroiling ourselves in debates about minor theological points, focusing on peripheral matters of doctrine and practice that too easily divide us. But in the cramped cabins of those greasy AAVs, it all seemed to so clear. Men in need, humbly and with a childlike faith, were seeking a God who never fails to provide for His children.

"Chaplain, is there a God who will help me when I'm afraid?"

"Chaplain, is there a God who will go with me through the firefight?"

"Chaplain, is there a God who will forgive my sins and meet my deepest need?"

They were desperate. And desperate men do not hunger for trivialities. They hunger for someone to point them to the One who is the Way, the Truth, and the Life. They long for a relationship with God.

How could I ever forget, for example, a young private first class from Second Tanks? I was conducting a prayer service one morning behind a berm that separated our forces from the eastern side of Ad Diwaniyah, which was still a danger zone. The young private, a Marine reservist from Trenton, New Jersey, had been called up to active duty with no more than two week's notice. He had been at work one day at his civilian job, and in a matter of forty-eight hours, he was mobilized at his reserve center, on his way to the front lines in Iraq.

He and his fellow tankers had already seen one of their own killed during the first week of the war, shot by an accidental discharge. And the young man had already seen his fair share of fighting too. His particular tank platoon almost always led the charge for our Marines wherever we went.

He had wandered into the service, and once it was over, he wanted to talk to me. I could immediately see that something was troubling him. His deep-set eyes looked frightened; his mouth was clinched, almost like he was holding back tears. He was clutching a crucifix that hung around his neck.

"Chaplain, you got a minute to talk?"

I nodded and asked him to sit down. He was visibly nervous and seemed to be searching for the right words to say. Only two words came out: "I'm terrified!"

When I asked him why he was so frightened, he explained that he had received a disturbing letter from an aunt—a relative whom he trusted deeply. It seems that she had consulted a psychic before the war to glean any important information that might help her deal with having her nephew serving on the front lines. She hoped to find out whether or not he would be injured or otherwise harmed. My eyes must have been widening in utter disbelief as he talked. I could hardly imagine a loving aunt going to a psychic and then writing to her nephew the results of her inquiry. But that is exactly what she had done.

"It's going to be at a bridge," the young Marine said, nearly trembling with emotion.

"What's going to be at a bridge?"

"That's where I'm going to get it. The psychic told my aunt that I'm going to be killed at a bridge." He looked away for a moment and then went on, "And our platoon just got tasked with taking a bridge the day after tomorrow. What am I going to do? Chaplain, this one's really scaring me."

I wanted to thoroughly castigate his aunt for her lunacy, for her lack of compassion for her nephew. But that wasn't the most important point. The young man was desperately afraid. Opening my Bible to Psalm 1, I asked him to read for himself the words that I knew he needed to hear:

> Blessed is the man
> Who walks not in the counsel of the ungodly,
> Nor stands in the path of sinners,
> Nor sits in the seat of the scornful;
> But his delight is in the law of the LORD,
> And in His law he meditates day and night.
> He shall be like a tree
> Planted by the rivers of water,
> That brings forth its fruit in its season,
> Whose leaf also shall not wither;
> And whatever he does shall prosper.
>
> —PSALM 1:1–3

For years, the private told me that he had been what he called an "on-and-off" Christian, attending church here and there with his family, but never having owned his faith for himself. I could tell that this crisis, while sparked by a discordant letter, was quickly becoming an opportunity. It was time for him to discover, perhaps in a way he never had before, the power and victory that a relationship with Christ brings. With my Bible in hand, I shared with him how Christ died not only to set us free from the power of sin, but from the power of fear and uncertainty . . . evil. "For God has not given us a spirit of fear," I read, "but one of power, and of love, and of a sound mind" (2 Timothy 1:7).

Hope dawned on his worried face. His eyes brightened, his countenance relaxed, and a smile began to form. Together we bowed in prayer and prayed that from this day forward he would not heed any voice or thought that came by the way of fear and terror; but that instead he would look continually to the One who had died and risen for him. We asked God to help him trust and believe that nothing in this world—no power, no threat, no false prediction—could ever frustrate God's perfect will from being accomplished in his life. With that, I laid my hands upon his shoulder and said, "Go now, and do your job. Just know that God will be with you, not only during the rest of the war, but for the rest of your life."

He had wandered into a service just an hour earlier with a burden on his back so heavy that it was literally crushing the life out of him. Now he smiled and walked away to his tanks and his friends with a lighthearted step, quiet confidence, and the assurance of victory that only God could bring.

And after six months in Iraq, where he saw five pitched firefights against the enemy, had countless bullets and rockets fired at him and his tank crew, and crossed more than twenty bridges, that private first class from Second Tanks grabbed his pack and boarded a jumbo jet. After taking one last look over his shoulder at Kuwait City International Airport, he smiled and flew home, very much alive.

I must have led hundreds of services back at Camp Pendleton, and even in Kuwait. And every one of them was a blessing to be a part of, because God always inhabits the praise of His people (see Psalm 22:3). But there can be no doubt that once we crossed the line of departure into Iraq and found ourselves in the midst of the battle, our worship services began to take on a whole new meaning and significance.

I would drive up in my Humvee to a platoon or a company, and there the men would be waiting. Sometimes there were ten. More often there were one hundred ten. And they were hungry for the Lord. We all were. "Blessed are those who hunger and thirst for righteousness, for they shall be filled" (Matthew 5:6). Time after time, we were filled.

Using the tailgate of my vehicle as an altar, together we sought the Lord. We prayed together, heard God's Word together, shared communion together. The men would come to receive the body of Christ with their heads bowed in reverence, their hands cupped together and lifted up—hands that were filthy, sometimes even bloody, but hearts that were pure. "Blessed are the pure in heart, for, they shall see God" (Matthew 5:8). And we saw God. We saw Him move in our lives.

One busy Sunday, Rufo and I had just driven away from leading our sixth worship service of the day. And even though the sun was quickly fading beyond the western horizon, there was still one other unit that we had not gotten to yet—the 81-mm. mortarmen. Earlier that day, I had already promised one of their radio operators, Lance Corporal O'Hanaka, that Rufo and I would be there for him and his guys before sunset. The problem: Rufo and I couldn't find their position. They weren't responding when we called to them over the radio, so up and down we drove along Route 1, searching the sea of Marines who spanned several kilometers. No one seemed to know where they were. Finally, feeling mildly defeated, we decided that it just wasn't going to happen. I wasn't too upset, except that I'd wanted to fulfill my promise to O'Hanaka.

"We'll have to find them tomorrow. Sun's almost gone and it's getting too dark."

Rufo agreed and turned our vehicle around to head back to our position. As our beat-up Humvee made the wide-sweeping turn off the road and momentarily onto the gravel shoulder, my eyes spotted Gunnery Sergeant Francisco. He was filling up water containers and loading supplies into the back of his Humvee, obviously heading somewhere. Although the 81s comprised their own section, Gunny Francisco was a part of their same company and probably knew where they were positioned.

I asked Rufo to pull over and hollered at Francisco. "Hey Gunny! Do you have any idea where the 81s are?"

He smiled, nodded and said, "Heading there right now. Why don't you just follow me?"

I looked at Rufo and laughed. "Looks like O'Hanaka and the 81s are gonna have a service after all."

Following Francisco's Humvee, our vehicle staggered and pitched over the uneven earth until we finally arrived at the remote front-line entrenchment that the 81s called home. I was thankful we'd had a guide because their position was even more out of the way than I had thought.

The first face I recognized was O'Hanaka's. His smile was visible from thirty yards away, and had a playful smirk to it as if to say, "You almost didn't make it, Chaplain." I winked at him and smiled right back as if to say, "What'd I tell you?"

Immediately O'Hanaka began spreading the word that the chaplain was there to do services. A steady stream of men began to gather around the back of my Humvee where Rufo had already set up our makeshift altar on the tailgate. In the center of the altar, stood a plain gold cross. To the right of the cross was the cup of wine; to its left, the bread. A simple setup, and yet every time I looked at our altar against the backdrop of desert, rubble, war, and death, its power and purity moved me.

I turned around to find that the steady stream of Marines was still trickling in to the semicircle "congregation" that had now formed. Their backs were to a high berm. On the other side of it was a massive desert field separating us from Ad Diwaniyah. The field was nothing short of a demilitarized zone. We were on the front lines.

Staff Sergeant Mainz, seeing there were still a few more Marines moving toward the gathering, did what only a Marine staff noncommissioned officer could do and still get away with it.

Bellowing from his lungs, he shouted, "Marines! Chaplain's here! If you want to go to services, get the —— moving! Chaplain ain't got all ——ing night!"

At that he smiled at me and joined the group that had gathered, gladly taking one of the field hymnbooks that Rufo was passing out to all the men. How could I not love these guys?

The order of worship we followed was usually the same, and that night was no exception. I always tried to plan the services to go no more than thirty minutes. So much can happen to pull the participants away, and yet we all very much enjoyed a general pattern or liturgy, if you will, that we could rely on each week.

After a brief, "How you doing?" I usually opened with a call to worship that signified the presence of God, His love, His protection, and His unchanging mercy. Then came the hymns.

For many, I noticed, this became a unique opportunity to vocalize their faith in a meaningful way. So often, young Marines, being at the bottom of the chain of command, don't have much to say or aren't asked to share their opinions. Worship, in a sense, removed those obstacles. It gave Marines of all ranks and phases in life a chance to "sing unto the Lord" and to "cry out from the depths to the One who always hears." We sang songs like "How Firm a Foundation," "Amazing Grace," "Holy, Holy, Holy," "O God Our Help in Ages Past," and "Father I Adore You." Those lamentations, assurances, and cherished promises filled the skies over the war-torn lands of Iraq. These were the truths that bound our hearts in worship day after day, week after week. To quote from a particular favorite hymn:

> When through fiery trials thy pathway shall lie,
> My grace, all-sufficient, shall be thy supply.
> The flame shall not hurt Thee; I only design
> Thy dross to consume and thy gold to refine.
>
> The soul that on Jesus hath leaned for repose
> I will not, I will not, desert to his foes;
> That soul, tho' all hell should endeavor to shake,
> I'll never, no never, no never forsake.[2]

Following the hymns, scripture was read, almost always, by willing Marines. There seemed to be an added power every time a warrior, standing in front of his own peers, spoke aloud the words of the Holy Scripture. I will never forget, when a young lance corporal, passionate about his faith, agreed to read the words of Jesus in Revelation 3:20.

> Behold, I stand at the door and knock. If anyone hears my voice and opens the door, I will come in and dine with him, and he with Me.

The young man was not necessarily articulate, but he was wholeheartedly determined that his brothers in arms knew the hope and joy that comes from a saving relationship with Christ. The men in the service that day were gripped by his reading. Looking back, I am certain that the great harvest of souls I saw reaped during the war was because courageous young Marines who were spread throughout the battalion, providentially placed in their platoons by the hand of God, offered a living testimony of knowing Christ to the others.

After the Scripture readings, I gave opportunity for anyone to share prayer requests or burdens. This was always a special time of release. We heard about buddies who were injured, family members who were in crisis, the need for courage, and so much more. These were the burdens that we "cast upon the Lord," as the Bible commands us. Of special significance each week was prayer for the families of those Marines and soldiers who had been killed in battle. After March 21 at Pumping Station 2 in Rumeilah, that prayer request became unceasing.

Following a brief sermon, in which I tried to allow God's Word to speak to the men's needs, we celebrated Holy Communion. As much as I enjoyed singing and preaching, communion was for me, and I believe I speak for most of the men, the most powerful aspect of our worship experience.

I had always heard my father-in-law, a thirty-year naval chaplain who also served with Marines, talk about the desperate need for Holy Communion that he observed in men who were facing battle or some monumental trial. I saw it as well. Our men yearned for something they could touch and taste, something they could visibly and tangibly share in the presence of others. They needed a sign and seal that we were not alone.

One after another, the men would come forward, their rifles over their shoulders, clanging against their gear, hands gnarled and faces filthy, and with outstretched arms and cupped hands, they would receive. Although I am Baptist and my tradition normally practices otherwise, the method we used was intinction—first passing out the wafer, and then allowing the men to come and dip their wafer into the chalice. What a profound blessing it was for me to look in the eyes of each Marine who dipped his wafer into the cup, to place a hand upon his shoulders and confer a blessing or a prayer. In truth, with each prayer, I partook of the blessing as well.

Marines expect their chaplains to inspire them, and of course I hope and pray I did that. But it was the men's humble love for God and simple faith in His power to heal, forgive, and protect, that became a source of unspeakable blessing for me in my own walk with Christ. Just as a prism, refracting a single beam of light, reveals the splendor of its many bright colors, Holy Communion, on the field of battle, made compellingly clear the real joys of being a part of the body of Christ.

In those services, I saw at least three reasons that I believe Holy Communion was so important to the men.

First, *communion reminded these warriors that Christ Himself knew something about battle, heroism, and sacrifice.* Sharing the sacrament of the body and blood of Christ reminded them that Christ Himself had stormed headlong into the teeth of battle, just as they had. He also knew the anxious moment of the heart before stepping foot into the lair of the enemy. He understood the costly price for others' freedom—that "greater love" whereby a man lays down his life for another. Communion reminded them that they were neither alone nor misunderstood as warriors. Their God had been one too.

Second, *communion was a way to partake of something spiritually concrete before rushing off onto a field of battle full of intangibles and uncertainties.* Jesus said in Mark 2 that true worshipers will worship Him in Spirit and in truth. And yet, knowing our need for experience, He also left us with a practice that would make the deepest spiritual realities—the unseen—come to life by being touched and tasted. How many times did these Marines head off to the fight wondering, hoping, praying all would go well? Communion was God's special gift to us all, during which we did not have to wonder or hope or merely pray that He was with us. Through the power of the sacrament, we saw Him with us. He was there.

Third, *communion fulfilled the deep longings that we all had, indeed that every human heart knows, for mystery.* We all understood that there are some aspects of the Supper that cannot be explained, that there is a deeper work of God transpiring when we receive the elements by faith, that there is a work of the Spirit that none of us can quite articulate. And this is vital in anyone's journey of faith, but especially to the one who is forced to gaze out upon the wasteland and carnage of battle. All around the naked reality of man's failure and evil intent is exposed. Every piece of rubble is a commentary, every stain of blood is an advertisement of the failed work of humanity. Communion is a bold contradiction, for within it lies a mystery suggesting that a different ending is possible for our world and for our lives. An ending that doesn't result in the death and destruction of the battlefield, but in the hope and the glory of the empty tomb.

After serving communion to the Marines of the Eighty-First Platoon, we sang a brief hymn and bowed for the benediction taken from Numbers 6:24–25, "The Lord bless thee and keep thee. The Lord make His face shine upon thee and be gracious unto thee. The Lord lift up His countenance upon thee and give thee peace . . . both now and in the life everlasting, Amen" (KJV).

By the time the service ended, the late afternoon sun had finally disappeared, revealing the faint half-moon and a few dimly twinkling stars. In the time between the opening prayer and the closing hymn, the breeze had gone from warm to pleasantly cool, just enough to reinvigorate our tired bodies. As I milled around for a few minutes talking and laughing with a few of the Marines, I noticed that a tall stocky one with glasses was waiting near the back end of our Humvee, which in a matter of minutes had reverted back from a sacred altar of worship to an olive drab tailgate. I soon learned that his name was Eli Schlueter.

"Chaplain," he said hesitantly, "I've never really gone to church much, but something told me to come tonight. I don't really know how to say this, but I've never become a Christian, and it's something I've always known I needed to do. So what should I do?"

There are few occasions when an earnest seeker seems to ask the perfect question, with the perfect disposition and posture of heart. Most of the time, as pastors, we hopefully ply our trade, attempting to persuade people just like us, people who are full of mixed motives, misunderstandings, shibboleths, and fronts. Eli Schlueter was exceptional. He didn't express a hint of reservation, mistrust, or effrontery. He just wanted to know what a man must do to be saved and what he had to do to be that man.

As he spoke, I couldn't help but notice that he seemed to have walked right out of the 1950s—he looked like he came from a perfect world of Mom and baseball and apple pie. But it wasn't so. Having grown up in Iowa, Illinois, and Wisconsin, Eli Schlueter had lived in fifteen different foster homes between the ages of eight and eighteen. He never knew his biological mother, and upon turning twelve, he had no contact with his birth father for the next six years. Eli and his younger brother, during the most critical adolescent years of their lives, were bounced from one family to another, at times allowed to live together, but more often than not separated.

One of Eli's childhood friends had a grandfather who had served in the army during World War II. Eli and his friend always looked forward to seeing the aging veteran, and Schlueter recalled later that it was the old man's stories that first got him thinking about joining the Marine Corps.

He graduated from high school in 2001, and soon after the events of September 11, he enlisted in the Marines. He believed it was something he needed to do, not only for his country but for himself. Military service would offer him the kind of direction and stability that he had never known as a child.

Along the way, as he had moved in with family after family, Eli had experienced minor encounters with church and faith, but nothing he could ever make sense out of or own for himself. In my opinion, he was already a walking miracle—a testimony to the love of a heavenly Father who, unlike many earthly fathers, never abandons His search for us.

After we had talked for a while, I grasped the side of one of Eli's big arms and asked, "Do you believe that Jesus is the Son of God . . . that He died on the cross for your sins . . . rose from the dead the third day . . . and lives right now through the power and presence of the Holy Spirit?"

He nodded, "I do."

"And do you want to trust Him with your whole heart and live for Him the rest of your life?"

"Yes," Eli responded, smiling from ear to ear.

In the moments that followed, it was my great privilege, my profound honor to lead the young Marine in a prayer in which together we asked God to send His Son, Jesus, into Eli's life, cleansing him from his sin, and forever making him a child of God. And with that simple step of faith, Eli Schlueter received the indescribable gift that God offers to everyone who looks to the Cross and believes.

When we lifted our heads from prayer moments later, there was a smile on his face that almost made his glasses look crooked. My eyes welled up with tears. I looked at Rufo and wanted to celebrate. And that's when the thought occurred to me.

Why not a baptism?

Admittedly, in the context of a local church, there is time for counseling and reflection, and baptisms can be planned more methodically. But this was war. None of us knew when we said, "Good-bye" or "See you later," what the next few hours or days might bring. Schlueter was a front-line infantry mortarman. I saw no point in waiting to baptize him.

I once read a powerful article by a navy chaplain serving with Marines in Vietnam—Eli Takesian. He said that there were a few occasions where the battles his men fought were so intense that he had baptized a few willing and sincere believers with his own saliva. Now, it wasn't my plan to try that one. But a baptism it would be.

Just then I remembered the Ethiopian in the New Testament book of Acts, who asked Philip the Evangelist on the spot, "Look, water.

What prevents me from being baptized?" I turned to Rufo who was watching the whole thing. "Do we have any water in the vehicle?"

"Just your canteen, sir."

It would do.

Filling my chalice to the rim with the potable water from my canteen, I asked the young Marine to lean back, and in the name of the Father, and the Son, and the Holy Spirit, Eli was baptized. The water streamed down his forehead and onto his flak jacket, and his fellow Marines, many of whom were brothers in Christ, watched with excitement in their eyes and joy in their hearts. Another soul had been born into the kingdom of God.

I looked over at Rufo, who was smiling from ear to ear. I know he felt the same thing I did—it wasn't only Schleuter who had received a gift. It was us too. God had allowed us to be in the right place at the right time, to help a young seeker discover the miracle of new life in Jesus Christ. I hugged the drenched Marine and said one last prayer with my arm around his shoulder. Then off he went, back to his fighting hole. And Rufo and I headed back to ours. A good day.

I HAVE OFTEN WONDERED how different that service might have been if I had not found Gunnery Sergeant Francisco loading supplies into his vehicle on the side of the road. Or what if Lance Corporal O'Hanaka had not relentlessly held me to my promise? Or suppose I had just decided to find the 81s platoon the next day? I guess I'll never know the what-ifs. But I have to believe that from the beginning, that worship service was meant for a Wisconsin boy, who, after never quite finding a home of his own, had decided to join the Marine Corps. It was a decision that inevitably brought him to manhood, to war, to the tailgate of a beat-up Humvee, and to the everlasting arms of a loving Father who would never leave him or forsake him.

It had only been ten days since we had crossed the line of

departure into Iraq, and already the men of First Battlion, Fifth Marine Regiment had witnessed the grim sights of war; had known the fear and trepidation of being in a dangerous land; had experienced the heart-breaking sorrow of loss and the ache of human suffering. All around us lay ruin and desolation, rubble, and a scarred landscape inhabited by men and women, boys and girls, desperate to believe a better day would come.

And yet, despite the reality of the world we looked out upon, God was quietly but powerfully revealing another world—a kingdom that would have no end; a kingdom that cannot be thwarted by death, disease, ruination and the machinations of men. It's a kingdom built not with human hands, but built by the Spirit of God and forged upon the anvil of faith within the hearts of men. Saint Augustine was right: there is a *city of God* that shall have no end.

> God is our refuge and strength, a very present help in trouble. Therefore we will not fear though the earth should change, and though the mountains slip into the heart of the sea; though its waters roar and foam; though the mountains quake at its swelling pride. There is a river whose streams make glad the *city of God*, the holy dwelling place of the Most High. God is in the midst of her, she will not be moved; God will help her when the morning dawns. The nations made an uproar, the kingdoms tottered; He raised His voice, the earth melted. The LORD of hosts is with us. The God of Jacob is our stronghold . . . Cease striving and know that I am God.
>
> PSALM 46:1–7, 10

The longing that I had seen in the life of Eli Schlueter was a parable of the longing that was sweeping the hearts and minds of our Marines. With tears in their eyes, they came. They came to hear God's Word, to receive Holy Communion, to pray for their brethren. They came to see a deeper reality shining through the reality of bullets and death and destruction. And God, who honors the simple faith of our most elementary steps toward Him, met us. He met us with the comfort of His Holy Spirit and the abiding peace of His presence.

Peace amidst war. After Schlueter's dramatic baptism, I remember thinking, *The audacity of it all!*

Peace amidst war.

The lesson had begun. It would not be the only lesson we learned.

7
Assa-lamu-alay-Kum

Our milelong convoy wound its way through the dusty village of Zubadiyah, and I leaned out my passenger-side window. Like a good assistant driver is supposed to do, I scanned over every corner and alley I could see, looking, searching for anything or anyone even remotely suspicious. It was to no avail. The more I looked out upon the crowds that had poured out of the mud huts and onto the streets of the tiny village west of the Tigris, the more I was gripped by their faces—their sincerity, their longing, their welcome.

But it was their children who really got my attention. Their eyes were bright with hope and all the unfulfilled dreams of childhood, yet they were visibly restrained, sad, even guarded. It was as if all the dreams of my own children were reflected in each little boy's or girl's face—all the hopes of being something, someone important or heroic. And yet there was a shadow, too; perhaps an awareness that those dreams might never come to pass. I had seen that same look countless times in the faces of adult parishioners I'd counseled or Marines who'd fallen onto hard times. It was the look of someone who has known tragedy or divorce or betrayal and has lost hope.

But why was this look in the eyes of such little ones? Was I just a dad missing my own family, reading into those children my own longings, fears, and heartaches? It did seem that several of the little boys and girls bore an uncanny resemblance to my own children. Or maybe I was moved by the poverty and squalor in which they lived, a primitive lifestyle that characterized Iraq's villages and towns, many of which had no running water or electricity. Men and women walked the roads barefoot while the elderly washed clothes in the same streams that provided drinking water. Perhaps it was the difficult living conditions, although for most of these people, this was all they had ever known. It's tough to miss something you've never had.

Just then I saw something that made me shudder, perhaps explaining the guarded looks of sadness on the faces of the children. In the center of that village stood a palatial compound, towering above every other roof in the village. Encircled by rows of barbed wire, this structure was not constructed of the mud-and-clay mortar that made up the rest of the dwellings. It was supported by marble pillars and gleaming stones. The compound, complete with its own satellite dish and antennas, gave off an air of serious intimidation. A heavy iron gate barred the front driveway from any uninvited guests, and a deep trenchlike moat lined the inside perimeter of the barbed fence.

I thought of history books in which I had seen illustrations of life in feudal times, where small farming villages run by peasants and serfs were overshadowed by the castle walls of the local petty king. To see streets lined with people who looked like they came right out of a Bible story picture book, and only moments later to encounter an opulent mansion hemmed in by fortresslike defenses just didn't make sense. Or did it?

Our unit, even as far back as late summer in Camp Pendleton, had been briefed that Saddam's regime had created a system in which the overwhelming number of people lived in poverty and desperate want. Only a few who cast their lot and loyalties with the governing authorities enjoyed power, privilege, or riches. Until our battalion had rumbled through the town of Zubadiyah, we had not really been exposed to this disparity between rich and poor. All we had seen up until this point was unmitigated poverty, or at best Bedouins who lived off the land as their fathers had undoubtedly done for millennia, tending their sheep along the fertile river valleys.

But now, April 2, 2003, our perceptions began to line up with the way things really were. Here the oppression was all too evident. Children and young men ran alongside our convoy, begging for any food we might throw to them. And when we did, it was a frenzy of violence as boys pushed aside girls to grab up the package, rip it open, and in a matter of seconds, gobble down its contents. Nobody was saving the rations for a rainy day. They ate the food on the spot. Sometimes they tried to trade cigarettes, liquor, ragged clothing, or even pornography for something to eat. They wanted food, and from the looks of their slight frames, that's what they needed the most.

Our troops took great pride in trying to help them. Nineteen- and twenty-year-old Marines and sailors demonstrated concern and compassion by offering both food and medical treatment all along the way. And the Iraqi people's reaction to our kindness was so ecstatic and emotional that I remember thinking they must have never before experienced real respect or esteem. Most of them hadn't.

Earlier, our battalion had passed through an intense firefight at the Saddam Canal, which saw dozens of Iraqi soldiers killed and dozens more taken prisoner. I had assisted our medical corpsmen and doctor while they labored furiously to treat an Iraqi soldier who had received a serious gunshot wound to the lower leg. For hours into the night, our corpsmen worked with the frightened young man, redressing his bandages, giving him water to drink, taking his vital signs, and holding his hand to assure him he was going to make it. I will never forget the look on his face. He couldn't understand why we were helping him. I watched as his abject terror gradually melted into a confused stare, and finally into the peaceable assurance that we were indeed trying to save his life.

Like other young men fighting in the Iraqi Army, he had no

doubt been told that we would brutalize him as well as his family. Of course, it didn't take long for the Iraqis who surrendered to see that we were not those kind of people. Yet it didn't surprise us that they believed such lies at first. Why not? Their own army had in fact committed unbelievable atrocities upon their enemies, especially the Kuwaitis and Iranians, not to mention upon their own civilian populations.

Just hours before providing medical assistance to the frightened Iraqi soldier, our unit had come across a family of four Iraqi men, four women, and four small children in their car, caught in the crossfire at Saddam Canal. When our men brought them over the canal and into a holding area, the battalion surgeon and I went over and tried to communicate with them. They were huddled together, the children shivering, the parents visibly terrified.

We offered blankets, food, and water, hoping to assure them that we did not intend to hurt them. Dr. Trivedi and I tried for about an hour to let them know that we were their friends and would let them go as soon as possible. Each of us had what we called a "walkie-talkie sheet," which had a hundred different Iraqi phrases and greetings along with their English transliterated equivalent. Over and over again we spoke the words *Assa-lamu-alay-kum*, which in Arabic means, "Peace be upon you." It was a phrase that all of us had been taught. Its etymology (historical origin) was religious, like the etymology of their entire culture.

Assa-lamu-alay-kum, we said to the frightened family that night, smiling in reassurance. With half-smiles, they nodded in agreement and tried to let us know that they understood.

The wooden conversation seemed to be going as well as possible, until one of our Marines, realizing that one of their men needed to relieve himself, offered to escort him to a spot a few feet away. In appreciation, the man nodded, "Yes," and off they walked, the Marine, naturally, with rifle in hand. Suddenly the man's wife started crying. Covering her mouth with her hand, watching her husband walk away into a nearby plot of grass, she began to sob. That's when it hit us that the whole thing looked like an execution:

an armed Marine walking off into the field, escorting a lone Iraqi detainee. After gesturing to the women as best we could what was really going on, in a matter of seconds she had calmed down with her husband once again at her side. Still, even after showing the family obvious kindness and good intent, the supposition remained that we wanted to kill them.

For most of the Iraqi people, authority simply implied brutality. Under Saddam, they had seen it for decades. When our battalion crossed into the southern Rumeilah oil fields, and encountered Iraqi civilians for the first time, many of us noticed that whenever we saw women, even at a considerable distance, they were sprinting for cover. Gunnery Sergeant Kirkham, who had served in the infantry for nearly twenty years, offered an invaluable perspective. "To these women," he said, "we're the plundering hordes, here to rape, kill, and destroy. And why wouldn't they think that about us? It's all they've seen in their own military leaders for the past three decades."

He was right. And as the days waned on in our push closer and closer to Baghdad, Marines and soldiers everywhere saw oppression at a level that we would never have imagined, including torture chambers, execution rooms, and mass graves. But nothing could have prepared us for what we found the day we pulled into the slums of Saddam City.

8 April 2003.

"CONTACT! WE'VE GOT ENEMY CONTACT!"

EVEN THOUGH BY THEN we'd heard the words too many times to count, the phrase still sent a chill down my spine and a sickening feeling in my gut. It was early afternoon, and our battalion had just entered the projects of Saddam City, a Republican Guard and Baath Party bastion, which was once again hallmarked by the strange contrast of mass poverty and military industry. As our rifle companies fanned out over the eight square kilometers that had been apportioned to our unit, they immediately ran into sporadic enemy forces firing rocket-propelled grenades (RPGs) and small arms rounds from the tops of buildings.

Captain Shawn Blodgett's voice came through over the net: "Contact! Contact! Taking small arms fire from across the river! Request permission to pursue and engage."

By now, the enemy was blanketing Charlie Company with heavy machine-gun fire, shooting from a rooftop just across the banks of the Tigris River. Blodgett's reaction was instinctual—he wanted to "Go get 'em!" The only problem was that they were out of our unit's zone, in a sector already being cleared by an adjacent battalion.

"Negative, negative, Cherokee 6. This is Hondo. Do not, I repeat, do not, cross river. Pull back to safe area and hold. How copy?"

Lieutenant Colonel Padilla's directive couldn't have been clearer. Getting tangled up in such a skirmish was too dangerous and would stretch our forces too thin. Besides that, if Charlie Company had crossed over, they might have been hit by friendly fire. Biting his lip, Blodgett answered, "Roger that Hondo, Solid copy. Cherokee 6 out."

Such was the condition of Saddam City for the first three hours after our battalion entered it, with sporadic firing from elusive enemy positions causing chaos, confusion, and the urge to fight back no matter the cost. Until now on our push northward we had not experienced such close-quarters urban combat. It was Day 19 of the ground war, and Coalition units were just beginning to enter the regions surrounding Baghdad, where innumerable political and military analysts had warned that we would take the heaviest casualties.

I was standing fifty meters from a huge military production factory that was engulfed in flames, and as I looked around I could see why those predictions had been made. Surrounding us on every side were buildings, apartment complexes, and walled-in compounds, all of which were potential ambush sites and sniper nests. The streets were filled with civilians, most of whom were not only cheering, but running from building to building looting, tearing down statues, and defacing murals.

Despite all the celebration, the security threat was high. Intelligence had reported clusters of Republican Guard units wandering the area, disguised as civilians, taking sniperlike shots at our troops. Already two of our companies had been dispatched to secure Baath Party compounds where tortures and executions had taken place for decades.

Just two hundred meters down the road, hundreds of Iraqi citizens crowded a traffic circle, cheering wildly, tearing down a billboard of Saddam Hussein that had marked the entrance to the city for years. We could all feel the adrenaline rush as we watched the first passions of freedom unleashed, still well aware that hard-core resisters were also present. In fact, the very next day, an intersection near that traffic circle would be dubbed "Dead General's Intersection" after an Iraqi Republican Guard intelligence general was killed by U.S. Forces to the overwhelming applause of the multitudes.

I wiped the sweat from my forehead and walked over to a platoon of Marines about to clear the burning military factory. I wanted each one of them to know they were being prayed for as they entered the building. "God be with you. I'm praying for you."

The men smiled back at me as I walked through them and placed my hand on each one's shoulder. They then moved slowly toward the building in a horizontal line, their rifles poised at shoulder level ready to fire. I watched as the last of them disappeared inside.

Only blocks away from where we were, Lieutenant Colonel Padilla and Sergeant Major Jones drove cautiously through a crowded city street, keeping tabs on where our companies were and checking out the area for the most secure place to set up a command center for the night. Just then a commotion broke out.

Padilla looked to his right and saw dozens of Iraqi civilians approaching his vehicle, frantically waving their arms back and forth up in the air as if something was desperately wrong. Sergeant Major Jones gripped his M-16 firmly in his hand and made sure the people could see its black barrel through the open window.

"Slow . . . slow," Padilla instructed his driver. "Let's see what they want."

As the civilians came to the right side of the vehicle, they began to make signs and signals with their hands and arms.

"What are they doing?" Jones asked, well aware that neither he nor Padilla had a clue.

Padilla watched them, keeping the corner of his eye on his own pistol. It might not be as effective as Jones's rifle, but it could, if the moment went south, mean the difference between his life and theirs.

By now the crowd was more frantic than ever. They all seemed to be pointing wildly in the direction of a building at the end of a dead-end road. Padilla searched the people's faces, trying to read them.

"Pree-zun, pree-zun, pree-zun!" Dozens in the crowd shouted the barely intelligible word while clasping their hands tightly around their wrists. They were indicating handcuffs or shackles or some other form of bondage.

"I think, they're saying 'prison,'" Jones exclaimed.

Several men, shouting the words, "pree-zun, pree-zun," held out their hands at knee level, palms facing down. A sickening thought ran through Padilla's mind: *Are they trying to tell us there is a prison full of children?*

The more he watched them gesture, the more convinced he was that this wasn't a wild mob. These were parents, pointing in the direction of a building where they believed their children were being held. Immediately, Padilla called the unconfirmed report in over the battalion's radio, requesting the Human Exploitation Intelligence Team (HUMET), along with a security platoon of riflemen, to get to the scene ASAP.

All along the way, HUMET had done their job, although most of us had never even seen them do it. Equipped with linguists, wads of hard currency, and nonconventional strategies, they had plied their trade in near secrecy. Because of their ability to communicate in local dialects, as well as to project a no-nonsense image of our battalion's capabilities to any potential doubters, their presence was invaluable.

Although Padilla felt like the frantic crowd was legitimate, he and Jones had only one rifle between them. He wanted to be sure they didn't find themselves fighting prison guards or other enemy forces that might have holed up in the facility. Still, between HUMET and a platoon of armed Marines, he had to believe they would all be safe enough. So he directed his driver to proceed slowly in the direction of the building.

Closer and closer he and Jones inched, hemmed in by the hysterical crowd, toward the iron gates that marked the compound's entrance. The edifice definitely looked prisonlike in its austere construction, with barred doorways and windows, raised walls, and stone walkways. Already a few of the men and women had begun to grasp and shake the gates with both their hands, peering down a darkened hallway, shouting and raving at the top of their lungs.

Suddenly there was the sound of screaming—not the screaming of adults or women, but of children. Then, like a river bursting through a weakened bank, as the iron gates swung open a mass of frail children came pouring out onto the stone terrace and into the arms of their waiting parents. They were malnourished and filthy, many of them wearing nothing more than rags for clothing. There were dozens at first; and then there were hundreds, mostly males between the ages of eight and fifteen. They flooded the lot in front of the building and soon were grabbing the necks of Padilla and Jones, crying, kissing them on each cheek, then jumping back into the arms of mothers, fathers, sisters, and brothers.

Padilla didn't know what to think or what to do. He couldn't help but feel emotionally overwhelmed. Little boys, many of whom were no older than seven or eight, were sobbing and clinging to their parents. He had never seen anything quite like it. Meanwhile Jones, in classic sergeant major fashion, bristled at all the overt affection. "Come on now, boy, don't go kissing on my neck. All right, all right, that's enough. Go hug on your daddy and mama."

Padilla couldn't help but laugh, and neither could Jones; but their laughter was mixed with tears. Indeed, whatever elation the two felt as they watched the celebration continue was soon overshadowed by a grim reality. In the hours after the release, HUMET specialists found out that the prison had been established years ago by the local Baath Party as a jail for the sons of parents who refused to support the regime. Many of the boys had been incarcerated for more than five years. As soon as they turned fifteen or sixteen, most of them were involuntarily conscripted into the regular Iraqi Army to man border posts, or to serve as cannon fodder in Saddam's wars.

In fact HUMET later discovered that many of the frightened conscripts we had faced in the southern Rumeilah oil fields were in fact just such men. They had been imprisoned as young boys, and after coming of age, they had been required by their military leaders to fight against the Americans. They were warned that they would be killed if they fled.

As the report began to circulate among the various sections of our battalion, we could hardly believe it. "What kind of place is this?" we asked each other. "A *children's* prison?" We had heard that Saddam's regime often jailed and murdered members of his own party who hinted at disloyalty. U.S. Forces everywhere had already seen the evidence of torture, mass executions, and clandestine assassinations. But children?

We already believed we were in Iraq for a just cause. Saddam's refusal to abide by the United Nations resolutions was enough for us. But now we were also responsible for freeing of hundreds of little prisoners. It became a symbol to us of our mission's significance. Much more was at stake here than merely enforcing resolutions or protecting America's borders. We were also defending the future of the Iraqi people.

Their oppression was not merely physical, socioeconomic, or political. It was also ideological. Fear, coercion, and the threat of abject subjugation were the day-to-day machinations Saddam's henchmen had used to rule the masses. They'd wielded power not merely to dominate, but to bring every discordant voice in line with one man's ideas and behaviors. "Operation Iraqi Freedom"— at first the term had sounded kind of benign, more a term of appeasement than anything else. But after finding the children's prison in the slums of Saddam City, and after releasing its young hostages, "Operation Iraqi Freedom" became real to me. And it confirmed something I was beginning to recognize more clearly each day.

Ever since our battalion had pushed beyond the sandstorm into day-to-day life in that Iraqi civilization, I had been awakening to a possibility that was at first too deep for words. It was dawning on me that things like oppression, captivity, and human bondage were more than physical realities. They were spiritual signposts. So were the Iraqi women.

That particular midday, the sun's afternoon heat had chased away any last current of cool air, making even the blowing wind outside our vehicle uncomfortably hot. I tugged on the collar of my twenty-five-pound flak jacket to try to ventilate my neck and chest. But it was to no avail. It was only early April, but the Middle Eastern heat had already arrived, casting its stifling blanket over us, nearly pressing the air out of our lungs.

For days I had seen slender figures shrouded in flowing black gowns making their way along the side of the gravel roads. Now there they were again, struggling along in the intense heat. One by one, their eyes furtively cut to mine and then turned back to the road. They passed in silence, their heads balancing enormous teetering baskets, held steady only by their thin arms and weathered hands. Ahead of them by nearly twenty yards strolled their husbands, laughing as they walked alongside other men, smoking their cigarettes, followed closely in line by skipping children.

Meanwhile, the dark figures behind the men carried their family's possessions and supplies, the weight of which sometimes pulled their shoulders nearly to the ground. They said nothing but simply trudged along in silence. No one offered a hand. No one even seemed to notice them. Of all the things we saw as we pushed ever closer to Baghdad, it was the sight of Iraq's women that told the most persuasive story. It didn't take us long to recognize the pattern behind it all.

Scores and scores of beautiful young Iraqi girls, who waved happily to us as we passed through their dusty towns, were living out their lives on a merciless timeline. From birth to adolescence, they played as cheerfully as the boys. Along with their brothers, they lined the streets as we passed through their villages, smiling, cheering, angling for any candy or rations we might give them. They ran in the fields, skipped stones at the brooks, and explored the riverbanks. And they were beautiful—their adolescent faces were clear and bright; their smiles modest; their hair, dark and flowing.

But by the age of twelve or thirteen, those pretty faces were gone, each one hidden behind a heavy, dark chador. They were victims of a culture where women exist as property, and their eyes provided the only window into their suffering. It grieved me—the father of daughters—that such sweet and lovely young girls eventually vanished into the oppressive landscape as nameless figures, owned by men for nothing more than usage.

The transformation was striking and tragic. I noticed that by the time the women were allowed to show their faces again, somewhere in midlife, their beauty was lost, hammered into a tired and haggard countenance. There was nothing reminiscent of those earlier days, when the innocence of girlhood still shone through their hopeful eyes.

Of course, it wasn't difficult to see why their feminine beauty had been driven out of them well before menopause. Day after day, as our convoys passed through the agricultural villages and mud-brick towns, we observed that it was the women alone who struggled and labored in the fields, who worked along the riverbanks, who carried the heavy loads. It was by and large the women who bore the brunt of the society's hard but necessary physical labor.

In that part of the world, the Islamic faith is a religion based upon strict adherence to Qur'anic (koranic) Law, also known as *shari'ah* law. For millions of Muslims, Islamic law requires its women to live suppressed lives as second-class citizens. While many Muslim people live under a modified religious ethos that grants varying levels of freedom to women, in almost every culture where Islam is practiced in rigid conformity to the Koran, or where the ruling government has attempted to impose the full weight of *shari'ah* upon its society, it is the women who bear the brunt of that weight in the form of great personal suffering.

Iraq, under Saddam Hussein, was not a theocracy. Saddam's government did not attempt to set up a Taliban-like religious regime. There is even a fledgling Christian church in Iraq that enjoys some measure of freedom and protection by law. But there are strains of Islam in Iraq that submit to its strictest interpretation. And after observing the women of Iraq, it was difficult for me not to equate their grueling way of life with the inherent bent toward rigid law within the Islamic faith.

I believe that one test of a religion's message is the way it manifests itself in the lives of its women. Does it give them the hope of equality and esteem that is due every human being made in the image of God? Or does it capitalize upon the physical disparity between women and men, causing women to live under the rule and prerogative of those which society deems as powerful?

"Come unto Me," Jesus said, "*all* ye who are weary and I will give you rest." In fact, Jesus Himself shattered his own society's religious and cultural customs and norms many times during his ministry. This was especially evident when he encountered an immoral Samaritan woman at Jacob's well. Here was a woman who, according to Jewish law, was considered unclean and outcast. Jesus not only initiated a conversation with her, but He went on to offer her the promise of eternal life (John 4). To women as well as men, Jesus exemplified grace.

But as our convoy continued to move slowly along the winding tributary of the Tigris River, we saw women all around us who were not treated with dignity and respect. Instead they were little more than veiled objects. Sadly, grace is often absent in Islam, which is based upon binding religious law, requiring strenuous adherence to every tenet of the "Five Pillars of Allah": the belief in Allah's greatness, daily ritual prayer, mandatory almsgiving, observance of the Muslim holy season of Ramadan, and a pilgrimage to Mecca. Rigid obedience to these dictates is the only way a faithful Muslim can hope to gain the rewards of heaven and eternal life. Even then, by some interpretations, the assurance of eternal bliss cannot be absolutely guaranteed unless a Muslim proves his devotion to Allah by martyring himself, or by committing jihad against infidels.

Certainly it can be said that it is only the extremists in the Islamic tradition who actually interpret jihad to mean violence against "unbelievers." However, extreme manifestations, such as the actions of suicide bombers and crazed gunmen, don't arise out of thin air. They are part of a religious tradition that from its very birth has used the edge of the sword as a means to convert or conquer those with different religious convictions. Chuck Colson, in his book *Being the Body*, raises the issue:

> Some moderate Muslims say the term *jihad*, which literally means struggle, is used figuratively as a picture of the individual's struggle to achieve holiness. That is doubtless so for millions of Muslims. Yet it was during an intense time of local wars that Mohammed, seeking to unite his people against aggressors, wrote of jihads. Many scholars believe that he meant it quite literally; indeed, the new religion Mohammed founded soon vanquished its enemies by the sword.[1]

Since September 11, 2001, millions of Muslims are commendably declaring Islam to be a religion of peace. Yet influential leaders in the worldwide Islamic community, including mullahs, ayatollahs, and political radicals, are demanding quite the opposite. In numerous mosques around the world, they continue to declare jihad against Americans, Christians, and Jews. And their impassioned summons has translated into an outbreak of suicidal martyrdoms and mass murders, the likes of which has rarely been seen in history.

As with the plight of women, the phenomenon of suicidal jihad is also a window into the essence of the Muslim faith. A religion that emerges from the soil of strict adherence to law as a means of gaining God's favor will always tend toward extreme self-sacrifice. If the rewards of heaven are given on the basis of how rigorously one has obeyed a legal code or how meticulously one has performed a prescribed set of good works, then the greater the deed or sacrifice that is carried out, the more God will be pleased.

In Christianity, it is not the grandeur of our sacrifice that earns us heaven. It is not our ability to strictly follow a rigorous religious code. Jesus Christ has already accomplished the single greatest act of obedience and self-sacrifice that this world will ever know. *He was* the martyr. *His* death, not our own, assures us of eternal life. His sacrifice, and no one else's, guarantees the promise of heaven.

If lavish sacrifices and rigorous adherence to a religious law are not necessary to gain God's favor, then what must we do to be saved? The answer is far easier (and perhaps far more difficult) than most people realize. We simply must receive. In Ephesians 2:4–9, the apostle Paul urges the new Christians in Ephesus to remember that salvation was never theirs because they "did, did, did" or "worked, worked, worked" for it. Salvation was theirs if they simply, and with the faith of a child, received the gift that Christ's death and resurrection provided for them. Paul wrote,

> But God, who is rich in mercy, because of His great love with which He loved us, even when we were dead in trespasses, made us alive together with Christ (by grace you have been saved), and raised us up together, and made us sit together in the heavenly places in Christ Jesus, that in the ages to come He might show the exceeding riches of His grace in His kindness toward us in Christ Jesus. For by grace you have been saved through faith, and that not of yourselves; it is the gift of God, not of works, lest anyone should boast.

The imprisoned children and the shrouded women we saw in Iraq had been betrayed by a society veiled off from the freedom Jesus Christ offers every man and woman and child alive. As we drove past them along the roadway, as our convoy wended its way through their villages, towns and cities, how I longed for the Iraqi people to know not only political freedom, but spiritual freedom.

I wanted them to know the joy that Eli Schlueter had experienced when he prayed a simple prayer of faith and asked Christ, the Almighty God of the universe, to abide in his heart.

I wanted them to know the peace and comfort that a frustrated Sergeant David Roza discovered when after prayer one night, I laid my hands on him and repeated over and over the words "grace, mercy, peace . . . grace, mercy, peace. . . ."

I wanted their little girls to feel the freedom and hope that the ten-year-old daughter of one of our Marines knew the moment I baptized her as a sister in Christ.

I wanted their little boys and young men to realize that life is not about keeping every aspect of the law or preparing oneself to die an early death in order to secure heaven. Instead I prayed their lives could be lived with the all the joy, discovery, and passion that Jesus introduced and modeled to his watching disciples.

I can still see the face of an Iraqi man I met just a few hours after we had released the children from their prison. He was allowing our snipers to stand guard on his roof—a particularly courageous act on his part since his home overlooked a suburb where Republican Guard units were known to operate and train. When I first shook his hand, he was alone on the front porch of his ramshackle house. He was smiling broadly, and I could see that he wanted to communicate with me despite the language barrier between us. Just then one of our snipers called down to me from the roof that the man had ten children, most of whom were in the house.

I motioned with my hand the sign of a child and pointed to his doorway. He nodded and before I knew it he had run into the house to fetch his children. One by one, they emerged from the front door. There must have been seven or eight there, the oldest perhaps eleven, the youngest, two—all with a handsome countenance like their father's. Still unable to communicate with each other in a meaningful way, I hastily pulled out a picture of my own family. I thought that if I could point to my wife and five children, reciting their names as I go, he might do the same with his children. By now the youngest, a little boy, was staring up at me with the biggest, brownest eyes I'd ever seen.

Down the line I went, pointing to the faces of my wife and children on the picture. "Caleb . . . Justice . . . Phoebe . . ."

He understood and, as soon as I was done, eagerly did the same. "Akmed . . . Fatima . . . Musaaf . . ."

Now we were communicating, not as strangers from foreign lands whose governments were at war with one another, but as men and husbands and fathers made in the image of God. We continued to talk about our children, my hands rubbing the heads of his. It was a happy moment, and one that seemed to transcend the rubble and ruination of the war zone that surrounded us on every side.

When it was time for me to go, I wanted to give him something to remember me by. I searched my vehicle looking for anything that might symbolize friendship, peace, brotherhood. All I could find was military issue gear and MREs, which I didn't think he really wanted. Then, with no agenda other than communicating friendship, I reached down into my assault pack and grabbed the only thing I could think of that meant a great deal to me. It represented the kind of peace that I wanted him to have. My fingers closed around the gold chaplain's cross insignia that I wear on the collar of my uniform.

I paused momentarily before I pulled it out. Before deploying, we were cautioned not to come across as if we were advancing any particular religion, since such an act might play into the hands of the militant Islamic world, which was already painting the war in those very terms. But gifts are just that—gifts. We give to others what we cherish the most. I knew this man would understand my gift to be nothing more than my own way of extending an olive branch of peace, brotherhood, and goodwill to him. It just seemed right.

I grabbed the cross and walked over to where he stood. When I handed it to him, he looked at it and immediately smiled. He knew that it was a sign and symbol of peace and that I was giving him a part of myself. Stretching out his arm, he took my gift, and said, "*Salem*," which means "peace" in Arabic.

"*Salem*," I responded, placing my free hand upon his shoulder.

I said good-bye to his children, playfully messing up the hair of the smallest one.

"*Assa-lamu-alay-kum,*" I said as I took my seat and closed the door of my vehicle.

"*Assa-lamu-alay-kum,*" he answered, waving good-bye.

Then it really hit me. *Assa-lamu-alay-kum* means "Peace be upon you."

God's purposes never change. Kingdoms may come and kingdoms may fall, wars may rage and nations may be in uproar, but God wants to bring all people—women and men, boys and girls—to know Him. It is God's will to bring His peace to everyone, everywhere. The Iraqis weren't a strange people from a strange land that had nothing in common with me. They were, like us all, made in the image of God. They were, like us all, a people for whom God had sent His Son into the world. And God loved them, just as He loves us all, whether they recognized it or not.

Later on, in light of our mission, I talked about these ideas with some of the men. When war is just, as we believed this effort was, it is good, right, and noble. But the opportunity for spiritual freedom we were providing for the Iraqi people made our cause even more significant, our hearts more determined, our resolve more intense.

I have always tried to remind our men that as military personnel they have a unique role in the world. Theirs is not merely a job but a calling, a vocation. I remember saying that the Bible only speaks of three institutions that are specifically *ordained* of God as having a special and sacred worth to society: the family, the church, and the government. Throughout the Bible government is elevated above all other institutions. I had even joked with a few interested men once, saying that when they'd joined the Marine Corps, in some sense, whether they knew it or not, they had entered the ministry. Of course, the ministry in that context is the *administration* of justice, order, and the protection of the innocent (as articulated in St. Paul's Epistle to the Romans, chapter 13).

While the military does not exist for the purpose of expanding any one religious belief or building any one notion of the kingdom of God, it does exist for the purpose of creating the kind of peaceable society where men and women may freely, and without fear of reprisal, pursue their faith. In this way, military personnel are in fact ministers, bringing the prospect of freedom—political and religious freedom—to whomever they defend.

We certainly didn't go to Iraq as crusaders, trying to convert anyone to Christianity or any other religion. We were there, however, to open doors of freedom that had not been opened for a very long time. The purposes of our nation in sending us to Iraq may have been justice and good. But the purposes of God transcended even those of our nation. Jesus said, "I have come that you may have life, and life more abundantly." He came to offer the peace of the kingdom of God to all the world. As we made our way northward in Iraq, we were able to see in a new way the part we were playing in the great drama of God's love for humanity.

His message to the Iraqi people—to us all—is *Assa-lamu-alay-kum:* Peace be upon you.

8
Arms Lifted Up

More things are wrought by prayer than this world ever knows of.
—ALFRED LORD TENNYSON

GET DOWN! GET DOWN! Don't know where it's coming from, but get down . . . now!"

Second Lieutenant Joshua Glover's urgent plea didn't fall on deaf ears, as every one of us either hit the deck or grabbed a weapon to fire back.

Stunned by the wicked melee of machine-gun fire, I lunged over and threw myself on the ground behind the front bumper of my Humvee. Rufo was right behind me. With his trembling hand on my shoulder to keep me down, he immediately made ready his rifle and prepared to engage. A hail of bullets was raining down around us. Where was it coming from? We had no idea, but it was close, way too close.

It was the morning of April 9. I had just been leading a worship service for a platoon of Charlie Company Marines on the banks of one of the lush Tigris River tributaries. Although the river was placidly beautiful, all around us lay the fly-infested outskirts of Baghdad—the neglected slum known as Saddam City.

That day it wasn't darkness and the stagnancy of oppression that was in the air, but the fresh winds of liberation. Only the day before we had discovered and set free those hundreds of children who had been locked up, some for four or five years. After that, impulses of freedom began to sweep throughout the slums like wild-fire. A new sense of liberty caused thousands of Iraqi citizens to take to the streets celebrating, looting Baath Party headquarters, gathering in groups, and singing in happiness. It was like nothing we had ever seen before.

Naturally we knew that lurking within those same crowds were imposters. However futile their efforts might prove to be, Saddam's loyalists would not hesitate to use any means necessary to terrorize our forces. So as we gathered under the shade of an AAV, the twenty men in our worship service had their rifles in hand and were more than ready to fling themselves into action in a moment's notice. Their readiness was about to be tested.

For twenty minutes we worshiped, sharing God's Word, singing His praises, and receiving Holy Communion. Then, only moments after I pronounced the concluding "amen" of the final prayer and benediction, just as my lips were forming the last words, "Go in peace," the barrage began.

The men scattered like billiard balls in a break shot. Although we couldn't tell where the bullets were coming from or where they were hitting, we knew the enemy was close. The sound of blazing gun barrels vibrated in the air around us, echoing its sickening "crack" off every structure and vehicle within sight.

"Just stay right there, sir. Don't move. I got you covered."

Resting his hand on my hunched shoulder, Rufo peered over the hood of our vehicle looking for the source of the firing. He was ready, I could tell, to let loose a not-so-friendly answer from his M-16, which by now was braced tightly into his clavicle, firmly resting on the vehicle's hood. I waited.

Seconds later, the firing stopped, and I could hear only the voices of our men yelling—what they were saying, I couldn't tell. Slowly, the Marines around me began to emerge, each with his rifle braced firmly against his shoulder, the sight held straight at eye level. Radios crackled to life as platoon sergeants and commanders began inquiring what had happened and whether there were any injuries.

The situation seemed to be under control, and thankfully there were no Marines injured. But the same couldn't be said for the seven Iraqi gunmen who had tried to attack us.

Lance Corporal Clay Anderson saw the Iraqis first. They were in a yellow, flat-faced work truck that was moving slowly toward our worship service. Anderson, who was manning a lookout point on the top of a building just a few yards away, could see that the truck was full of men, so just as a matter of protocol he pointed them out to his platoon sergeant, Staff Sergeant James Gominski, who was roving the rooftop as well.

"Keep your eyes on them," Gominski said. "They might just be workers, but you never know."

Anderson nodded and continued to watch the slow-moving truck. Then he noticed their guns. He was positioned only twenty or thirty yards away and was quite sure about what he saw. Bunched up like sardines in the compartment of the moving vehicle, every one of them was holding an assault rifle.

"Staff Sergeant Gominski! They've got weapons, and they're motioning for people to get out of their way. Somethin's going down!"

By now Anderson's heart was racing, and his palms were beginning to sweat.

Just then, the eyes of the hostile driver locked with Anderson's, and in that split second, they both knew what was going to happen.

Gominski, an experienced veteran, didn't even hesitate.

"Fire, Anderson! Fire! They're trying to take our checkpoint out! Fire *now!*"

Anderson laid into the trigger of his two-hundred-round squad automatic weapon (SAW) and unleashed a volley of lead into the windshield of the truck. As the glass-shattering rounds impacted, the truck swerved wildly. One of the gunmen, his legs splintered from Anderson's salvo, held his assault rifle out the rear window and shot aimlessly, hitting the shallow brick ledge just below where

Anderson lay prone. Tenaciously the Marine fired again, and this time there was no enemy answer. The blood-smattered truck jerked off the side of the dirt road and rolled to a stop under the rubble of a burned-out building. It was over. The earsplitting noise that had sent our worship service into a horrific postlude fell silent.

Of the seven gunmen who were in the truck that morning, one was killed instantly, three were critically injured, and the other three came through remarkably unscathed. Later that day, interrogation revealed that all seven men carried in their wallets official identification cards of Saddam's elite Republican Guard.

There was no doubt about their intent that morning. It was a suicide mission planned to take out our checkpoint, and they weren't the least bit concerned that we were gathered in worship. Thankfully, the vigilance of the watching Marines had thwarted the attack and saved our lives.

And yet, we all knew that something more than our own watchfulness, strength, and courage was protecting and defending us from our enemy. Across the ocean, thousands of miles away, untold numbers of Americans—probably millions of them, not to mention supporters all over the world—were hitting their knees and lifting us up in prayer to God. People were praying for us day and night, hour by hour, moment by moment. One letter I received just days after the attempted attack on our worship service in Saddam City came from a dear friend of our family.

Dear Carey,

It's Sunday night in Virginia Beach, and I've been thinking about you and all that has happened. We are hearing so much information that it's impossible to digest it all. However, our hearts are with you and your mission there in Baghdad . . . American Christians are having prayer vigils and special prayer meetings to pray for our troops, our leaders, and for the war effort. I pray that you feel our support and are strengthened by the force that only prayer can bring . . . Remember, the Lord is your Helper and He will sustain you. You have what you need. We love you, and are praying for you daily.

"Strengthened by the force that only prayer can bring." It was true. The first payload of life-breathing letters and packages arrived on April 8, just one day before we entered Saddam City. Not only did the words of our families, friends, and even complete strangers cheer us up and remind us of home and apple pie, but much more than that, their words revealed another kind of boldness that was being demonstrated during the war. Theirs was not the conspicuous valor of clearing an enemy bunker, or flying a dangerous mission. It was the quiet heroism that only God sees—the hard and sometimes lonely work of intercessory prayer.

That same quiet heroism had supported another army many thousands of years before, who also faced a cruel enemy bent on the destruction of all that was good. In the Old Testament book of Exodus, chapter 17, we read about the armies of ancient Israel, who found themselves face to face on the battlefield with the pagan armies of Amalek. As long as Moses lifted up his hands toward heaven in prayer, the battle swayed in favor of Israel. But whenever his arms grew tired and weak and began to fall, the tide turned, and the Amalekites would begin to prevail.

Aaron, Moses's brother, saw what was happening. He and Hur, another faithful Israelite, immediately rushed to Moses's aid. They physically lifted up his arms to God and held them there. And so, the Scriptures tell us, on the last day of the great conflict between the two nations, these three servants of God—Moses, Aaron, and Hur—could be seen by all, standing atop the mountain, overlooking the fight, and lifting up holy hands in prayer while the battle waged on. Because of their faithfulness, because they tirelessly stood together in prayer, God gave their army an overwhelming victory.

It has always been true: when the faithful fight the spiritual battle in prayer, those shouldering the burden of combat are given the strength to prevail. This was the awesome story of the home front during our war in Iraq. Prayer was the unseen force behind every victory, whether tactical or spiritual, that we experienced. Once we read the first delivery of mail after crossing the line of departure, that fact became as real to us as the Middle Eastern sand beneath our boots. While we fought the physical battle against flesh-and-blood enemies, it was our mothers, fathers, wives, children, friends, churches, schools, Girl Scout troops, and countless others who were fighting the spiritual battle on our behalf. Around the clock, from the moment our wheels touched down into Kuwait to the moment we crossed the line of departure into enemy territory, and to the moment we entered the dangerous outskirts of Baghdad, the American people were with us. They were like the strong arms of Aaron and Hur, and the holy hands of Moses, lifting us up in prayer to Almighty God.

Here's what some of them wrote.

From a homemaker and mother of two:

March 15
Dear Marine, Sailor, Soldier, or Airman,
   No words can describe what we feel. We know you are where you should be. Our hearts are heavy with the impact of this effort, but we stand on the promises of God. There are reasons for a "just war." God has allowed you to participate in this moment in history. We believe the Shield of God is upon you. Put on the full armor of God in prayer every day! You will have discernment, strength, health, empowering. God promises. "He will do it!" I will be praying for you daily.

From Jared in San Diego:

Dear Soldier,
   I do not know the specific role you are playing in this war, but I do know that whatever it is, it is contributing to the protection of my freedoms and my rights as an American to not fear terror-

ist acts against me and my family and to live a long happy life. I
am praying daily for you and for all the other men and women of
the Coalition forces to return home safely and unharmed. When
you do finally come home, I promise you that even when this war
has left the front pages of the newspapers, my family and I will
not forget the price you paid for our victory. Thank you so much!

The following prayer was offered up just hours before our
battalion was blinded by one of the worst sandstorms in recent Iraqi
memory. As I described earlier, we were not able to see our hands in
front of our faces, and we were stranded for hours in total darkness,
breathing out of respirators, knowing all the while that enemy
forces were only a few kilometers to our east and west.

From a grandmother of eight:

March 24
Dear Marine or Soldier,
    We know God is with you. We carry you in our hearts in
prayer day and night. We believe that God is equipping you in
every way that you need. You will come home forever changed.
The scenes you have seen . . . We are anguished in what you
must be enduring. We are crying out to God and when His people cry out, He delivers! People are all over the U.S. praying for
you . . . Be strong, be not afraid. The Lord your God is with you.
You are God's vessel. He is near to you.

The day the next letter was written, our battalion was moving
north on Route 1 in the midst of extremely dangerous territory.
Already a sniper had killed a Marine from a sister battalion just
kilometers away, and the day concluded with us witnessing an F-14
air strike on an enemy position that we had driven by not long
before and had never seen.

From a mother of three from Mt. Pleasant, South Carolina:

March 27

We are so blessed as a nation to have men like you—and those with you—to protect and defend the values and ideals of this country! Please know that you are in our thoughts and prayers, and we are so thankful that the Presence of the Lord is there with you on the battlefield. May He protect you with His Mighty Hand! May He who is able to do all things, protect you and give you peace.

From my wife, Charity, on the same day:

The nerves of many of the wives are on edge. This is a faith-shaking and hopefully building time for many people. I can't imagine not knowing the Lord. He is all I have to cling to . . . Please be careful and wise. Stay alert. I need you. Let all the guys know that literally thousands and thousands of people are praying for them. I love you . . . I miss you . . . I need you . . . Be careful. Angels all around . . . Psalm 37:7

From a Vietnam veteran to his son:

March 26
Son,

Know that we fill in the bulk of our time in prayer, while watching continuously the events as they unfold. Only you can know the excitement and anticipation that is there, but you must know that in my heart, I have been there, and would go again. It's what we do. It's the only thing we can do. It's just. It's good versus evil, and we are finally reasserting the moral imperative that brought this nation to its present state . . . Take excellent care in what you do; be alert and always know the situation in your presence and in the ones around you. Take care of them. He will of you.

The following was happening at roughly the same time our worship service in Saddam City was being stalked by the seven men in the yellow truck.

Prayer of an organist in Oceanside, California:

April 8

All of us here at home think of you and your comrades con-stantly. With every breath we take, we are uplifting a prayer for you and all involved.

From a mother and father in Tennessee:

March 3

Dear Marine or Soldier,

You know how much we remain in prayer over the upcoming events. You are in the right place, with the right people, with the right aims . . . and you are held by the right arms—outstretched, embracing you day after day, night after night . . . holding you, carrying your burdens, empowering you to give! His strength prevails always.

From the mother of a Marine from Alexandria, Virginia:

March 31

Dear PJ,

I pray to God every day that God will protect you and all the military personnel . . . helping in the war against terrorism. I know that God will protect you and that you will complete your assignment and will be safely back in the U.S. when your duty is completed. Don't forget to pray Psalm 91. Always pray and always trust God. He is our Guardian and our Protector. His wish above all things is for us to prosper and be in good health as well as our souls prosper. Always pray . . . I can do all things through Christ who strengthens me. No weapon formed against me shall

prosper . . . Believe in God. Don't doubt. He will protect you all
. . . Everyone is praying for you. Don't forget that prayers can
move mountains, and don't forget to pray for yourself as well. I
pray that God will protect all the military personnel from all
harm. In Jesus name, Amen.

From Rachel in San Diego:

April 14
Dear Soldier,

I ask the Lord for your safety and soon return . . . your work
and loyalty to our country and its people finds me without words,
incapable of explaining my awe and gratitude. You are doing
more than "serving" your country, you are providing life. I thank
you for protecting mine, and I promise to pray for you everyday,
as that is my greatest gift to those I care about most.

From a major in the United States Marine Corps:

April 6

I'm there with you in spirit. I'm not a religious man, but I'm
praying for the battalion's safe return as soon as the mission is
accomplished. Semper Fi!

From the wife of a front-line commander of infantrymen:

March 1
Dearest,

Please know that I am so proud of you and have the utmost
confidence in you and your abilities to lead your men down
whatever path lies ahead. God goes with you and is with you in
every step, did you know that? He loves you so much, and He is
guiding you through all of this—just as He is guiding me. Please
stay strong in mind and spirit, and know that God is with you.

From Mary in Illinois:

Dear Soldier,

I hope you are safe as you receive this letter but know that God leads this movement to free the Iraqi people and He will be with you and your fellow alliance forces through even the worst of conditions. News media report many good and some difficult situations the last six days since the war started. I listen constantly. You are a very brave person for what you do this day. I cannot imagine how difficult it might be for you over there. I am a mother of eight children so I know your family is proud of you (as we all are), even as they worry. Know that millions of people in America support and pray for you, as do people all over the world. The students at school pray for your safety and quick return. And now a short prayer for you: Father, thank You for Your presence in the midst of the anxieties and conflicts of our daily lives. Help us to realize Your love for us, and to be reminded of it with the dawn of each new day. Just as the blossom comes out of the dark ground, so out of the night, a morning appears. God bless America!

From Ben a young boy from Hanahan, South Carolina:

Thank you for protecting our country as well as helping the people of Iraq get food and water and other supplies. I hope you all get back safe and soon. The whole country, America, depends on you our soldiers. Remember the force is with you always.

From Alex, a simple card with a hand-drawn picture of the American flag with these words over it:

It's still standing.

From Carla in Shelby County:

Dear Soldier-Friend,

Thank you so much for your sacrifice on my behalf! My family and I are sending you our love and prayers during this time . . . The only encouragement I can cling to at this time is that God is sovereign, and none of this took Him by surprise, and ultimately, He will bring all things about to get glory for Himself. This letter is a prayed-over missive. I've prayed for your safety and well-being, for comfort when you're lonely or sad, for courage and strength, for personal stamina, and that God would undertake in any areas I would forget to mention.

As our battalion, along with every other unit in northern Kuwait, was just being awakened in the middle of the night to head to the border of Iraq for the ground invasion, the following was being written.

From a California school teacher:

March 17

I am praying throughout the day and into the night. The Lord has been waking me up to full alert several times a night to pray. You are covered by His shield. Fear no evil, for the Lord is with you.

From Nick in Tennessee:

April 2
Dear Brave Soldier,

We will win the war no matter what. My grandpa was drafted into the Army. He made it, you'll make it too.

During the time the following prayer was offered, Marines and soldiers all across the northern border of Kuwait were rushing into chemical gear as four Scud missiles were launched at Saddam's orders into Coalition areas in Kuwait.

From Anne at Germantown Baptist Church:

March 18

 I am praying for you and your family. May the God of all ten-der mercies give you strength, peace, guidance, comfort, and pro-tection. I pray the full armor of God on you and your family. May you stand firm in God's mighty power and strength. I pray for safety, strength, and good health. I plead Psalm 91. May God bless you with His love and grace.

From a volunteer children's worker:

March 28

Dear Marine or Soldier, American or British,

 Our thoughts and prayers are never far from you. We have yellow ribbons around the trees and poles at the chapel. We are waiting and praying for your safe return . . . On the Internet, the Presidential Prayer Team had "adopt-a-Marine to pray for." They had such a big response, the computer couldn't handle it and went down . . . thousands of Marines are adopted by name . . . You are not forgotten . . . God be with you.

During the late afternoon hours of March 26, our battalion was heading north into an extremely hostile area. The wind from the previous night's storm was still whipping and artillery batteries were pounding away right next to us on Iraqi enemy positions. That night many men shared with me their fears. As the convoy was leaving to head north, I stood in the middle of the two columns of departing vehicles, praying with each group of men as they moved out.

From an author:

26 March

Dear Marine or Soldier,

 I am on my knees for you today, believing God's Hand rests upon your shoulders.

From an airline consultant:

Dear Sailor,

Your service is noble and selfless. Your spirit is filled with care and concern for others . . . Your physical and emotional being will weather the harshness of the elements. Through it all, and regardless of the dangers, know that your real strength and defense are in Him; your prayer support is strong and continuous.

From an unknown child:

Dear U.S. Soldier,

There are millions of people in the world thinking about you and lifting you up in their prayers. Even more importantly, God is holding you in His hands.

From a little boy:

Dear Marine,

My name is Isaiah. I am four. We are proud of you.

I play G.I Joe at home. The good guy always wins.

The good guy always wins. Indeed, when the good guy wins, it's because somewhere, somehow, good people have bowed their heads and hit their knees, and with arms lifted up have given the battle into the hands of Almighty God. And this, we soon found, was the deeper story, the hidden subtext, that like a sacred fiber, weaved its power throughout the lives of the men facing the dangers of war. Churches, classrooms, offices, flight-lines, hospitals, kitchens, automobiles had become the catedrals, the places of prayer, the holy ground where millions of faithful believing Americans tire-lessly lifted us up night and day, hour by hour, moment by moment into the hands of an awesome God.

Strengthened by the force that only prayer can bring . . .

How true it was for the men of First Battalion, Fifth Mariness.

Already, by April 9 we had seen the power of God, in answer to those prayers, save us from hidden enemies, empower us to fight, and give us the courage to persevere.

But nothing could prepare us for what lay ahead.

A time of great fear and uncertainty awaited us in Baghdad. But there, too, we experienced God's help in answer to prayer. In fact, it was in the battle for Baghdad that we saw His power exhibited in ways none of us had ever seen before.

9
April 10th

April 10th

GUNNERY SERGEANTS are a breed apart. Most of them walk with a slight limp due to the decade and a half of forced marches and grueling runs that their bodies have already endured. Their faces are weathered, their hands gnarled, their eyes wrinkled at the corners. They are, without a doubt, the toughest men in the Corps, and the Marines know it. Called "gunnys" for short, these able veterans understand the system, know their men better than their men know themselves, drink lots of strong coffee, and command respect in a way that leaves no doubt as to who is in charge.

More than once back at Camp Pendleton, while I was counseling a married couple, the eyes of the wife widened in surprise when one of the gunnys started barking at somebody outside. "Oh, don't worry, ma'am. It's just the gunny," I would remark.

The Marine sitting next to his wife would smile as if to say, "You see, honey, this is the world I work in."

But that was who the gunnys were. They led by toughness and expected the same spirit in their men. And yet, I believe their toughness was grounded in love. Now admittedly, *love* is not necessarily a word that one hears thrown around much in an infantry battalion. But when a gunny barks at his men to keep them in step on a forced march, or when he demands that they do the smallest things correctly, or when he rails a young private for not obeying orders, severe as he may sound, his reaction could save that Marine's life in combat. Staying in step, getting the details right, obeying orders—it all translates to split-second decisions on the battlefield.

Gunnys know this. Most of them have been around long enough to see the grim consequences of less-than-instant obedience: the Marine who thinks twice about his squad leader's orders and gets shot by the enemy. The Marine who doesn't pay attention to the exact grid coordinates and wanders into a firefight. In the end, the tenacity and toughness of our gunnery sergeants was a form of good, fatherly authority, and yes, it was grounded in love.

That same love for their men and concern for their welfare undoubtedly drove all our gunnys to make a courageous decision on the evening of April 9, 2003. It was a decision that, for one, would cost him everything.

"SO DO YOU GUYS WANT TO GO?" Gunnery Sergeant Jeffrey Bohr's question seemed to hang in midair like a thick cloud, its implications swirling before the eyes of his men, forewarning them of danger. For a moment, no one said anything. They just looked at one another, back at Gunny, and then down at their boots.

Gunny put it to them again, and this time, he explained it clearly. "We don't have to go. The battalion commander's given those who don't ride in an armored vehicle the choice to stay back with the logistics trains. And I'm not gonna lie to you . . . it's gonna be bad . . . real bad. So . . . do you guys want to go or not?"

Gauthier spoke up first. "I'm in."

Moments later, the other three—White, Bonner, and Cash—joined as well.

"Good," Gunny firmly responded, not trying to conceal his half-smirk of instant approval.

They all knew the answer from the moment he asked the question. He was the Alpha Company Gunny, and 160 Marines depended on him for ammo, water, and chow. And even though he framed the question as if it were an option, in reality there was only one right answer in his mind—his boys needed him, even if it meant heading into the "belly of the beast."

A strong-willed Iowan who had served as an army ranger before joining the Marine Corps, Gunny Bohr knew what combat was all about. A sturdy workhorse of a man with dark blond hair and piercing eyes, Bohr had seen the likes of Grenada, Panama, Desert Storm, and Somalia, all within the first decade of his service to his country—a decade that would see him leave the army for the ranks of the Marines. And it would be his service as a Marine that would bring him face to face with the vast majority of his combat episodes. Although he rarely talked about them, those episodes added to the almost mythical ethos that surrounded him.

His young Marines feared him, but it was a fear interwoven with a kind of reverential awe that is given a man who has seen the opposing end of a muzzle flash. Perhaps one good indication of how closely the young Marines in his company watched and respected him was the way they imitated him the night of the talent show. Of all the Marines impersonated that evening—and there were many—Bohr was by far the most imitated. The young Marines had him down to a T, and the few who braved the stage that night caricatured him in such a way as to leave no doubt as to just who this man was—a tough warrior with a disturbingly calm manner of speaking and a dry sense of humor. Bohr had the uncanny ability to strike the fear of God in young grunts without ever having to raise his voice. And for the most part, he did it by employing the third-person voice: "The gunny is about to place his boot up your — if you don't get moving!" It was a style that seemed to add enormous weight to his disturbingly calm manner of speaking.

The Marines never doubted for a moment where he stood and

what he believed. And despite his leathery appeal, he was also a man of deep faith. Baptized and confirmed a Roman Catholic, Bohr almost never missed Mass when the battalion was back at Camp Pendleton. Every Sunday he slipped into the worship service at the School of Infantry's Catholic Chapel. On several occasions, he helped the priest with lay duties during and after the gathering. I will never forget watching a Mass at Twentynine Palms in which Bohr was participating. As the Marines lined up to receive Holy Communion, I noticed that when it was Bohr's turn to take the Sacred Host, his head was bowed in reverence, and his hands were cupped together lifted up over his head.

It was a powerful symbol, and I'm sure he wasn't even aware of it. There he was, a tough Marine gunny, known for his no-nonsense approach and rigid adherance to the highest of standards. And yet, in that moment, he was a symbol of childlike faith—trusting, accepting, receiving all that God gives us. In the months that followed, his sacrificial spirit and simple devotion to what is right would be imprinted upon us all in a way that would mark us forever.

ON APRIL 9, our battalion had received an order from the division's commanding general to seize the Al Azimiyah Presidential Palace in the center of Baghdad. For days we had been locked in sporadic small-arms conflict in the filthy outskirts of the city. But this was different. We had been tasked from the highest level to take hold of one of Saddam Hussein's presidential palaces, situated on the banks of the historic Tigris River deep within the heart of the city. The palace was a royal jewel in the scepter of one the most notorious tyrants of our age.

Assuming that a well-armed and determined enemy force would be waiting for us at the palace, Lieutenant Colonel Padilla did something that up until now he had not done before. He ordered all of our non-armored vehicles (mainly the soft-skinned Humvees and seven-ton trucks that comprised the combat train of which I was a part) to proceed with the convoy only as far as the outskirts of the downtown Baghdad area. There they would await further orders.

Intelligence reports indicated that the enemy defending the palace would be more dangerous than any we'd faced thus far. Those of us who drove in vehicles unprotected by armor plating would be at serious risk. Our intelligence officer had already briefed Padilla that we could expect somewhere in the neighborhood of an entire battalion's worth of enemy forces (roughly a thousand). These were not merely Iraqi soldiers, he went on to say. They were Fedayeen militants, largely foreign mercenaries who had been lured to Iraq from places like Syria, Saudi Arabia, and Egypt. This time we weren't dealing with grudging conscripts. Our adversaries would be a well-armed group of radical terrorists looking to collect a healthy paycheck at our expense.

Furthermore, these were men who, days earlier, had already fought in other areas of Baghdad and had shown an instant willingness to use civilians as human shields—women, children, and anyone who might serve as a protective barrier. To them, the ends justified the means. And they knew how to blend in. Wearing civilian clothes, often black pajama-style pants, they could move invisibly through the city streets until they poised themselves at just the right position to lob a grenade or fire an assault rifle into an unsuspecting vehicle full of Coalition troops.

It was because of this threat that Padilla had ordered our nonarmored vehicles to remain behind. Except for the gunnys, that is. They had a choice in the matter. Not surprisingly, just like Bohr, every one of them made the decision to go with their guys. Each company gunny's unarmored Humvee was chock-full of immediate resupply materials (ammo of all shapes and sizes, water, MREs, spare parts, even extra weapons) that could sustain that company for a couple of hours in the middle of a firefight. While they didn't have nearly the volume of resupply that our combat train carried, they did have enough to help their Marines in the short term. Of course they would go.

Walking back to my vehicle from the command tent where the order had been passed, I looked up at the fading sky. A warm breeze stirred the air, sporadic gunshots cracked in the distance, and the faint sound of looting crowds still lingered. In the quiet of those moments, I began to pray.

I prayed for Lance Corporal Jeff Guthrie, who at the age of thirty had decided to enter the Marine Corps to find direction and a sense of purpose for his life.

I prayed for Corporal Zebulon Batke, a self-proclaimed seeker, who more than anything else, wanted proof to know that God was really there.

I prayed for First Sergeant Luke Converse, whose wife had a new baby girl on the way.

I prayed for them all. And I wondered what the battle would be like. What would the next hours bring for our men? Would it turn out that intelligence had overestimated the enemy? Were the Marines going for a walk in the park? Or were they heading into serious danger?

I think all of us knew it would be unlike anything we'd experienced yet. As it turned out, we were right. The men of First Battalion, Fifth Marines, were about to enter into one of the most ferocious and unrelenting barrages of firepower ever unleashed in the streets of Baghdad.

Our intelligence reports proved all too true. More than one thousand mercenaries, dressed in civilian clothing, armed with heavy machine-guns, and shouldering more rocket propelled grenades (RPGs) than we could ever hope to defend against, were about to amass in the shadows and the alleyways of Route 2, the only viable route leading to Baghdad's Almilyah Presidential Palace. Acting with an almost eerie foreknowledge of our movements, for hours they waited, watched, and readied themselves for one final stand.

For the next five hours, we drove slowly, methodically, watchfully. The occasional sound of sniper fire from a rooftop or abandoned factory kept many of us awake; but as always, there were those few who could sleep through a landmine explosion right underneath them. Leaning back against the vibrating steel interior walls of his AAV, Bravo Company's Rob Hart was busy snoring away with a look of peaceful contentment on his face, causing some of his fellow riders to playfully place the two-fingered "bunny ears" over his head. Hart had prayed, and he firmly believed God would take care of everything. Why not sleep?

Corporal Hardy placed his hand on the pocket Bible sitting on the radio mount, and he reminded Dickens, Batke, and Beavers, "God is with us. Just remember, we don't have to be afraid. He'll protect us all." They all recalled how God had brought their lost Bible back from the raging storm, and they honestly believed, or at least *wanted* to believe, it was a sign of His protection.

First Sergeant Luke Converse, sitting in the top hatch of his Charlie Company AAV, stole a quick glance at the picture of his wife, Colleen—pregnant with their second child—and their little girl. He knew everything was in God's hands—his family, his hopes and dreams, his life. Over and over, as his AAV wound through the lonely roads outside the city, the same Scripture verse came back to his mind: "For me, to live is Christ, and to die is gain" (Philippians 1:21).

For Staff Sergeant Bryan Jackway in his counter-mech vehicle, it was Psalm 91 that offered the greatest assurance. Its words had carried him through Desert Storm in 1991, and through the bloody streets of Somalia. Its promises had been his strength just days ago when enemy mortars had nearly taken his life at the Saddam Canal: "A thousand may fall at your side, and ten thousand at your right hand; but it shall not approach you . . . for you have made the LORD, my refuge . . ." (Psalm 91:7, 9).

Looping around the eastern side of the great city, we arched over the northeast corner, and finally stopped just shy of the northern end of Route 2. The fifteen vehicles in our combat train pulled off the side of the road to let the armored convoy pass. We watched them disappear, one after another, down Route 2's shadowy four-lane highway.

They were out of sight, but not out of mind. And in the long hours that followed, we did our best to hear and understand what happened to them after they left us behind. It would take us several days to put the picture together.

Riding in one of the lead AAVs, our battalion's intelligence officer, Captain Stean Maas, began frantically looking for a photo of his wife. For the last three weeks it had been taped up to the wall directly over his console. Now it was gone.

For about a minute, Maas violently tore through his papers and field journals, lifted up his gear, ripped open his pack. Every single day until now he'd been able to see her face, and if ever there was a time he needed her picture, it was in the moments that he now faced. Finally, with a sigh of relief and half a smile, Maas felt the waxy surface of the photo underneath his seat. "There it is! I knew I'd find it!"

A few Marines smoked down the last dregs of their cigarettes, a few cut the ice with off-the-cuff humor, and a few clutched their crosses and rosaries. All of them knew that this would be the enemy's last stand. Wherever their enemy was, and whatever he had left to throw at these Marines, they were definitely headed into harm's way.

The silence was eerie as the massive convoy entered Baghdad's city limits and began funneling into the narrow streets, which were cluttered with trash and lined on both sides with darkened buildings. The city's electricity had been disabled because of the intense bombings that had begun more than two weeks earlier. Now the Marines, standing atop their AAVs, turned on their infrared PEQ-2A lighted scopes mounted on their rifles. Like a silent laser lightshow, hundreds of green, light beams, invisible to the naked eye, fanned from right to left. Looking through their night-vision goggles, they poured infrared illumination into every dark corner and window.

The only sound to be heard was the strange hydroelectriclike cranking and squeaking of the gigantic AAV tracks rolling over the uneven surface of the road. For machines of their size, they were rolling fast. Padilla wanted to get through the city and into the palace as soon as possible, so he had directed the lead tanks to pull the rest of the convoy along at a blazing 25 mph. It was a column of more than seventy vehicles, stretching nearly a mile in length, running as fast as a mechanized convoy can go. It was 4:15 a.m.

Alpha Company's lead AAVs had just cleared the apartment complexes on the inside of the city limits. All at once, with a gut-wrenching crack, the first .762 round of enemy AK-47 fire broke through the silence of the night. It slammed into the side of Second Lieutenant Andrew Terrell's AAV. Jeff Guthrie jumped up as if the round had pierced his body.

Just as suddenly, the darkened windows of the surrounding buildings burst to life with such earsplitting noise and muzzle flash that Marines near the front of the column said it looked like a battle scene out of *Star Wars*. Green tracer rounds, like nightmarish beams of molten steel, were being shot from every angle. The bright red flames from the contrails of dozens and dozens of rocket-propelled grenades (RPGs) assaulted the convoy. Explosion followed explosion, unabated.

Corporal William "Willy" Fairweather of Bravo Company was sitting deep inside his AAV when the crushing sound of metal striking metal began. He looked through the airhatch and saw hot tracer rounds filling the night sky above him. In an instant, a blast from an enemy RPG rocked a civilian truck parked just feet from his AAV.

Fairweather recalls, "Every Marine standing up, all nine or ten of them, was flung across the top of our vehicle and came crashing down on top of us. They were followed by a massive wall of fire that seemed to just leap into our compartment."

The Marines pointed their rifles in every direction, firing wherever they saw enemy muzzle flashes. Major Pete Farnum recalls, "Bullets were literally whizzing over our heads. And then came the RPGs."

The AAVs of Alpha, Bravo, and Charlie Companies became engulfed in the deafening sounds of RPGs smashing into the thick outer layers of their armor. The armor was built in a zigzag ruffled pattern to deflect high-velocity rockets or antiarmor missiles. But rockets were already penetrating some of the vehicles, erupting into hundreds of jagged pieces of twisted metal and steel, which ripped into the arms, shoulders, and faces of the exposed Marines who were firing from the top.

Platoon commanders and radio operators started echoing the same words across the battalion's radio net: "Contact! Contact! Taking heavy fire from the left side . . . right side . . . RPGs everywhere! Casualties!" Within minutes of the first shots, the entire convoy was nearly suffocated in a blanket of hot lead and exploding RPGs. And the casualties continued to mount.

Bryan Jackway and his counter-mech team could see the tidal wave of bullets working its way from the front of the convoy to the back, where he was stationed. Just then, a fuel truck just a few feet away was hit by machine-gun fire. It exploded in a fury of white-orange flames and poured a wall of fire and debris all over Jackway's vehicle. "Keep driving! Keep driving! Don't stop moving!" Jackway yelled to his driver.

At about that time, Jackway's gunner, manning the .50 caliber machine-gun on the roof of his armored Humvee, began letting loose. Chips of building and brick spit outward, showering the sidewalk. The gunner pounded away on every burst of light coming from the dark windows and shadowed rooftops where the enemy was hiding.

For Gunny Bohr and his boys, keeping their vehicles moving was a matter of life and death. Since they had no protective armor on their Humvee, their only defense against the enemy's rockets was to drive like maniacs in and out of the convoy, herking and jerking the vehicle this way and that. Fortunately, Bohr had been in urban combat before. He knew what to do.

"It's hard to hit a moving target! Keep moving!" he yelled, as Corporal Gauthier pulled the steering wheel of their Humvee back and forth. With his radio handset rigged to the inside his helmet, Bohr shot his rifle unceasingly out the passenger-side window.

"I got two of them!" somebody heard him yell.

In the back of their vehicle was Corporal Mike Cash, who was all too aware of the zinging rounds skipping off the pavement next to him. With the cloth sides rolled up, he too emptied clip after clip into the blurry outlines of gunmen running back and forth in the shadows. The enemy was everywhere.

Indeed, in little more than an hour of fighting, the casualty list had grown to more than forty wounded Marines, and there was no end in sight.

Then things got worse.

The tank platoon that was leading the charge was taking heavy fire from a mosque. They took a wrong turn at a circular intersection. The map said "right," but there were in fact two "rights," one hard and one soft, and in a matter of minutes, almost half the convoy had doubled back and was now heading in the wrong direction, increasing the threat of friendly fire. It was just about the worst thing that could happen, given the high volume of enemy fire and the confusing architecture of Baghdad's side streets and alleyways. It meant smaller, more isolated sections of the convoy could be trapped and destroyed.

Alpha Company was heading down a road lined with high-rise apartment buildings. Not only were they lost, but they soon found themselves approaching a gigantic bridge spanning across the Tigris River. Captain Blair Sokol didn't like the looks of it. Neither did Second Lieutenant Nick Horton, who was riding near the front of Alpha's column.

Horton was the leader of Alpha's Third Platoon, a unit that was tight-knit, well-led, and tenacious. The son of a career fire-fighter, Nick Horton grew up in the small logging town of La Pine, Oregon, and was a stand-out varsity athlete in virtually every sport his small high school participated in. The strapping six-foot, 190-pound Horton entered college in 1997 on a naval ROTC scholarship, but had specified the Marine Corps option. He didn't have the brash, extroverted personality that many Marine officers do; his demeanor was quieter, more reserved and intense. But given a moment of danger and decision, Lieutenant Horton's quiet exterior quickly evaporated into a commanding presence. Such a presence would be crucial in the hours that followed. But for now, all Horton or any of his platoon could do was hang on for life.

As Alpha's lead AAV approached the base of the bridge, a violent frenzy of enemy machine-gun fire and RPGs began pouring out of the windows and balconies of the buildings on both sides of the road. Sokol, who was several vehicles back when it began, recalls that there were too many muzzle flashes to count. He knew the lead AAVs in his company were in the middle of it, but he also knew that it would have been suicide to try and turn the company around right there. He gave the order for all vehicles to press through and onto the bridge. It was his only option.

One by one, Alpha Company proceeded through what Sokol later found out was a prepared enemy ambush point. When he saw the intensity of the attack and realized that his entire company was going to have to go through it, he felt sure that many of his Marines, standing at the tops of their vehicles firing back, would not make it.

Corporal Kyle Menze, riding a few tracks behind the lead vehicle, watched as an RPG made a direct hit on the back of the AAV in front of his. A wall of fire and black smoke consumed the struck vehicle and sent waves of heat and shrapnel everywhere. He prayed that nobody had died. Injuries continued to mount as shrapnel ripped into the faces, arms, and hands of Marines who were exposed from the shoulders up. Still they stayed in place, refusing to stop firing back from atop their AAVs.

Lance Corporal William Bonner, who was driving the soft-skinned Humvee directly in front of Gauthier and Bohr, saw bullets whizzing over his head and even through his compartment. Corporal Brandon White, in the passenger side of Bonner's vehicle, just kept shooting. He was firing multiple rounds toward every muzzle flash he could see, cringing at the whizzing snap of rounds flying back his way. Bohr and Gauthier were doing the same thing, ducking and firing, but not for one moment stopping their vehicles.

Then a voice on the radio crackled through, "White's hit! White's hit! Apache 7, this is Bonner. White's hit!"

Brandon White threw down his weapon and seized his right arm in agonizing pain. He could see blood soaking from under the still-smoking hole just above his wrist. The enemy round had entered the side of his hand and exited two inches above his wrist, completely severing his main artery. His arm immediately went rigid as a steel shunt. He couldn't move it an inch.

Immediately Gunny Bohr started calling for a medevac. With his radio in his left hand and firing his M-16 with his right, he was a picture of steel grit and leadership under pressure. Gauthier later recalls that when the firing first began he thought he saw a smile on Gunny's face.

"It was his element," Gauthier remembered.

Indeed, it was. During the few minutes before White had been hit, when Sokol's vehicle had gone down, Bohr gathered all his logistics guys together in a huddle—Gauthier, Cash, Bonner, and White.

"You're doing great guys. I'm proud of you. Just hang in there, and don't stop moving. We'll get through this together."

Gauthier said that coming from Gunny, a combat veteran, those words of assurance in the midst of a fight meant everything. *If Gunny is this confident,* Gauthier reasoned, *we're all going to be OK.*

Just after White had been hit, first light began to break over Baghdad's smoke-wreathed buildings. "Bullets were flying everywhere," Gauthier told me later. "I could see enemy gunmen to my immediate left, some of them running around firing, others standing still and hoisting RPGs on their shoulders. One moment I look over, and Gunny's calling in a medevac for White and shooting his M-16 with the other arm. He wasn't even flinching. He was calm and cool, shooting his rifle as he was calling in the casualty. The next moment I look over, and he's slumped forward on the dash. My first thought was, *"He's knocked out."*

A couple of seconds later, Gauthier was able to swerve the Humvee to a relatively safe place behind the armor of the surrounding AAVs. He could hear the swish of bullets all around him, and he knew the only way he could stop and check Gunny was if he got in behind the massive vehicles. When he did, he pushed Bohr's upper body back against the seat. Unbelievable as it was, there was no doubt in his mind. Bohr was gone. He had taken a shot to the head that had killed him instantly. Gunny Bohr never knew what hit him.

"There was no life in his body . . . and his face . . . I'll never forget the look on his face. It was then," Gauthier remembers, "that fear . . . fear like I'd never known began to kick in."

With his hands trembling, Gauthier worked frantically to pry the blood-soaked radio handset from out of Gunny's helmet. He had to keep the Humvee rolling—there were too many rounds in the air. Holding the slippery radio against his own face he made the call that sent all of Alpha Company into shock: "Apache 7's down, Apache 7's down."

Mike Cash hopped out of the back to see if he'd heard what he thought he'd heard. Gauthier wasted no time. "Cash, get back in the back, Gunny's dead! We've got to keep moving!" Cash jumped back, firing murderously at every gunman he could see.

It had been exactly twenty days since Alpha Company had lost Shane Childers in the barren wasteland of southern Iraq. Now the Marines were beginning to process the reality that their gunny was gone too. "Apache 7 down," it inflicted what felt like an incurable wound in every man who heard the words.

For many young Alpha Company Marines, it was Gunny Bohr who had taught them what being a Marine was all about. He did everything wholeheartedly. Whether it was dilgently getting supplies to his men in the field, leading them on a grueling conditioning hike, teaching them the finer points of weapons handling, showing them the proper way to wear a heavy starched set of cammies, or attending weekly Mass, it didn't matter. He had lived his life deliberately and with absolute thoroughness and attention to detail. One of the men who knew him said, "Bohr died the same way he lived . . . fighting for what was right, serving his country, leading Marines."

And still the battle raged on. As the first wave of AAVs rolled over the joints of the bridge's entrance, a whole new enemy appeared, firing from underneath the pylons that supported the bridge's weight. Bullets and RPGs erupted from the lower sides of the bridge's entrance, sending fireballs underneath the moving AAVs and more shrapnel cutting into the armor, sending Marines reeling inside. Any one of those RPGs, if impacting in just the right spot, could have killed every Marine inside the AAV. As for the Humvees, their drivers were fully aware of their outcome should one of the rockets impact them.

In that moment, unexpected help appeared. The elusive army special forces (SF), who had been attached to our regiment from the beginning, appeared as if out of nowhere. All at once a group of them jumped out of their civilian SUVs and ran to the railing of the bridge. We knew they were supposed to accompany our lead AAVs to the palace; however, until that instant, no one had noticed them. Now they began hurling grenades over the side of the bridge, directing them right where they needed to go—onto the heads of the clustered militants.

It was a scene right out of a movie, but there was no screenplay. It was chaos at its deadliest—enemy crossfire, jagged RPG chards raking the air, Humvees spinning wildly in circles, AAVs hammering away with their .50-caliber machine-guns, SF soldiers lobbing grenades on the Fedayeen—acted out on the banks of the historic Tigris River. Meanwhile the men of Alpha Company kept moving, kept firing, kept praying.

Our battalion commander, Lieutenant Colonol Padilla, knew all too well that his unit was spread all over downtown Baghdad, taking fire from every quadrant. At almost every minute, new casualty reports were coming over his radio. The reports were nonspecific, but they made him cringe. He was beginning to think the worst. These were his Marines, and more than anything else he wanted to take them home alive.

As he looked out from the overpass where his vehicle was temporarily positioned, Padilla could see enemy tracer rounds blazing from every direction. Rockets exploded continuously. The convoy stretched back as far as he could see, and yet he knew he was only looking at part of his battalion. Alpha, at least, had become separated from the rest and driven into a wicked ambush. Who else was separated and cut off? The message that Gunny Bohr had been killed had just come over his radio. How many more of his men would die in the Baghdad streets?

There was just too much volume of enemy fire. Padilla knew that Marines standing at the tops of their vehicles just don't come through a gauntlet like that one unscathed. By now there were so many casualties that he'd lost count. He had seen enough fighting in the streets of other Third World countries to know what happens to troops that get trapped in an urban environment. Padilla's battalion was in serious trouble.

It was then that the words came across his mind: *issue in doubt*. Those are three words no commander ever wants to speak over his radio in battle. *Issue in doubt* means that, in all likelihood, victory is impossible and defeat is imminent. It means unless something or someone finds a way to change the battle's momentum, the only recourse is—at best—to pull back, regroup, and rearm.

Those three words were spoken by Major General Julian Smith off the coast of Tarawa, November 20, 1943, as he looked out on the hundreds of dead Marines floating along the seawall of the bloody shore and saw that the Japanese defenders were only becoming more emboldened by the American deaths. Those words were only uttered twice in all of World War II; and both times by commanders who believed that the end of the line had come for their men.

Issue in doubt. Dear God, has it come to this? Padilla asked himself. But he never spoke the words.

Meanwhile, Bravo Company, led by Captain Jason Smith and the rest of his 170 Marines, was headed for the overpass Padilla was on. An infantry officer whose father was a retired Marine colonel, Smith had led Bravo Company in a successful attack on the Saddam Canal only a week before. Pushing across the canal's well-guarded enemy bridge, Smith had taken a barrage of mortar and machine-gun fire, and yet he had managed to secure the canal without taking any casualties. In the end he had rounded up more than forty prisoners of war. His leadership was simple but direct, and never left any room for his men to doubt either his intentions or his courage. The last words he spoke to Second Lieutenant Tyler McGaughey before the convoy began its audacious push into the city were, "Whatever you do, never stop moving."

As Smith approached the overpass and realized that the convoy was bogged down in the midst of intense fire, he checked his own map and noted that there was a way to the palace that, while not the original route, could get the struggling convoy to its destination. It was a risky and unknown alternative but the only option.

"Hondo, Hondo, this is Blackhawk 6, I've got a route to the palace, I repeat, I've got a route to the palace . . . follow me."

Within minutes, the vehicles in the convoy found their place in line and began the push forward to the palace. Alpha Company, still reeling from the staggering ambush they had just endured, had in fact begun to find their way to the palace themselves. Staff Sergeant Kinser had decided to go ahead and take a narrow road along the side of the river, hoping and praying that it would get him and the rest of Alpha to their destination. His decision proved right.

In the distance, Bravo's McGaughey could see the approaching walls of the presidential palace. Standing over fifteen feet high, the brownish concrete barriers were intimidating, especially in contrast with the shantytown appearance of the surrounding buildings. The streets around the palace were disturbingly quiet. There was no one in sight, trash was blowing along the pavement, and the only cars in sight were parked, as if abandoned on the side of the road. There was no gunfire.

After the earsplitting chaos they had just driven through, the new sound of silence was almost worse. All the Marines could hear were the AAV tracks slapping down on the uneven pavement of the road. It looked as if the only thing between the men of Bravo Company and the brownish walls of the massive citadel was a lone traffic circle surrounded by grayish-brown buildings that were casting midmorning shadows down upon the empty street. Bravo Company's "Track 1" never saw what hit them.

A Syrian militant, dressed in the familiar loose-fitting, black pajama trousers, stepped into sight only momentarily. Then, with an almost gentle puff of white smoke, he disappeared again, vanishing behind the back-blast of the rocket he'd fired from his shoulder. In a moment of surreal horror, the rocket, screaming full speed, ricocheted off the right hand of Corporal Kavir Dawani, and hit Corporal Chad Shevlin square in the jaw, only to bounce yet once again before exploding into a brick wall behind them.

Shevlin had taken the brunt of the rocket to his face and never felt it. With his jaw literally hanging from its ragged hinges, he felt the blood spilling out onto his flak jacket. Dawani thought he was dead.

The voice of one of Shevlin's fellow Marines snapped across the radio, "Doc, Doc! Shevlin's been hit—Three wounded in Track 1!" One of the corpsmen, Doc Gage, heard the report, climbed over all the Marines in his AAV, and ran outside under fire to attend to the fallen corporal. Shevlin was alive, but barely recognizable.

Private Moore's wound seemed less serious. In reality, it would almost cost him his life. A piece of red-hot shrapnel had pierced his right arm and had plunged through both lungs, causing them to begin to collapse within minutes. Whereas Shevlin was a bloodbath, Moore had only a barely visible entry wound; yet the others recalled later that within moments of being injured, his face began to turn a squeamish pale green. He was barely breathing.

In the thirty minutes it took Bravo Company to lead the charge into the palace gates, they saw more than twenty of their Marines injured by another explosive ambush of machine-gun fire, RPGs, and even mortars. The enemy certainly had no intention of allowing the Marines to enter the palace compound alive. And as with the opening volleys earlier that morning, what started as one lone shot fired from the top of an adjacent building soon erupted into a maelstrom.

Still, one by one, the vehicles in the convoy converged behind Bravo Company and managed to roll through the deadly traffic circle and into the gates of the palace. First Lieutenant Jeremy

Stalnecker and his heavy guns from the counter-mech platoon soon formed a phalanx around the eastern side of the palace and began to fire relentlessly into the windows of the surrounding buildings, allowing the battalion to make it through. Stalnecker's barrage continued for an hour.

Meanwhile, as the Marines from Bravo Company cleared the rooms and terraces of the palace complex, the casualties were brought to a holding area in the back, toward the riverbank. By this time, every company had its share of injuries. Most of them involved shrapnel or gunshot wounds to upper bodies, arms, hands, and even faces. Second Lieutenant Tavis McNair from Charlie Company was one of the worst. Having taken shrapnel from an RPG that virtually exploded in his face, the tissue from the base of his neck all the way up to his cheekbone was filleted wide open. Corpsmen and Marines who attended to him said they could see his jugular vein throbbing.

There were many more. Some men were able to walk, some were fading in and out of consciousness, some were so bandaged up they were almost unrecognizable. The enemy fire had still not ceased. In fact, as the injured Marines were lying in the designated casualty holding area, enemy gunmen and snipers from the other side of the river started firing into the complex. There seemed to be no safe place, even for the wounded.

It was then that Captain Shawn Basco became another of that day's real heroes. An F-18 fighter pilot who had been attached to our battalion as a forward air controller (FAC), Basco was responsible for talking to overhead pilots and arranging with them either casualty medevacs (by helicopter) or air strikes to destroy enemy positions. His leg had been injured by an exploding RPG. It didn't stop him.

Basco knew that if didn't get medical help for some the most severe casualties, they would not survive. There was only one thing to do—call in helicopters. The injured Basco climbed to the roof of the palace and began radioing for help. Exposing himself to enemy fire on every side, the athletically built pilot began bounding from roof to roof, calling in the grid coordinates to several navy CH-46 helicopters nearby. Within minutes, the deep chop of the helicopters' rotors could be heard flying low over the city's rooftops. As they approached, Basco waved wildly to flag them down. One after another the choppers circled around, touched down, and began taking the injured Marines out.

The enemy was relentless—a barrage of RPG fire began streaking toward the lurching helicopters as they lifted off. One Marine who was evacuated remembers feeling much more safe in the palace than in the helicopter. While the giant birds yawed and dipped to avoid being hit, their side-gunners pounded away with .50-caliber machine-guns. A rocket clipped the rear fuselage of one of them and the explosion sent the helicopter reeling sideways, nearly flipping it over from the percussion. It was nothing short of a miracle that the thinly skinned CH-46 wasn't blown out of the sky and every Marine inside killed. Finally Basco, weakened by his own injury, along with the last of the wounded, collapsed aboard a rumbling aircraft and was lifted off to safety.

After three hours of fighting to get into the palace, the entire battalion had finally made it.

Captain Sokol, however, along with the rest of Alpha Company, was only able to enjoy a brief respite. Almost immediately after entering the gates and beginning the arduous task of getting their wounded and dead to the casualty evacuation site, Sokol received an urgent order from Padilla. He was to take his men back out. Their orders were to seize the Abu Hanifah Mosque where there had been a reported "Saddam sighting" only hours before.

For some of the Marines, hearing the new order was no big deal: "Hey, if we got through the first fight, we'll make it through this one." For others it felt like the kiss of death. Many Marines sincerely believed that they had only a very definite and fixed number of firefights or days of combat "in them." If they happen to transgress that number and fight one more day, or venture out on one more mission, it would simply be "their time." I don't really know how many in Alpha Company felt that kind of trepidation when they heard the order to go back out and seize the mosque. But based on what I had already seen in other Marines before and during the war, I am sure that some felt like this would be their last battle.

Nevertheless, Alpha saddled up and headed back out into the dangerous streets of Baghdad. Curiously, except for a few sporadic shots here and there, the first few minutes en route to the mosque were relatively quiet. The Marines used the time to make sure their rifle magazines were fully loaded.

Sokol had only a sketchy intelligence picture of what kinds of enemy forces were thought to be there—reports suggested at least a company-sized element. All the units in First Marine Division had been given specific instructions not to fire on places of worship or shrines of any kind. Our commanding general wanted to make sure the Iraqi people understood that this was not a war against Islam.

However, the caveat was clear—if ever we received fire from a holy place or shrine, we were given full authority to use whatever means necessary to engage and destroy the enemy. Already, on Route 2 earlier in the morning, our battalion had taken heavy machine-gun fire from another mosque along the way. Sokol and the rest of his lieutenants fully assumed that this mosque would be no different. They were right.

Sweeping around the northeast corner of the gated holy site, Alpha's lead AAVs suddenly drew a barrage of machine-gun fire. In an instant, bullets began screaming down at them from gunmen in the upper portals of the mosque and the surrounding buildings.

"Here we go again," Horton said to himself.

Metal collided with metal and the men inside Horton's AAV braced for the worst. Horton, looking to his immediate left, spotted an open blue door leading into the outer courtyard of the mosque. He noted that only minutes before, the door had been closed. Moments later a Fedayeen militant, wearing those too-familiar black pants and a loosely fitting grey tunic, appeared to the left of the door. He was holding an RPG. In an instant his outline was gone again. Horton knew he had only seconds before the man would fling himself into the open and fire his weapon. Horton's AAV was just five feet away from him. It might well be obliterated.

"Sir . . . sir . . . did you see him? He's right there! We've gotta get him!"

The voice of Corporal Kyle Menze raised itself above the machine-gun fire. Menze, who was standing in the back of Horton's AAV, had seen the Fedayeen warrior too and immediately began firing his M-16 in the direction of the doorway. After squeezing off about ten rounds, Menze's rifle jammed.

He still recalls the fear he felt. He knew that the assailant, now unimpeded, could step out at any moment and send his rocket into the side of the AAV. Frantically he worked his weapon over, trying to get it to fire. No luck. Now what?

Horton had carried a grenade with him throughout the war. As a platoon commander, he never really thought he would have to use it. In fact he admitted later that there were several times when he almost got rid of it. For the most part, grenades were carried by grunts who put them to good use in the "front end" of a bunker clearing. Horton later explained, "Something just made me keep it . . . I never knew why."

Pulling the grenade off of his chest where it had hung for over twenty days, Horton jerked free the pin and let loose on the handle. He knew that he only had three to five seconds left before it blew. He counted, "One one thousand, two one thousand, . . . three . . . "

He gently tossed it over the side of his AAV and watched it roll back toward the Fedayeen militant. Peering out the bulletproof glass of his AAV's hatch, Horton eagerly watched to see the outcome of his effort. It wasn't quite what he had in mind.

The gunman, no doubt realizing it was over for him, stepped out from behind the wall and pointed his RPG at the side of Horton's AAV. Just as the grenade exploded, the gunman pulled the trigger and the rocket knifed its charge into the AAV's steel hulk. The enemy's rocket of choice was a shape charge, designed not to explode so much as to pierce completely through the armor of a tank or AAV, destroying or killing anything or anyone in its path.

Piercing the outer armor of Horton's AAV, the charge sent a

molten beam of lead all the way through the vehicle and embedded itself in the other side. The force of the impact was so great that Menze was shot several feet straight up in the air, landing on top of the vehicle. Shrapnel from the shredded interior of the AAV exploded outward into the small compartment, which was loaded with Marines. Unbelievably, the charge missed every one of them, although tiny pieces of steel rained down on the huddled group and wounded several of them.

The blast caused the vehicle's Halon fire retardant system to engage, pouring noxious chemical fumes into the lungs of the shell-shocked Marines. Choking, gasping for air, vomiting, they crawled up and out of the hatch, falling on the ground, oblivious to the continual enemy fire around them. They didn't care—they had to breathe.

A couple of days earlier, someone had been smoking and had inadvertently set off the Halon system, emptying its bladder of over half of its supply of fire retardant. Horton recalled later that, if the providential smoking mistake had never happened, some of those Marines would never have made it out of the compartment before choking or being suffocated.

Just then a burning Iraqi troop carrier exploded, sending shrapnel and debris all over the Marines who by now were positioning themselves to kick down the front door and storm the mosque. Lance Corporal Benjamin Wetzel took a piece to his face, leaving a burning hole in the side of his jaw. He fought on, not realizing that his face was smoking.

Guthrie took cover as the red-hot shards of a second explosion peppered the men, badly injuring the arm of his squad leader, Corporal Mejia. Seeing the condition of Mejia, Staff Sergeant Nerad looked at Guthrie and yelled, "Okay, Guthrie, you've got the team. They're yours now!" In an instant, Guthrie was responsible for the lives of five other men.

Always having managed to find his share of trouble in the platoon, Guthrie had never been given a great deal of responsibility. But this was different. It was urgent. So Guthrie, who was still reeling from the explosion that somehow hadn't put a scratch on his body, rose to the occasion and took charge.

While Guthrie and the others started assembling themselves against the side wall for the breach into the mosque, Captain Ray Lawler was busy calling for an air strike that would, if on target, effectively destroy the enemies who were still firing from the row of buildings just across the street. Lawler, or "Spanky," was, like Basco, a pilot who had been assigned to the battalion as a forward air controller.

When he wasn't serving with infantry Marines, Lawler flew the famous KC-130, a hulk of an aircraft that is almost indestructible. It can fly in almost any weather, get shot up by enemy rounds, and still deliver the troops or equipment in its payload to remote areas where the only landing strip is a dirt road. Lawler's demeanor was as tough as the aircraft he flew. It would have to be. The kind of air strike he was about to call in would put five-hundred-pound bombs and supersonic armor-piercing bullets within only a stone's throw of the hunkered down Americans. It went against all Marine Corps aviation doctrine, but Lawler knew, as did Sokol, that it was the only choice they had.

"This one could get a little squirrelly," Lawler was heard saying as he confirmed the enemy grid coordinates with the A-10 pilot who was by now screaming toward the mosque.

The Marines, who had just busted into the inner courtyard of the Islamic holy site, were startled by the growling sound the A-10 made as its 30 mm cannon roared to life. As for the enemy militants, they never knew what hit them. Fragments of concrete and slab were chewed up and spit upward like the brittle heads of ripe wheat in a combine. Smoke and fire leapt out of the buildings as the A-10 armor-piercing rounds struck power lines and gas outlets. The precision strike could not have been more effective. Nor could it have come at a more crucial time. Lawler later received a special decoration for his gutsy call.

By noon, the mosque was all but secured, and while Saddam was nowhere to be found, Alpha Company had taken more than forty enemy prisoners of war. Most of them were finely dressed and well armed, suggesting that they may have, in fact, been protecting someone of importance. The tenacity with which the enemy fought was enough to convince many in the intelligence community that Saddam, or at least one of his high-level advisors, had actually been there.

The battle of April 10 was virtually relentless until the mosque was secured. For me, and for the other men of the combat train, located only a few miles back on the outskirts of the city, it was a day filled with confusion, fear, and at times unbearable tension. Early that morning, just after the first of our companies ran into enemy fire, we started hearing patchy radio reports of enemy contact and even casualties. Constant static kept us from understanding the specifics. We knew our boys were in a fight, we knew that some were wounded, but we had no way of knowing just how bad it was. Then a Marine CH-46 helicopter landed at our site with awful news.

The pilot's words were few. "I'm not sure how to say his last name," he said, "but his name is spelled B-O-H-R."

I felt like a dagger had plunged deep into my gut.

I wondered what the men were going through right now. Certainly grief and confusion must be gripping many of their hearts; and yet grief is something that tough Marines are reluctant to reveal. I'd seen them bite their lips when Lieutenant Childers was killed. I knew their hearts were breaking now that Gunny Bohr was gone too.

"Were there others?" I asked the pilot, who by now was fumbling through a green notebook he'd pulled out of his right cargo pocket.

There had to be more. I had already counted a handful of casualties while listening to the garbled radio reports. But I was hoping and praying that there weren't too many. The pilot began quickly flipping through the oil-smeared, spiral-bound pages, and I knew he was looking for names. I braced for the worst.

"Moore . . . shrapnel in upper body . . . Dumas . . . gunshot wound in the neck . . . Peyton . . . gunshot to the lung . . . Shevlin . . . shrapnel to the face . . . McNair . . . shrapnel to the neck . . . Keenen . . . gunshot wound in the arm . . . ."

On and on he went, reading off the names like some kind of

awful roll call. He had flown out many of the men himself. And I could tell that he was holding back from telling me what some of them had looked like. As the day went on, the first official roster of our wounded was printed out by the regimental administrative office just a few hundred yards away. Like the pilot's initial report, it was not encouraging.

Dr. Trivedi and I snatched the perforated paper from the hand of the regimental aid and immediately pored over the names. In all, seventy-six Marines had been injured in the hours between 4:00 a.m. and 1:00 p.m. that day. My heart sank. Not only where these men I had shared my life with for the past year and a half, but many were men whom I had baptized as new Christians just weeks earlier in Kuwait. Others had recently made life-changing decisions to renew their faith in the Lord.

"Doc Williams . . . shrapnel in the leg . . . Corporal Dawson . . . shrapnel in the hand . . . Lance Corporal Newman . . . gunshot wound in the lower body . . . Lance Corporal Henry . . . gunshot wound in the arm . . . Corporal White . . . gunshot wound in the arm . . . Lance Corporal Quintana . . . shrapnel to the body/gunshot wound to the hand . . ."

I knew their faith, like mine, was being tried and tested. I knew they were probably questioning everything. I so much wanted to be with them, to be a presence in the midst of the agony they were experiencing. They weren't just names. They were men whom God had given to me as a chaplain to love and encourage, to strengthen and to bind up, to comfort and to heal. But all I could do was pray. And I prayed as I'd never prayed before.

"Dear God . . . they're Yours . . . all of them. I commit them into Your hands. Please breathe the assurance of Your presence and love into their struggling hearts and minds right now."

In truth, I needed that same assurance myself.

As the Middle Eastern sun made its final descent over the western horizon, there was no pretending what this day had been— a disastrous, deadly ambush. In just over nine hours, seventy-six of our men had become casualties, and at least one had been killed in action. A third of the wounded were so critical that they had already been evacuated out of Baghdad for good. And none of us knew if there was an end in sight.

Perhaps Oliver North, who stood just feet from me that night, said it best. Reporting live to millions of watching Americans, he announced, "Tonight has been the worst night of the war for U.S. Marines."

Lying down on top of my sleeping bag at the end of that day, all I could think about was how right he was.

10
A Mighty Fortress

A QUICK LOOK AROUND BAGHDAD the next morning told the tale. Even the most uninformed civilian, strolling up and down the sidewalks and side streets of Route 2, would have been in no doubt about the kind of violence that had taken place just hours earlier. Machine-gun holes riddled the concrete sides of buildings, shops, and overpasses. The blackened and charred remains of burnt-out vehicles still smoked and reeked of burning steel, electrical wires, and even human flesh. Blood smattered the ledges of window sills and balconies. Stray dogs rummaged through the twisted metal and trash that lined the streets.

But the Marines of the First Battalion, Fifth Regiment woke up that morning to a world that had suddenly become a place of peace, where the song of birds and the sounds of ordinary traffic had replaced the deafening sounds of missiles, bullets, and gut-wrenching distress calls. They were as safe as could be inside the fortified walls of Saddam Hussein's Almilyah Presidential Palace.

Truthfully, there was more than safety on their minds. The Marines felt a growing sense of wonder. In fact, when Rufo, White, and I arrived at the palace from the outskirts of the city where we had spent the night, it was as if we had stumbled into a kind of celebration. It was no riotous laughter or wild partying, but the deep and quiet joy reflected in the eyes of men who had seen something come to pass that they had desperately prayed for. And that answered prayer had exceeded their greatest expectations.

How could I forget the look on Corporal Ayani Dawson's face when our Humvee drove through the gates of the palace? Smiling from ear to ear, he was sitting behind a stack of sandbags that served as a machine-gun guard post. A rifle in one hand and thick white gauze wrapping the other, he waved proudly. He wanted our incoming vehicle to see his injury, but not because he was looking for sympathy. For him that injury symbolized the triumph that he and so many others had experienced. His radiant smile was far more than a benign look of relief. I had baptized Dawson as a new Christian just weeks earlier, and he and I both knew in that instant what he was communicating as his eyes met mine. God had saved him.

"Chaplain," Dawson grinned, "remember those angels, the ones your wife talked about . . . the legions? They were there, surrounding us, protecting us, defending us. I should be dead, Chaplain, but God was with me."

The young African-American Marine was referring to a worship service I'd given two weeks earlier about eighty miles south of Baghdad. In the service, I had shared with the men a prayer that my wife, Charity, as a third-grader, had learned from her parents. Their family said it when they headed out on road trips together. It went something like this:

Dear Lord, please make the driver awake, aware, alert, and aggressive; and surround us all with four legions of angels wherever we go. Amen.

It was just a little girl's prayer, yet it conveyed a promise of God's protection—"For He shall give His angels charge over you, to keep you in all your ways" (Psalm 91:11)—that has breathed courage and faith into warriors for thousands of years. I could never have imagined how many men had been clinging to that promise when the rounds started flying on April 10, 2003. But they believed it.

And the *angels* were there.

All day I listened to the stories. Alpha Company's Lance Corporal James Miller and countless others recalled that they saw waves of RPGs screaming straight for them, shot from point-blank range. Yet, at the last second, the missiles curved wildly, as if they had been batted away in midair. Sailing completely around the AAVs, the RPGs struck buildings on the other side of the road, buildings that were teeming with enemy gunmen.

Private First Class Timothy Pawloski recalled an RPG that was heading straight for him. The missile was coming so fast that Pawloski didn't even have time to close his eyes or duck for cover. At the last second, when it was only feet from where he was standing, it suddenly jerked upward and to the left. As if it were being pulled by an unseen rope, it split a tree wide open instead of striking the frightened young man.

The Marines of Weapons Company watched in disbelief as RPGs, hurtling directly toward their Humvees, were seemingly pushed down into the street pavement. Like smooth rocks bouncing across a glassy pond, the missiles skipped along without exploding underneath their vehicles. They finally blew up when they hit the curb or storefronts along the road.

Adam McCully's AAV was the first to enter the ambush at the Tigris River Bridge. McCully recalled the innumerable muzzle flashes coming from each side of the street. Captain Blair Sokol, riding three vehicles back, concurred. After watching McCully's AAV full of Marines moving through the raking fire, he said, "In that moment, I felt certain that many of my men were gone. There were too many muzzle flashes to count."

Sokol should have been right. McCully's men were standing atop their AAV firing back, completely exposed to the sheets of enemy fire from the shoulders up. But for some reason not a single man was hit during the melee. Staff Sergeant Bradley Nerad, who had lost his lieutenant just three weeks earlier, said, "There is no way they should have gotten through that ambush like they did. Someone must have been there with us, providing air-watch."

Corporal Mike Cash, who was riding in the back of Gunny Bohr's soft-skinned Humvee, showed me the ragged entry and exit holes where enemy AK-47 rounds had passed through the green cloth coverings on each side of him, and where he had been hunkered down. Neither Cash nor I nor any one else could explain why the rounds did not strike his body. A newly baptized Christian, Cash, with tears in his eyes, could only believe that he had been protected by the angel of the Lord.

Nor could anyone explain how Lance Corporal Ryan Harnish survived. Standing atop his AAV, the young warrior rattled off his rifle at every gunman he could see, but there were too many to keep up with. Just then, an RPG was launched from the shoulders of a hidden militant crouched in an alleyway. It struck Harnish full force in the side of the head, throwing his body back against the plenum of the AAV like a rag doll. He never knew what hit him. It is no overstatement to say that he and all ten Marines standing up next to him should have been instantly obliterated.

But God had other plans. The rocket never detonated. And even though the force of the blunt impact alone should have killed him, Harnish remains very much alive. In fact, he suffered no serious injury. Later on, at the palace, his fellow Marines pointed out to him the large chunk of Kevlar blown out of the side of his helmet where the missile had struck.

And then there was Staff Sergeant Russi of Weapons Company. As he peered out of his AAV, he could see that the firing was coming from every angle. Even though he was sunk down in his hatch, there was no way to get away from the gunmen on the rooftops. And he didn't. As the AAV tracked through the melee of fire, Russi felt a blow on the side of his Kevlar helmet, like he'd been hit in the head with a baseball bat. He immediately blacked out.

When he awoke moments later, he could still feel the throbbing of the percussion echoing in his head. He had no idea what had happened; he only knew that he was still alive and not bleeding profusely. Ducking below, he took his helmet off to check the top of his head from where the pain was radiating. He found a minor scratch and a dab of blood—nothing more. Then he inspected his helmet for marks or punctures; and what he saw made his heart skip and brought tears to his eyes.

An enemy round had entered his helmet just above the top of his right ear. But as if its path were marked out in advance, the round had curved up and over his head, still underneath the Kevlar skin of the helmet, and finally lodged itself on the left side, about the same place where it had entered on the right.

As I continued to make my way through the palace compound and listened to more and more stories, I realized that our men had been shielded in ways none of us could fully understand.

"Chaplain . . . you know how I'm always saying that I won't believe it 'less I see it? Well, I believe it now 'cause I can't explain what happened to me out there yesterday. I . . . I should be dead . . . but there was something with me . . . something real . . . Someone real . . ."

Zebulon Batke's voice sounded a little shaky as he struggled to describe what had happened to him just hours before. A half-smile played around his face. Clearly he'd seen something in the streets of Baghdad that was, for him, miraculous.

Positioned well to the rear of the convoy, Batke, Dickens, Hardy, and Beavers had their radio dialed into the battalion's main net. At 4:15 a.m., they heard the familiar but dreadful word: "Contact!"

Their stomachs tightened. "Here we go again," Dickens said.

Up until then, the pattern hadn't been so bad for them. Because they usually traveled near the rear of the convoy, they could count on the forward rifle companies to stir up the enemy's nest. By the time their vehicle arrived on the scene, the enemy had either been defeated or had already fled. This time, however, was different.

Like so many dominoes falling, every vehicle in the armada began, one by one, announcing "Contact" over the radio. "Apache has contact . . . Cherokee, contact . . . Blackhawk has made contact . . . Tomahawk is receiving fire . . . contact."

Meanwhile Batke, who was sitting atop the hardback shell of his Humvee, could see enemy tracers coming closer and closer. With the convoy moving at nearly 25 mph, it was like driving toward a gauntlet of flaming steel. All Batke could do was wait his turn. For the first time in the war, real fear gripped him.

At six-feet-five inches, Batke knew he was an easy target atop the vehicle. And yet, what could he say? It was his turn. Beavers had manned the mounted gun for the several hours it took to drive from Saddam City to the outskirts of Baghdad. This was Batke's moment and he knew it. He also knew that any of the others in the vehicle would have manned the gun if he'd asked them to. But that's not why he joined the Marines—to give dangerous duties to others.

By now, the fire was coming so close that Batke could see the sparks of rounds hitting vehicles just a few meters in front of his. He pulled back the charging handle of his roof-mounted Mark-19 grenade launcher to chamber a round that just might save his neck. The round wouldn't load.

"What's going on? This thing has worked the whole time in this God-forsaken place . . . and *now* it quits on me!"

He worked and worked on the jammed chamber until finally, just as the first red-hot tracers began shrieking past his head, he yelled down to Beavers below, "My M-16! Just get me my rifle!"

As he reached down to grab up the rifle from Beavers, Batke could hear their driver's voice, as if they were in a quiet room together. "We're going to be OK," Hardy reassured him. "Just trust in God. Believe, and He's gonna get us through it. Remember the Bible in the storm? It was a sign. He's our shield. It's gonna be OK, man . . . just believe."

How could Hardy be so calm and peaceful in the middle of such a wicked assault? Batke thought to himself, *God must be whispering something in that boy's ear.* He grabbed the rifle from Beavers and started shooting at every muzzle flash he could see.

Just then an RPG shot across the hood of their vehicle, blanketing the front end with a sheet of fire and smoke contrails. Batke reloaded his rifle and started firing again—at anything. He'd never felt so vulnerable in all his life. Streams of lead were passing over him; rockets were exploding to his right and left. He was totally out in the open, a two-hundred-pound, seventy-seven-inch target waiting to be obliterated, or at least maimed beyond recognition.

"It got so bad, I could literally feel the overpressure from the bullets whizzing by me. I knew I was going to get hit at any moment. I could see the shadowy outlines of men running all around me, above me on rooftops, everywhere. But something just kept me going."

There was a momentary pause in the firing, and shaky as his hands were, Batke was finally able to get his Mark-19 unjammed. The convoy began to funnel into a narrower street, making the vehicles slow down and increasing the chance of getting raked by enemy fire. Then came the heartstopper. "Something told me to look to my right, and when I did, I could see the silhouette of a man . . . couldn't have been more than twenty-five feet away. He was kneeling with an RPG, and it was pointed right at me."

The moment stretched into eternity, and the fear of death riveted Batke's insides. Hardy saw the man too, and keeping his eyes on the road, he prayed. They both knew that in an armored AAV, they might have a chance. But a direct RPG impact upon a Humvee would leave nothing behind but a little puff of smoke.

What happened next was simply unexplainable.

As soon as Batke could whirl his Mark-19 around and start shooting, the man, for no good reason, stood up as if he'd seen a ghost. He looked at another gunman standing close-by, waved his arms frantically, and together the two ran full-speed into a darkened alleyway. They never once looked back in Hardy and Batke's direction. It was nothing short of bizarre.

The enemy gunman had had every opportunity to launch his RPG into the side of the stopped Humvee. Yet instead of taking the point-blank shot, he simply ran. Yelling something to his cohort in Arabic, the two fled for their lives.

It happened so fast that Batke didn't even have time to process what was going on. Wheeling his weapon around, he simply pulled the trigger and showered the alleyway with a half-dozen grenades. The gunman and his companion were gone—for good. But what on earth had the man seen? What caused him not to shoot his missile? Why did he turn and run away? Those questions tugged at Batke's mind, but there was no time to search for answers. They all had to keep moving.

When they finally drove through the iron gates of the presidential palace, Dickens recalled having an overwhelming desire to fall to his knees and thank God. Tears of emotion and gratitude streamed from many of the men's eyes. Hardy just kept smiling and pointing to the worn leathery Bible that still sat unmoved on the radio mount. "I knew it . . . I knew it when we found it in the storm. God was going to protect us. What'd I tell you? He did it!"

As I listened to Batke's account, I could tell that there had been a glacial shift in his heart. Here he was, a self-proclaimed atheist who, like so many of us, needed proof. His questions betrayed the kinds of doubts with which we all struggle but perhaps lack the courage to voice. It occurred to me that not only he, but I too was witnessing something remarkable. Here was a man who had doubted all his life, who had searched for answers, who had demanded evidence. And he'd gotten it!

Oh, the love of God, I thought to myself. He meets us wherever we are. He doesn't turn away the cynic or the skeptic. He knows that we all need a dose of the miraculous from time to time, a burning bush to remind us that He lives. In His great love and patience, He will do whatever it takes to bring us to a point of childlike and simple faith, in which we finally we cry out, "Yes, God, I believe." For Batke, it was a Bible in a storm, a friend with simple faith, and an unseen Power at work around him that led him to faith.

For Staff Sergeant Bryan Jackway and the three other men in his Humvee, it was something else.

Having already survived a near-fatal mortar explosion days earlier at the Saddam Canal that had launched his body fifteen feet in the air and nearly shaken his teeth out of his head, Bryan

Jackway knew that God's protection was no pie-in-the-sky dream. Simply put, the mortar round should have killed him, if not by the percussion alone, then by the raking sheets of shrapnel which ought to have shredded his body.

Jackway, whose father had served two combat tours as a door-gunner for an army helicopter in Vietnam, had joined the Marine Corps at seventeen without even realizing it was a paying job. He told his recruiter that it didn't matter where he went in the Corps, as long as it was where he was needed. His recruiter, predictably, sent the willing and eager youngster straight to the trenches as a machine-gunner in an infantry battalion. It was a tough and, at times, physically grueling job, but before long it became more of a calling for Jackway than a duty. He began to believe that his decision to enter the military hadn't been so much a boyish fancy as a deep desire to serve something greater than himself. For Jackway, the idea of a calling was given further meaning by his deep religious faith.

"God ordains and chooses the government and the military for a high and noble purpose," Jackway told me after the war. "And the man who chooses to enter its ranks, whether he knows it or not, is serving more than his country; he's serving God. I knew even before entering the war that God had a plan and purpose for my life, and that if His plan was for me to live and continue to serve my country, nothing—no power, no enemy, nothing at all—could stop it."

Jackway's survival at the canal was noteworthy. But it was eclipsed by what happened to him on April 10. Like the rest of the convoy, Jackway (who rode on the passenger side), his driver Lance Corporal Lo, his radioman Lance Corporal Rosales, and his roof-gunner Lance Corporal Hayes were trying to find their way to the palace. Their armored Humvee had already taken incoming .762 AK-47 rounds, all of which had thus far ricocheted off the steel sidepaneling of the vehicle.

But now the battle was intensifying. The volume of fire was growing at such an earsplitting rate that with every shot each man checked his doorway or body for an impact or a wound. Everyone knows that surges of adrenaline can, at least for a few moments, obscure even deadly injuries. But the most disheartening aspect of it all was that they had just passed the same traffic intersection for the third straight time. By now it was 5:00 a.m. in the morning, and the convoy was a tangled mass of AAVs, Humvees, and tanks, moving wildly in every direction, doubling back, rolling on and off overpasses and on-ramps. The lead elements were still searching for that elusive right turn to the palace.

"Finally," Jackway recalled, "Charlie Company found what seemed to be the right way. We immediately jerked our Humvee around to get in behind them, hoping it would take us to the palace."

It was at that very moment when every man in Jackway's vehicle should have been killed. Without warning, from point-blank range, an RPG struck the driver's side door frame, twelve inches from where the driver, Lo, was sitting. It sent waves of fire and shrapnel rippling through the cramped compartment. It was the kind of direct hit that often leaves no human remains in the aftermath. In short, a high-explosive rocket exploded with all of its force *inside* the cabin of an armored Humvee, manned by four men.

As the rocket struck the door frame, it was as if an unseen hand channeled its force. The brunt of the round's explosion passed through the driver's open window and impacted, with full force, the inside of the front glass. The windshield exploded—from the inside out. In a millisecond of deafening sound and overpressure, the thick bulletproof front glass windshield disintegrated into a fireball. Thousands of jagged chards showered the paved road in front of Jackway's still-moving Humvee like a deadly rainstorm. All four men were engulfed in a scorching wall of heat and flames.

Marines driving behind Jackway's Humvee saw the hit. They knew beyond a doubt that America had just lost four boys. Calls burst through the radios and headsets of the other vehicles. "Tomahawk One is down! Tomahawk One's down! Docs . . . we need docs now!"

There are moments in battle so profound that the warriors who face them recount a peaceful, momentary pause in the violence of the bombs and bullets exploding around them. Such moments are almost quiet, although perhaps accompanied by a slight ringing sound. Voices and other noises are muffled, actions are reduced to slow motion, and the lines between life and death seem blurred. Time literally stands still. It was into such a surreal realm that Jackway and his men were plunged the moment the rocket exploded in their vehicle. Perhaps it was death, they thought. It should have been.

Opening his eyes after the blinding flash, Jackway grabbed his chest and arm. He kept pounding and squeezing to make sure he was still there. "Dear God . . . I'm alive!" he shouted.

Without looking at Lo or at the other two Marines sitting behind him, Jackway immediately picked up his radio and started calling in casualties. "This is Tomahawk One . . . I have wounded! I have wounded!"

He didn't bother to look at them. He knew very well that one couldn't have emerged from such an explosion alive, much less unscathed. But as he pulled away his handset from his ear, he glanced beside him and behind him anyway. And there sat the others, fully alive and uninjured.

Jackway looked over to Lo, who was still driving with a smile on his face.

"Are you hurt?" he screamed. "Where did it get you?" Like a worried parent, Jackway began frisking the body of his driver. He knew that it's not uncommon for men who are mortally wounded in battle to go for a few seconds, or even minutes, and not realize that they've been hit or are dying. Lo had been sitting precisely where the blast had occurred. He *had* to be wounded.

"I knew he probably just couldn't feel it," Jackway told me. "I started running my hands down his back, on his legs, up his neck, patting him down, looking for an entry wound, an exit wound where shrapnel had hit . . . nothing . . . there was nothing. I couldn't believe what I was seeing."

Finally, Jackway commanded the now rejoicing Lo, with no windshield in front of him, to keep driving through the fire. "Don't stop! Don't stop! Press on! We're gonna make it!"

As they drove, Jackway couldn't seem to get the words of a psalm out of his head—a scripture he had read time and time again in preparation for going off to war. His heart leapt as he experienced its newfound power and meaning as never before: "I will set him on high, because he has known My name. He shall call upon Me, and I will answer him; I will be with him in trouble; I will deliver him and honor him. With long life I will satisfy him, and show him My salvation" (Psalm 91:14–16).

As Bryan Jackway described the vivid events of the day before, even as much as I attempted to understand his experience, I knew he was trying to describe for me something indescribable. He and the others in his vehicle had seen and experienced things that, by every governing principle of combat and physics, should not have happened. But those things *did* happen, impossible as they were.

As I continued to walk the palace grounds, late in the day I found myself in a giant circular rotunda, a throne room of sorts, where our battalion command staff sat exhausted, still reflecting on so many unexplainable events of the last twenty-four hours. That's when I talked to Major Cal Worth, the battalion's executive officer and second-in-command.

Positioned near the middle of the giant convoy, Worth's command AAV had been in the heart of the chaos when the convoy took the wrong turn and started doubling back on itself. Worth and the others in his vehicle had worked nonstop, under unceasing small-arms fire, to try and realign the battalion and find the right way to the palace. "It couldn't have been worse," he admitted. "We were all over the place, moving in every direction. It's the last thing you want to happen in a fight like this one."

And yet as terrifying as those hours were, he said, "In the end I think our getting lost like that and being spread out all over the place may have worked in our favor. In fact, I think that more than anything else, it actually worked to confuse the enemy. Instead of driving down one narrow street, there we were coming at them from every direction. Even though there were only a thousand of us, I'll bet they thought they were facing an entire regiment!"

Overhearing our conversation, Padilla chimed in, "Or a whole division!"

As I thought about what Major Worth was saying, I felt as if I had heard his story somewhere before. Something about a ragtag and weary group of warriors, facing overwhelming odds, yet appearing to the enemy a far mightier force than they really were. Yes, I had heard his story before—in Sunday school.

In the Hebrew Scriptures—2 Kings 6—is the story of Gideon's army. Three hundred faithful men were transformed by the power of God to appear as tens of thousands before the eyes of their enemies, the Midianites. Armed only with trumpets and pitchers, Gideon and his faithful band of warriors had spread themselves around the enemy's camp in such a way that when they blew their trumpets and shattered their pitchers, they appeared not as three hundred, but as legions of conquering soldiers. The story has been one of my favorites since childhood, because it demonstrates that God can take the most unlikely circumstances and use them to reveal His power and His protection.

Perhaps we weren't a mere battalion on that day; but like Gideon's army, we had become an all-consuming flood of men and machinery, surging from the north, rolling in like an unstoppable tide. It was too clear to miss. And it went a long way toward explaining the utter confusion and chaos that so many of our men witnessed among the forces they were fighting.

Yes, our men were lost and separated. But our God was not confused. Just as He had from the very beginning of the war, He was providentially working all things together for the good of a cause that was just and true.

Major Steve Armes, our unit's operations officer and third-in-command of the battalion, said that during the worst part of the fight, he remembered looking up at an overpass just ahead of him and saw that it was lined with AAVs from end to end, like a steel wall. But something caught his attention that made him take a second look: the AAVs were not marked. Whereas all of our battalion's vehicles had the distinct and clearly visible markings of our unit painted in bold white letters and numbers, the ones Armes saw had nothing painted on them at all. As the operations officer, he of all men in the battalion knew exactly where the various units were positioned and what they looked like.

But he had no idea to whom those strange AAVs belonged. They were unmarked and out of place, and none of it added up, except for the fact that their position on the bridge provided a perfect shield from the incoming enemy rounds that were hailing down from surrounding rooftops and balconies.

In the heat of battle, Armes simply sloughed it off and kept fighting. But days after the battle he had to think twice. Going back to that same intersection, Armes tried to relocate the overpass on which the strange AAVs had been lined up in a steel column. But he searched to no avail. No matter what direction he looked—north, south, east, or west—the overpass simply wasn't there.

As Armes described all of this to me, he didn't offer any conclusions. He neither tried to explain it away nor forced an interpretation. He didn't demand that it be anything other than what it was—something he knew he saw with his own two eyes that he will never be able to comprehend. He left it there.

But I couldn't.

What had he seen? Was it a figment of his imagination? Was it mental misfire in the midst of a nightmarish experience? The truth is, his account wasn't the first time something like that happened in a war. Again, the Hebrew Scriptures relates a similar story. Second Kings 6 describes what the prophet Elisha's servant saw thousands of years ago, during a moment when two armies were squared off against each other on a field of battle.

> Therefore he sent horses and chariots and a great army there, and they came by night and surrounded the city. And when the servant of the man of God arose early and went out, there was an army, surrounding the city with horses and chariots. And his servant said to him, "Alas, my master! What shall we do?" So he answered, "Do not fear, for those who are with us are more than

those who are with them." And Elisha prayed, and said, "LORD, I pray, open his eyes that he may see." Then the LORD opened the eyes of the young man, and he saw. And behold, the mountain was full of horses and chariots of fire all around Elisha." (2 Kings 6:14–17)

Is it too farfetched to believe that a God, who never changes and who upholds the cause of justice and freedom, could not or would not do the very same thing for a weary major in the United States Marine Corps? The truth is that the God of the Bible is a God who fights for what is right, a God who contends with those who plot evil against His own.

The Scriptures call God the "Lord of Hosts," which is a name reserved for a captain or general who commands an army. He is also called "Mighty Fortress," "Strong Tower," "Shield," and "Defender." And despite what so many well-meaning people say today, His place is not only in the quiet corners of the human heart, divorced from the raw reality of a blood-and-guts world. God's presence descends into the valley of the shadow of death, is revealed in the sweep of world events, and has for centuries been mightily demonstrated wherever courageous warriors, inspired by a worthy cause, have stepped foot on the field of battle and marched against the forces of evil and tyranny.

That day, in Saddam's palace, we all knew it. We needed no convincing, because we had been eyewitnesses to events that could only be explained as evidence of the hand of God. Indeed, as the Middle Eastern sun began its descent on April 11, 2003, perhaps the battalion commander's words summed it up best: "There is no doubt in my mind, Someone was watching over us the entire time."

I slugged down a big gulp of my canteen water and bid good-night to Lieutenant Colonel Padilla, Major Worth, and the rest of the command. We were all more than ready to bed down for the evening. If the day before had been marked by battle and bloodshed, this day had been one of discovery and celebration. I walked out the arched hallway of the ornate domelike room and stepped over a pile of rubble made by a five-hundred-pound bomb that had been dropped into the palace days before we attacked. The sun had completely disappeared behind the horizon, and the sounds of Muslim muzzeins could be heard droning their Qur'anic dirge over the loud speakers of the city.

What are they saying? I asked myself. *What kind of hope are they offering?*

I didn't know. But one thing I was sure about—our battalion commander was right. Someone had been watching us while we stormed the gates of the palace. Just ask the ones who were there, the ones who tried to describe the indescribable, the ones who should be dead, but are alive today, and giving glory to God.

Yes, Someone was watching over us all. So many of us believed it. And it wasn't luck, or good fortune, or some cosmic play of chance. It was One who is a warrior Himself, who knows something about battle. It was the One who fought against Satan in the wilderness and defeated his schemes. It was the One who fought against sin on the cross and was victorious over its power. It was the One who fought against death at the tomb and burst its bonds.

That night the significance of what I had heard began to warm me to sleep. I still remember the feeling, the exhilaration, and the lyric that was beginning to be sung in my heart. I am sure that one way or another, that new song was heard by hundreds of young heroes that night, within the palace walls.

I waited patiently for the LORD; and He inclined to me, and heard my cry. He brought me up out of the pit of destruction, out of the miry clay; and he set my feet upon a rock making my footsteps firm. And He put a new song in my mouth, a song of praise to our God; many will see and fear, and will trust in the Lord. (Psalm 40:1–3 NASB)

11

Semper Fidelis

O God our help in ages past, our hope for years to come,
our shelter from the stormy blast and our eternal home.

Eᴀʀʟʏ ꜰʀɪᴅᴀʏ ᴍᴏʀɴɪɴɢ, April 12, as I made my way around
Saddam's palace grounds, I felt compelled to keep talking to the
men and listening to their stories. I sensed in them a deep need,
even a compulsion, to articulate their wonder and amazement at
what God had brought them through. And this wasn't true of only
a handful of Marines. From the youngest private to the oldest
veteran, every man seemed to have a story to tell. Every one of
them had a view of the firefight that was uniquely his.

Their stories seemed to have one common thread—they all
believed they had been in the midst of a modern-day miracle. As
they told me what they had seen, their eyes lit up and their faces
glowed. It was clear to me that I wasn't merely in the company of
warriors but of witnesses. No matter how different and diverse their
faith backgrounds were, whether they had always attended worship
services or had never darkened the door of a church, no one could
deny that something extraordinary had taken place—something
beyond human explanation.

These men hadn't merely been in combat; they felt as if they'd
walked through the Red Sea. They might as well have seen the
waters part, stepped onto dry virgin ground, heard the terrifying

rumble of Pharoah's chariots behind them, and watched in awe as the hand of God destroyed their foe right before their eyes. As they spoke, with tears in their eyes and bullet holes through their clothes, I realized that I, too, was a witness. These were not men who had "found religion" momentarily, or who were courteously acknowledging the practical aspects of prayer or faith in times of need. These were men who had stumbled onto something historic, something they had to share with family and friends—a message, a lesson, a story that had to be told.

Sensing their desire to give thanks and offer praise to God, I planned a service of worship for early that evening. And worship God we did.

At 5:00 p.m. on April 12, the burnt-orange warmth of the afternoon sun had already begun to give way to twilight. The great river, only a stone's throw away, rolled between its lush banks, hemmed in by waving bullrushes. Two hundred Marines who had, only forty-eight hours before, experienced the worst that this fallen world had to offer, gathered together. Many of them were still tearful, and with one mind, one heart, and one purpose, they gave thanks and praise to Almighty God. Our worship that evening was not so much planned as it was forced out of our souls by some inward pressure, by what we could only explain as the deliverance of God. I especially remember the sound of the men's voices as they sang:

Before the hills in order stood, or earth received her frame,
From everlasting You are God to endless years the same.
A thousand ages in Your sight are like an evening gone,
Short as the watch that ends the night, before the rising sun.

Time, like an ever-rolling stream, bears all its sons away.
They fly forgotten as a dream dies at the opening day.
O God, our help in ages past, our hope for years to come,
Remain our Guard while life shall last, and our eternal home.[1]

As we sang and praised God, each of us resonated with the comforting words of Holy Scripture. We shared our stories of God's power and presence, able to save and deliver us. Yes, there were tears of sadness as we mourned the loss of our two fallen brothers. Lieutenant Childers and Gunny Bohr were men we loved, men who had died fighting for all that we believed in. Yet mingled with sadness and heartache were tears of profound joy as we celebrated a God who, through the very chaos and carnage of war, had revealed Himself to us—His love, His power, and His plan for our lives.

In those quiet, fading moments after the service, when the last of the men had begun to head back to their platoon for the night, Rufo and I were enjoying the cool of the early evening as we collected the pocket-sized worship books that the men used during services. That's when it dawned on me.

Semper Fidelis . . .

Semper Fidelis is the official motto of the United States Marine Corps, and it means "Always Faithful." For generations it has been the very ethos of the Corps, shouted by every raw recruit, sealed on every official letter of correspondence, woven into the fabric of the institution's every plan and purpose. Semper Fidelis describes the commitment to personal integrity and honor to which every Marine must swear. It embodies the legacy of generations of brave men, faced with the terror of battle and the prospect of individual sacrifice, who did not turn back. They remained faithful and true to the orders of their commanding officers and to their nation.

Of course I knew it meant all that, but now it took on a deeper meaning as well. I began to understand that Semper Fidelis also describes our God's faithfulness to us.

In the throes of battle, God had never once turned back or turned away. He had never ceased to remain true to us. He had provided for our every need, protected us from evil, and empowered us with strength and courage each new day. A handful of young men, we had been thrust into one of the most perilous corridors in the world—danger, violence, and hatred had surrounded us. Yet our fear and uncertainty, grief and anxiety had been overshadowed by Another. As King David said in his most famous psalm, "Yea, though I walk through the valley of the shadow of death, I will fear no evil. For Thou art with me, Thy rod and Thy staff, they comfort me" (Psalm 23 KJV).

God had indeed been with us. He had been *always faithful* to us every step of the way.

First, *God empowered us for battle and gave us strength far beyond our own natural talents and abilities.*

I cannot count the number of young infantrymen and officers who told me that in the most agonizing and demanding hours of the war, it was God alone who gave to them the strength, wisdom, decisiveness, and courage to do their jobs.

Lieutenant Josh Glover's experience on April 4 serves as a memorable example. Glover, a young Charlie Company platoon commander, had only graduated from the Marine Corps' infantry officer course nine months before when he was tasked with providing security for a section of our artillery southeast of Saddam City.

In a twist of providence, one of his men spotted an Iraqi soldier on the horizon observing their post and ducking down to avoid being seen. Glover, not knowing what lay ahead, led his fifteen men, on foot and in broad daylight, into a surprise attack on an Iraqi armored troop carrier (BMP). His men headed into that dangerous patrol armed only with rifles and two AT-4 shoulder-fired antitank missiles.

After moving out for a quarter of a mile or so from the artillery encampment, one of Glover's men spotted something that made his heart stop. About one thousand yards away, underneath the fronds of a palm tree, were what looked like wheel tracks—not familiar American tracks, but the distinct brownish-beige tracks that characterize Iraqi vehicles. It turned out to be an Iraqi armored troop carrier equipped with an enormous machine-gun turret. If that turret wheeled around in time, it would surely mean death for the exposed squad in that open field.

Worse, surrounding the Iraqi vehicles were more than a dozen enemy soldiers.

Glover, his men completely vulnerable, had only one option. They had to charge the enemy position on foot and hope that one of their AT-4 rounds could score a direct hit before the enemy turret turned and fired.

With an explosion that all but woke the dead, the first AT-4 round was launched, falling several yards short of the target. That removed the element of surprise; now the Iraqis knew they were under attack. Every second meant the difference between life and death. Glover ordered the second and last AT-4 missile fired. He could already see enemy soldiers running back and forth around the grove of palm trees that concealed the vehicle. Glover prayed for a direct hit. He got it.

The round screamed into the side of the armored vehicle and blew the turret off like a trash can lid. What followed was a scene straight out of a World War II newsreel. With rifles blazing, Glover and his fifteen men charged the enemy position. They ran, they fired, and they hit the dirt every time an Iraqi rifle was leveled in their direction. The band of American warriors spread out in a concave line and quickly closed in on the overwhelmed enemy, creating chaos and confusion. Disoriented Iraqi soldiers fled in every direction, firing wildly as they ran.

Even after reaching the smoldering Iraqi vehicle, Glover was still taking sporadic fire from the enemy, so he ordered a grenade dropped into the hull to ensure that no Iraqi soldiers emerged from the ashes. After the grenade had done its worst, Glover enveloped the fleeing fighters and finished off those who refused to surrender. He and his squad of fifteen had won the day, destroying a hidden and well-armed Iraqi troop carrier that could have easily launched an attack against our artillery crew, located only a few thousand yards away.

Josh Glover, a bright young officer and tactician, had orchestrated a victory that no doubt saved American lives. Yet recalling the event months after the war, he continued to say that it was God alone who gave him the courage and decisiveness to do what he had to do. It was God who enabled him to put away his fear and to defeat the enemy.

But he saw something else at work as well. From the beginning of the war to the end, what impressed Glover the most was that the actions of his men in battle demonstrated a mental toughness, courage, and sacrifice. That, according to Glover and many other men, were more than personality traits, but evidence to them of man being made in the image of God—God, who is the source of all heroism, the bulwark of all courage, the foundation of all sacrifice.

I've always said that God has the heart of an infantryman. In the Old Testament, when His Spirit came upon a man, more often than not one of the defining characteristics of the encounter was that the man was given great strength and courage to fight against his adversaries and to gain victory in battle. Samson against the Philistines, Gideon against the Midianites, Elijah against the pagans on Mount Carmel, King David against the Amalekites—all of them were chosen by God to lead God's people. All were animated by the Spirit of God to wage war for the cause of truth and righteousness. The blessing of God in their lives did not make them timid and reserved, weak or afraid. Instead, it made them powerful in spiritual and physical strength, singular in purpose, and unswerving in their mission to eradicate evil and injustice.

About Samson we read,

And they bound him with two new ropes and brought him up from the rock. . . . *Then the Spirit of the* LORD *came mightily upon him;* and the ropes that were on his arms became like flax that is burned with fire, and his bonds broke loose from his hands. He found a fresh jawbone of a donkey, reached out his hand and took it, and killed a thousand men with it. (Judges 15:13–15)

And about Gideon we read, "But the Spirit of the LORD came upon Gideon; then he blew the trumpet, and the Abiezrites gathered behind him" (Judges 6:34).

Scripture tells us that God has the heart of a warrior. He equips those who find themselves on a battlefield with every bit of physical, emotional, and spiritual strength necessary to defeat the Enemy. Perhaps the Psalmist says it best:

> For who is God, except the LORD? And who is a rock, except our God? It is God who arms me with strength, And makes my way perfect. He makes my feet like the feet of deer, And sets me on my high places. He teaches my hands to make war, so that my arms can bend a bow of bronze. . . . For by You I can run against a troop, by my God I can leap over a wall . . . You have armed me with strength for the battle; You have subdued under me those who rose up against me.
>
> —PSALM 18:31–34, 29, 39

We saw it in Josh Glover in his courageous assault upon the Iraqi troop carrier.

We saw the same power in Nick Horton's showdown with the Fedayeen gunmen at the mosque.

We saw it in Captain Blair Sokol's ability to lead his company and remain calm in the throes of a chaotic ambush.

All of them, and so many others who experienced victory in Iraq, acknowledged that God was their source of strength and courage. It was God who fitted them with the skills of weaponry and leadership. It was God who helped them discern how and when to use a weapon; how and when to employ the lives of their men in the face of danger. King David said it himself thousands of years ago: "Blessed be the LORD my Rock, who trains my hands for war, And my fingers for battle. . ." (Psalm 144:1).

Second, *God strengthened our spirits in the loss of our fellow Marines*.

Unquestionably, losing two of our own was probably the most difficult trial our battalion faced. Admittedly, our losses were far less overwhelming than the losses previous generations of Marines and soldiers have experienced. Nearly six hundred men were killed in one day alone on the island fortress of Iwo Jima, and far more were lost at Normandy. However, in a sense, the loss of only two made their deaths even more poignant.

I have read many accounts about battles fought in World War II, Korea, and Vietnam, where the number of dead was so high that there was, at least for the moment, almost a sense of normalcy about it. Horrible as it was, death became something of a known quantity, a temporary but manageable shock. It was a reality that, at least in the immediate future, warriors simply did not have time to ponder.

"Bloody Tarawa" provides a brutal example—the assault of the Second Marine Division on Betio Island, Tarawa Atoll, which took place November 20–23, 1943. As the landing crafts opened up, historians depict men literally having to step over or move aside the bodies of their fallen comrades. Few completely grasped the horror they had faced until days later, when the beach was finally established and secured.

For our battalion, losing Lieutenant Shane Childers on our first day of combat was particularly difficult because, for the next five to seven days, the amount of fighting we experienced was minimal. Most of our time was spent in ten- to twelve-hour convoy movements along the desert highways of southern Iraq. Not only was it a grueling trek, but it gave us more time to think than we wanted. For the many young men who served under Shane, as well as many of us who were his contemporaries, his death was the foremost thought on our minds.

The same can be said of Jeffrey Bohr. We lost the gunny on a terrifying day of battle, and yet for all intents and purposes, it was our last major firefight of the war. We spent the next ten days at the palace and the next month in the southern Iraqi town of Ad Diwaniyah. Again, that meant we had more time to think, to ponder it all. In fact, after April 10, I heard very few conversations among the men that didn't at some point mention the names of either Childers or Bohr.

Still, we were not alone in our pain. God continued to strengthen our hearts and bind up our brokenness. More than a few

Marines shared with me how the very moment they heard we had lost one of those men, it seemed as if a voice literally spoke from heaven into the quiet of their hearts, assuring them that everything was going to be okay.

Lance Corporal Dave Cecil was a young Marine in Childers's platoon. He told me later, after realizing that his lieutenant had been killed, that he had never felt the presence of God like he did at Pumping Station 2. "When the word got passed that he was gone, a surreal feeling seemed to sweep over the platoon. I mean this was the first day, and already we'd lost our leader. I know guys were worried. You could see it on their faces. But for me, it was like God, in that very moment, strengthened me as never before. Talley (a fellow Christian) and I just got even closer and began to encourage one another each day. God took care of us, and as hard as it was to lose our lieutenant, when I look back on that morning, I remember it as a moment of newfound strength and spiritual growth."

Staff Sergeant Bradley Nerad, Shane's second-in-command, told me later that the moment Childers died, he immediately knew God was with him and that God would strengthen him in the difficult days ahead. "We knew," said Nerad. "We just knew that none of this was out of God's control, that we weren't alone."

Corporal Cliff Gauthier, who had to take the fallen Bohr to the palace after he had been shot, said that while he never knew fear like he did in those agonizing moments, he distinctly remembers the words of Psalm 91 coming into his mind, "You shall not be afraid of the terror by night, nor of the arrow that flies by day. A thousand may fall at your side, and ten thousand at your right hand, but it shall not come near you."

He was comforted. Even with the sound of bullets ringing overhead, the emotions that assailed him on every side were calmed.

For me, the comfort of the Lord came through a trusted friend and an MRE.

Just after finding out about Bohr's death, I ran into my close friend and fellow chaplain, Erik Lee, of the Secnd Battalion. Erik and I had arrived at Fifth Marine Regiment only a few months apart, and immediately had become good friends. His faith group was Nazarene, and the fact that I had served as a youth pastor of a Nazarene church during seminary only made our connection that much deeper. By now all the chaplains in the regiment—Holley, Tanis, Lee, and I—had begun to bond together in a way that I suppose only a war can make happen.

The ground war had been rolling for twenty days, and Erik and I hadn't seen each other for weeks. We had last met in Northern Kuwait, before receiving the word to move out. Grabbing an MRE, the two of us headed for the second floor of the abandoned house that our regiment had commandeered for use as a command post. We had a lot to talk about that afternoon—close calls, comical episodes, the morale of our men. But for me, it was more than that. I had reached something of a breaking point.

After hearing about Bohr's death, and breaking the news to many of the men in our combat train who knew Gunny well, my heart was heavy not only for my own loss, but especially for the men of Alpha Company. As chaplains, part of our job is to remain strong for our men and keep our own emotions at bay. For ourselves and for our men, we both wept that afternoon.

We wept for the horrible sights war had brought into all our lives. We wept for our families so far away, anxiously watching the daily reports of men being killed. We wept for the loss of life that we had both seen—good men who had fallen at the hands of the enemy. They were heroic men; men with wives and children, mothers, and fathers; men with hopes and dreams and goals in life. We both believed that this was a just war and a noble cause, and as always, in such an effort, sacrifices are demanded and lives are lost. But on that quiet afternoon, the two of us grieved for all those whose lives, and their families' lives, had been changed forever by the deaths of our fellow Marines.

Those moments with my friend were a gift from God, an oasis of spiritual fellowship and burden sharing. When God offers us His comfort, it does not necessarily mean He removes our pain and sorrow. Instead, He grants us His companionship *through* the pain and sorrow by providing a fellow soul to bear our burden with us.

As I reflect upon those moments Erik and I shared over an MRE, I have come to see that this afternoon was deeply symbolic of the same companionship God offered all of us throughout the dura-tion of the war. God offered His own presence, and was willing to listen to our grief, bear our burdens, and lift our spirits so we could be strengthened, persevere, and not lose faith.

His Word says, "Trust in Him at all times, you people; pour out your heart before Him; God is a refuge for us" (Psalm 62:8). What does *refuge* mean? It is a shelter or protection from danger and trouble; a place of safety; a place of recourse for aid, relief, or escape. In our grief and sadness, God really had been our refuge. He had listened to our questions, had given us the freedom to struggle, and in the end he had lifted our spirits to a place of strength and fortitude, enabling us all to press on bravely in the fight. "From the ends of the earth I will cry to you, when my heart is overwhelmed; lead me to the rock that is higher than I" prayed the psalmist (Psalm 61:2). For the men of First Battalion, it was more than a prayer. It was a promise from a faithful God, who never once failed to uphold us in the darkest moments of our lives.

Third, *God shielded us from the danger that constantly surrounded us*.

The ways God protected our men on April 10 were, by every assessment, beyond our comprehension. And yet the supernatural covering of the Lord had always been there, shielding us, protecting us, defending us. Who could forget Corporal Matthew Hummel of Weapons Company?

Just as our battalion was crossing the line of departure into Iraq, Hummel had been tasked with providing security in the middle of the night for a section of our convoy. While lying prone, he was run completely over across the midsection of his back by a rolling Humvee. Not realizing what he'd done, the vehicle's driver backed up and rolled over Hummel a second time. The young man should have been killed on the spot. But not a bone was broken on his body.

When Hummel found me days later to share the events of that night, the smile on his face was from ear to ear. "I should be dead,

Chaplain. But God protected me. I don't know how or why I wasn't killed, but here I am without a scratch."

Or what of First Lieutenant Jeremy Stalnecker, who on the second day of the ground war, March 21, drove his Humvee directly over an antipersonnel mine. The explosion erupted from underneath the vehicle, blowing out all four reinforced tires, cracking the gas tank, and sending bits of shrapnel up through the floorboard and into the cabin. It was an explosion that could have and should have taken lives.

Not one of the four men aboard was injured or even scratched in the explosion. Lieutenant Stalnecker, a devout Christian and a tremendous leader in his platoon, went on to distinguish himself with great bravery throughout the duration of the war. When others in the battalion heard of his run-in with the mine, and the fact that no one in his vehicle had been injured, one of his fellow lieutenants, who knew Stalnecker well, remarked laughingly but somewhat seriously, "That's got to be his good living paying off for him." Upon returning home to the United States, he left the Marine Corps and entered full-time pastoral ministry.

And then there was Staff Sergeant Antonio Rivera's backpack. On April 8, as our battalion pushed into the outer-lying slums of Saddam City, Charlie Company began receiving sporadic machine-gun and RPG fire from the rooftops of apartment buildings. Rivera and his men were hunkered down in their AAV, awaiting orders from higher up about how to proceed. Then, in a blinding flash, an RPG struck their vehicle on the left rear side, sending a wall of heat and fire up and over the top of the AAV that leapt into the open hatch where several men were standing. No one was seriously injured. Somehow the round, even though fired from virtual point-blank range, had not penetrated the vehicle's armor. On further inspection, the men saw why.

The rocket had hit directly in the center of Rivera's giant pack, which was hanging on the outside of the vehicle. It impacted where Rivera's sleeping bag and foam warming mat were balled up, and in truth couldn't have struck a more absorbent area. Although the blast still sent a few tiny fragments of shrapnel into the compartment, it was so muffled by the pack that no one was seriously injured.

Ever since our battalion crossed the border into Iraq, the men had realized that the best place to put their massive bulky packs was strapped to the outside of the AAVs. It gave them more room inside, and for Rivera and his men, the pack was in the perfect place. A Marine was sitting right where the high-explosive round would have entered the compartment. Of course Rivera's pack was destroyed (his toiletries were floating all over Saddam City), but had it not been hanging right where it was, several men could have died that day. When I found the platoon later that afternoon at the same site, all of them were smiling from ear to ear and thanking God (and Rivera) for the pack that saved lives.

And then there was Lance Corporal Ortiz, one of our logistics Marines, who along with two others were caught in a surprise mortar attack southeast of Baghdad. The mortars were shot at our men from well-hidden Iraqi soldiers, thousands of yards away, who had stopped along a road to refuel and replenish their supplies. When the mortar round impacted, two Marines—Evans and Rodgers—were standing just feet from the explosion and were instantly thrown back from the sheer percussion of the blast. Both sustained injuries to their feet and legs and would have to be evacuated to a medical facility in Kuwait, where they would eventually be flown back to the States to begin their convalescence. When I found Ortiz the next day, he showed me where a piece of shrapnel from the blast had entered the top shoulder portion of his protective flak jacket, only to stop at the base of his neck—a mass of razor-sharp steel, tangled in his green undershirt.

His words to me that day were, "Chaplain, God protected me, cause I've been faithful to Him."

God had protected him, and all of us. And even those who were injured went on to talk about the awesome hand of God shielding them from greater injury or even death. I heard about mines that should have killed but didn't; RPGs impacting vehicles fully loaded with men and not injuring anyone; bullets raining down around Marines striking everything within an inch of their lives; sandstorms that halted enemy counterattacks and revealed hidden mine fields. There was no question that God had literally reached down from the heavens and raised up a hedge of protection around us, a wall of angels that defended us from "the arrow that flies by day . . . the pestilence that walks in darkness . . . the destruction that lays waste at noonday" (Psalm 91:5–6).

Yes, from the very beginning, God had been *always faithful* unto us. He empowered us with strength to fight against our enemies. He lifted our spirits when we grieved the loss of fellow Marines. He supernaturally protected us from the perils of war and the snares of a relentless foe.

Most important of all, *God never once, even amidst the chaos of war, stopped pursuing our own hearts*.

In truth, Semper Fidelis describes far more than God's faithfulness to empower, encourage, or protect. It describes nothing short of God's unyielding faithfulness to never give up His relentless pursuit of our lives.

Semper Fidelis. Perhaps the most closely related word in all of Scripture is the Hebrew word *hesed*. Nearly untranslatable in English, it is a word used to describe the unending faithfulness that God has for His people; a faithfulness that, even when rejected, remains true; even when snubbed, He is not offended; even when forgotten, does not forget. *Hesed* describes God's undying commitment never to cease pursing our hearts, never to cease desiring our best, never to cease employing whatever means necessary to gain our loving companionship so He can grant us the indescribable blessings of abundant and eternal life.

God's faithfulness will not rest until a man or woman rests in Him. God's faithfulness never gives up the search for the lost and counts no sacrifice too costly to redeem a man's heart. God's faithfulness will even use the excruciating ordeal of war to bring a man to the point of recognizing his eternal need for a Savior. Why? Because when all is said and done, *that is* the ultimate desire of God.

Does not the apostle Paul say as much in his ancient letter to young Timothy? "For this is good and acceptable in the sight of God our Savior, who desires all men to be saved and to come to the knowledge of the truth" (1 Timothy 2:3–4).

Indeed, reflecting back upon the war, I could see—and I think we all could see—this powerful subtext giving an even greater meaning and significance to our purposes for being there. Yes, we were there to depose a ruthless tyrant. Yes, we were there to seek and destroy weapons of mass destruction. Yes, we were there to protect our own borders from the threat of terrorism. Yes, we were there to bring stability and peace to a rogue part of the world. But there was a deeper, more transcendent purpose behind it all.

Not only had we been brought to Iraq to fight a war, but even more so, each of us had been brought there to discover the boundless love of God. We had been brought there not only as a battalion of Marines and warriors, but as individual men, made in God's image. We were men who, like everyone else, had hopes and dreams, disappointments and regrets. We were all men who needed the forgiveness and new life that God grants unto all those who look unto His Son and believe.

Just ask Lance Corporal Jeff Guthrie of Alpha Company, Second Platoon.

It was Saturday morning, April 12, and I was still moving around the palace compound, trying to talk to anybody I hadn't yet seen since the firefight. Many of the platoons were patrolling the city, keeping suspicious men at bay and building rapport with the local populace. Others were strewn out on the palace lawn fast asleep or huddled together eating MREs, still going over the harrowing events of April 10. There was a rumor spreading throughout the battalion that we were going to leave the palace at sunset and move north to Tikrit for more combat operations. It wasn't definite yet, but I knew then that if I wanted to see all the men before we moved out, the next few hours would be my last chance for at least a couple of days.

When I first saw Guthrie, I could tell immediately that something was wrong. The open door of his AAV had been lowered all the way to the ground like a ramp, and there he sat. The rest of his platoon was scattered around the big steel beast. Some were eating, others were lying in the grass, still others were laughing and joking about what I could only imagine. All around the landscape were the symbols of war. Rifles were bunched together and pointed to the sky, small fires were being stoked to heat water for coffee or soup. The men were still weary, with dirt-smeared faces, flak jackets, and helmets, many with gauze wrappings around their hands and heads.

And then there was Guthrie.

Like a still photograph in the midst of a motion-picture, he sat, an expression of sadness on his face, staring off into nowhere.

I had gotten to know Guthrie fairly well over the last year and a half, while serving as the First Battalion's chaplain. Despite the fact that there were nearly one thousand men in the unit and I knew I could never get acquainted with them all, Guthrie was one man I'd spent some time with. Part of the reason for my knowing him so well was because his platoon commander, Shane Childers, cared about his men. He cared so much that anytime they experienced problems, whether professional or personal, he always tried to get them help. That caring attitude translated into Childers walking Guthrie to my office on more than one occasion. Beyond that, I always seemed to be running into him.

Guthrie and I first met while his company was out in the field on a weeklong training package at Camp Pendleton. During those exercises men stormed up mountainsides, crawled through dried-out riverbeds, and took out mock enemy strongholds. As a matter of fact, I heard Guthrie before I saw him. While a group of men moved up the slope of a small hill, I could hear one of them complaining about something—perhaps the length of the movement, the rocky terrain, or the heat of the afternoon sun. I couldn't tell.

I quickly noticed that it wasn't the kind of complaining that a senior Marine necessarily tries to nip in the bud, the kind that spreads like a bad attitude throughout the ranks. This was almost refreshing, a bit of comic relief on a long, hot afternoon. It sounded like a grandfather griping and groaning about having to finish a project his wife had been nagging him to complete—faithful to the end, but affectionately begrudging along the way. And the other Marines didn't seem to mind. They just kept moving along toward their objective, chuckling to themselves as if it was all quite benign. Jeff Guthrie's complaining was something they were used to.

Guthrie was a thirty-two-year-old private when I'd first men him nearly two years before. Standing at least six feet tall, with blond hair and blue eyes, he had a weathered look to his face that made you want to ask where he'd been in life, what he'd done, and what he'd seen. And compared to most privates who were no more than eighteen or nineteen years old, Guthrie had definitely seen his share of life experiences long before he had even decided to join the Marines.

Somewhat estranged from his divorced parents as an adolescent, Guthrie had made a spur-of-the-moment decision in the spring of 1988 to leave home for good. Having just completed his GED, the eighteen-year-old grabbed his skateboard, a duffel bag of his favorite clothes, and fifty dollars, and he caught a cheap flight to Europe where he hoped to find the German exchange student whom he had dated while a student at Wando High School in Mt. Pleasant, South Carolina. The relationship with the girl never worked out. Neither did his plans to return home. Meeting a friend at a youth hostel in Germany, Guthrie decided to stay with the friend's family just long enough to get on his feet, make some money, and decide what to do with his life.

Eight years later Jeff Guthrie picked up the phone to call his mother and tell her he was coming home. It was the first she'd heard from him in a very long time.

All those years, Guthrie had wandered the countries of Europe, staying with friends and kind strangers; sleeping on the streets of Paris, London, and Rome; finding odd jobs to keep food in his mouth and clothes on his back. Finally, with nothing to show for his years but sordid experiences, bittersweet memories, and more than a few regrets, the lonely Guthrie was ready to come home. His mother wired him the money for the ticket.

For the next three years he tried to collect himself and find some sense of direction for his life. But moving back and forth between his mother's home in South Carolina and his father's in Kentucky, Guthrie still couldn't seem to settle down. He tried college for a year or so, but after a few semesters and less-than-average grades, he left.

In 1999, life began to change for Jeff Guthrie. One day he walked into a Marine Corps recruiting office and decided that active-duty military might be his only option for getting his life together, and for finding the sense of purpose and direction that for so many years had eluded him. Several months later, after boot camp at Parris Island and infantry school at Camp Lejeune, the thirty-year-old Guthrie joined the First Battalion, Fifth Marine Regiment as an infantryman.

When Guthrie and I met in 2001, it had been more than three years since he had joined the Marines. Although by then he'd found a wife and had seen his share of deployments, in truth, he was still searching. But for what? He didn't know. Later he was willing to say that it had something to do with God. In fact, he had confided in me that while growing up there were several times, sitting a church, when he had given serious thought to the prospect of going forward after the sermon, as is the practice of many Protestant churches, and praying with the minister to become a Christian.

"But I could just never do it," Guthrie told me one day. "I knew I needed to get my life right with God. But I was always afraid of what others might think seeing me walk down that aisle. I always believed in the existence of God, and I even believed there was a Jesus. But that's where I left it—just kind of a distant belief that never had any real impact upon my life."

Guthrie's moment was about to come, and in a way neither he nor I could ever have expected.

When I walked up to Guthrie sitting on the back of the AAV ramp, I immediately noticed that he was on the verge of tears. Still, on that particular day, looking broken up wasn't that surprising. Many warriors were still reeling from the emotional load of April 10, especially those who had known Gunny Bohr.

Sitting down on the grass in front of Guthrie, I asked what was wrong.

"Sir . . . I'm, I'm just so sorry," he said, tears welling up in his tired eyes.

"Sorry for what, Guthrie?" I had no idea what he was talking about.

"It's just what I've done in my life. All I can think about is that I've just been through the worst experience of my life, and yet, God protected me through it all. But why did He do it? How could He do it after all the things—the bad things—I've done? I don't know what else to say, what else to feel. I'm just so sorry."

By now, the tears were streaming down his face. Guthrie's fellow Marines, all twenty of them who were seated around the same ramp, stopped everything. They were listening intently, watching everything. He and I could feel their gaze, but it didn't matter. He was overcome.

It reminded me of the story of Peter in the New Testament. After having seen Jesus perform a miracle right before his eyes—a miraculous catch of fish—Peter was literally undone, overcome with remorse. . . "Depart from me, O LORD," he said, "for I am a sinful man" (Luke 5:8).

Or the prophet Isaiah in the Old Testament, who in a vision entered the heavenly temple and gazed out upon the majesty of God. The first words out of his mouth were, "Woe is me, for I am ruined! For I am a man of unclean lips, and I live among a people of unclean lips, my eyes have seen the King, the LORD Almighty" (Isaiah 6:5 NIV).

Or Paul, the greatest of all apostles. After reflecting upon the grace that God had shown him throughout his life, he referred to himself as not merely a sinner, but as "the *chief* of sinners" (1 Timothy 1:15).

So Guthrie was in good company. He had just come through the most frightening experience of his life and perhaps one of the single worst firefights of the entire war. Like many others, he was uninjured, unscathed, and unharmed. And the only thing he could think about was his sinfulness. His mind was fixed on the things he'd done wrong in life, the regrets and failures that he was ashamed of, the disappointments that he'd caused others.

I was looking into the face of a man who, for the first time in his life, was truly encountering the power of God. "Jeff," I said gently. "Do you realize that God sent His Son, Jesus, for no other purpose than for forgiving all those things you or I have ever done wrong in life?"

He nodded.

"And that when Jesus died on the Cross, He died for you, Jeff Guthrie, for everything you're ashamed of, or that you regret?"

He continued to nod, as the tears mixed freely with the mud and grease smeared all over his face. Although the Marines around him hadn't moved a muscle, I felt as if Guthrie and I were the only two people in the universe.

"Jeff, do you believe that God loves you and that He sent His Son, Jesus, to die for you?"

"Yes I do," he said, his voice broken and trembling.

"And do you want to experience the joy and peace of knowing that all your sins are completely and forever forgiven?"

"Yes, I do," he answered.

"Then why don't you bow in prayer with me right here right now? Ask God to do just that—to send His Son, Jesus, into your heart and life and cleanse you from all your sin and give to you the promise of heaven."

We bowed together as twenty watching Marines stared in disbelief.

Our prayer together was brief, but it was rich with life and meaning. For there on the lawn of Saddam Hussein's Presidential Palace, Lance Corporal Jeff Guthrie, a man who had wandered the path of the prodigal son for years, who had avoided God because of his fear of what others might think, who had spent all he had searching for happiness, meaning, and fulfillment, bowed his head. And with all of his fellow Marines watching, he asked the Lord Jesus to come into his life and make him a child of God.

The next morning, April 13, 2003, was Palm Sunday. In

Saddam Hussein's palace, in the courtroom of one of the century's most notorious villains, I baptized Jeff Guthrie, a new creation, in the name of the Father, the Son, and the Holy Spirit. As the waters of baptism poured over his head and onto the marble floors of the palace, the symbolism wasn't lost on anyone. Here we were in the inner chamber of a place known for oppression and tyranny, vice and unspeakable cruelty. Yet that sacrament proclaimed to us all the greatest freedom and victory that a man can experience. There before our eyes, the courts of evil had become nothing less than the courts of the Lord. A place that had been known for the presence of darkness and treachery had become a place of the presence of God—*a table in the presence*.

Jeff Guthrie's baptism was no mere spectacle. It was not just a display of "dark versus light" or "good versus evil." It was a vivid picture of what God wants to do in every human heart. As the other fifty-seven Marines and sailors baptized by the end of the war came to understand, God wants to invade *our* dark lives, get behind *our* own palace walls, and find the inner courtroom of *our* own hearts, and there, through the power and victory of the Resurrection, proclaim spiritual victory forever.

The truth is, whether we are infantryman in Baghdad or civilians safe in our own hometowns, all of us need to claim this victory as our own, because in the end, we all face the same enemies. Fear, worry, doubt, discouragement, despair, temptation, the rising power of unbelief—these things attack us constantly. And they are often just as destructive, just as fierce, and just as unrelenting as evil men lurking in the streets of Baghdad. But if God can deliver an isolated, cut-off battalion of U.S. Marines surrounded by enemies in the belly of the beast, can He not deliver us from the enemies that assail us in our daily lives?

Thou preparest a table for me in the presence of mine enemies.

In the end, those words are not just poetry to be memorized or part of a beloved psalm to be read at funerals. That simple, ancient portrait of an unlikely feast is a promise to be believed and a bedrock upon which we can build our lives. King David believed it. A battalion of U.S. Marines experienced it. And its power is offered to us all, who in the midst of our trials, and when surrounded by enemies, can find that relentless courage, that reckless faith, that undying hope we need to look unto God—and believe.

Epilogue

SEVERAL MONTHS HAVE PASSED since our battalion returned home from deployment in support of Operation Iraqi Freedom. Thousands of other troops who returned with us have told strikingly similar stories of God's abundant provision and protection amidst the chaos of war. In the writing and researching of this book, it has been made abundantly clear to me that my experience represents all those Marines, sailors, soldiers, and airmen who have fought in wars past and present, and who have witnessed in their own fiery ordeal what can only be described as the miraculous hand of God. I thank God for allowing me to give voice to these stories, and can only pray that this book is a worthy offering and a shining witness to others' testimonies as well as mine.

As long as wars rage, as long as good men are confronted with evil, troops will continue to proclaim what God has done for them amidst the terrors of war. Yet, in the last year, despite the declaration that major hostilities are over in Iraq, and despite the capture of Saddam Hussein, the world has watched as hundreds of United States and Coalition troops have continued to be killed in ambushes, suicide bombings, and malicious attacks. Almost nightly, as we watch the news, our stomachs tighten and our hearts are broken once again as still more defenders of freedom pay the highest price.

I am well aware that a book like this raises a difficult and painful question in the hearts and minds of all those who care about our troops: "What about those who are dying almost daily? Where was God's supernatural protection for them?"

It is a valid question, and in all honesty, it is one that our battalion also struggled with. I don't know that there's an easy answer or a textbook explanation to it. Even if there were, I'm not so sure we'd want to hear it or that it would bring the comfort we need. I struggled myself with the implications of hearing so many describe how God had miraculously protected them, yet seeing two good and heroic brothers fall. I didn't necessarily find a perfect answer, but I did stumble across a comforting parallel, which I found in the biblical accounts of two men: Daniel, the great apocalyptic prophet, and Stephen, the first Christian martyr.

Those two men lived hundreds of years apart from one another, and without a doubt, they were cut from the same spiritual cloth. Both were men of integrity and strength, men of leadership and action, men of heroic virtue. Both were faithful, both served God, and both did what they thought was right in the face of the evil forces that conspired against them. Daniel was ordered not to pray to his own God, but instead to submit to the pagan religion of the land. He refused. Stephen was falsely accused of blasphemy and ordered to renounce his faith in Christ as the Messiah. He too refused.

Both men, full of courage and inspired by a just cause, met their adversaries with calm determination and indomitable will. Both men were exactly where God wanted them to be when they met their great ordeal. But in the end, there were two very different outcomes.

For Daniel it was the supernatural deliverance of God from a den of hungry lions.

But for Stephen, "And they stoned Stephen as he was calling on God and saying, 'Lord Jesus, receive my spirit.' Then he knelt down and cried out with a loud voice, 'Lord, do not charge them with this sin.' And when he had said this, he fell asleep" (Acts 7:59–60).

Daniel's supernatural deliverance and Stephen's death, as different as they may seem, both point to God Himself.

Daniel's story encourages us that God is our great defender and that in Him abides all power to save us from our enemies. Stephen's story however, strikes even deeper. For in it, we are not merely encouraged, we are confronted. Steven provides us with a vivid picture of the "greater love" that God demonstrated before the entire world when He sent His only Son, Jesus, to die on the cross.

Perhaps that is why, moments before Stephen breathed his last, the Scriptures tell us that he looked up to heaven and saw Jesus. And Jesus was not seated at the right hand of the Father, but He was standing—standing in approval of the ultimate price Stephen was willing to pay.

Daniel and Stephen both remained true to their calling; both walked faithfully no matter the cost. For one, that calling would be affirmed through the power of divine protection. For the other, it would be illuminated through the heroism of sacrifice. Daniel's account becomes a living testimony, and because of it, many will come to believe in the reality of God's miraculous intervention. Stephen's account is more than a testimony; it is a memorial through which humanity comes face to face with a picture of God's perfect love.

And so the comfort may lie here: in life or death, in miracle or sacrifice, in unexplainable deliverance or the sad loss of a fallen brother, God remains in the center of it all. He is the power behind every miracle. He is the source of all heroic sacrifice. Psalm 62:11–12 sums it up aptly:

> *Once God has spoken;*
> *Twice I have heard this:*
> *That power belongs to God;*
> *And lovingkindness is*
> *Thine, O Lord . . . (NASB).*

Notes

The people whose stories you read in this book have graciously given us permission to include them.

Preface

1. A. W. Tozer, *The Pursuit of Man: The Divine Conquest of the Human Heart* (Camp Hill, PA: Christian Publications, © 1979). p. xii.

Chapter 6

1. *Marine Corps Devotional Field Book,* "My Morning Offering," p. 17. Used by permission.

Chapter 7

1. Reprinted by permission. *Being the Body,* Chuck Colson, © 2003, W Publishing, Nashville, Tennessee. All rights reserved.